EYEWITNESS TRAVEL GUIDES

BARCELONA
& CATALONIA

EYEWITNESS TRAVEL GUIDES

BARCELONA & CATALONIA

Main contributor: ROGER WILLIAMS

DK PUBLISHING

LONDON • NEW YORK • MUNICH
MELBOURNE • DELHI

Project Editor Catherine Day
Art Editors Carolyn Hewitson, Marisa Renzullo
Editors Elizabeth Atherton, Felicity Crowe
Designer Suzanne Metcalfe-Megginson
Map Co-ordinator David Pugh
Picture Research Monica Allende
DTP Designers Samantha Borland, Lee Redmond,
Pamela Shiels

Main Contributor
Roger Williams

Maps
Jane Hanson, Phil Rose, Jennifer Skelley (Lovell Jones Ltd),
Gary Bowes, Richard Toomey (ERA-Maptec Ltd)

Photographers
Max Alexander, Mike Dunning, Heidi Grassley, Alan Keohane

Illustrators
Stephen Conlin, Isidoro González-Adalid Cabezas
(Acanto Arquitectura y Urbanismo S.L.), Claire Littlejohn,
Maltings Partnership, John Woodcock

Reproduced by Colourscan, Singapore
Printed and bound by South China Printing Company Limited, China

First American Edition, 1999
6 8 10 9 7 5

Published in the United States by DK Publishing, Inc.,
375 Hudson Street, New York, New York 10014

Reprinted with revisions 2000, 2001, 2002, 2003

Copyright 1999, 2003 © Dorling Kindersley Limited, London

See our complete product line at
www.dk.com

**The information in this
Dorling Kindersley Travel Guide is checked annually.**
Every effort has been made to ensure that this book is as up-to-date
as possible at the time of going to press. Some details, however,
such as telephone numbers, opening hours, prices, gallery hanging
arrangements and travel information, are liable to change. The
publishers cannot accept responsibility for any consequences arising
from the use of this book, nor for any material on third party
websites, and cannot guarantee that any website address in this
book will be a suitable source of travel information. We value the
views and suggestions of our readers very highly. Please write to:
Publisher, DK Eyewitness Travel Guides,
Dorling Kindersley, 80 Strand, London WC2R 0RL, Great Britain

Contents

Introducing Barcelona and Catalonia

Jaume I, "El Conquistador",
ruler of Catalonia 1213–76

Putting Barcelona
and Catalonia
on the Map *10*

A Portrait of
Catalonia *14*

Catalonia Through
the Year *30*

The History of
Catalonia *36*

One of the many popular cafés in
Barcelona's redeveloped Old Port

Barcelona Area by Area

Barcelona at a
Glance *46*

◁ **Previous pages: Bench, Parc Güell, Barcelona; Miravet on the Riu Ebre, southern Catalonia**

The small, whitewashed town of Cadaqués on the Costa Brava

OLD TOWN *50*

EIXAMPLE *66*

MONTJUÏC *76*

FURTHER AFIELD *84*

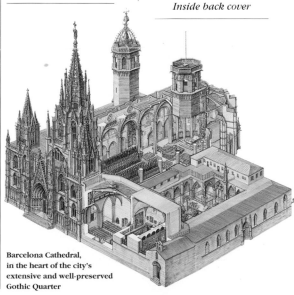

Spectacular stained-glass roof of
the Palau de la Música Catalana

CATALONIA

LLEIDA,
ANDORRA,
GIRONA,
BARCELONA PROVINCE,
TARRAGONA *90*

TRAVELLERS' NEEDS

WHERE TO STAY *114*

RESTAURANTS, CAFÉS
AND BARS *122*

SHOPPING IN
BARCELONA *134*

ENTERTAINMENT IN
BARCELONA *136*

OUTDOOR
ACTIVITIES *138*

Barcelona Cathedral,
in the heart of the city's
extensive and well-preserved
Gothic Quarter

SURVIVAL GUIDE

PRACTICAL
INFORMATION *142*

TRAVEL INFORMATION
150

STREET FINDER *156*

GENERAL INDEX
166

ACKNOWLEDGMENTS
173

Pa amb tomàquet – bread rubbed
with tomato, garlic and olive oil

CATALAN PHRASE
BOOK *175*

BARCELONA METRO
AND TRAIN ROUTES
Inside back cover

HOW TO USE THIS GUIDE

THIS GUIDE has expert recommen- dations and detailed practical information to enrich any visit to Barcelona and Catalonia. *Introducing Barcelona and Catalonia* puts the area in geographical, historical and cultural context. *Barcelona and Catalonia* is a six-chapter guide to important sights: *Barcelona at a Glance* highlights the city's top attractions; *Old Town, Eixample* and *Montjuïc* explore Barce- lona's central districts in more detail; *Further Afield* views sights outside the city centre; and *Catalonia* delves into the region's four provinces. *Travellers' Needs* covers hotels, restaurants and entertainment. The *Survival Guide* provides vital practical information.

BARCELONA AND CATALONIA

The region is divided into five sightseeing areas – the central districts of Barcelona, sights outside the centre, and those beyond the city. Each area chapter opens with an introduction and a list of sights covered. Central districts have a Street-by-Street map of a particularly interesting part of the area. The sights further afield have a regional map.

Sights at a Glance lists the area's key sights (great buildings, art galleries, museums and churches) by category.

Each chapter of *Barcelona and Catalonia* has a different colour-coded thumb tab.

Locator maps show where you are in relation to other parts of Barcelona or Spain.

1 Area Map of the city
Sights are numbered and located on a map, with Metro stations where help- ful. The sights are also shown on the Barcelona Street Finder *on pp156–65.*

2 Street-by-Street map
The area shaded pink on the Area Map *is shown here in greater detail with accurate drawings of all the buildings.*

A suggested route for a walk covers the more interesting streets in the area.

A list of star sights recommends places no visitor should miss.

3 Detailed information on each sight
The sights listed at the start of the section are described individually and follow the numbering on the Area Map. *A key to symbols summariz- ing practical information is shown on the back flap.*

CATALONIA

LLEIDA · ANDORRA · GIRONA
BARCELONA PROVINCE · TARRAGONA

There is a wealth of natural beauty in Catalonia's four provinces, plus the small Catalan-speaking country of Andorra. They offer rocky coasts and mountains, fertile plains and sandy shores. Many who visit don't stray far from the coast, but the rewards for venturing further afield are immense.

4 Introduction to Catalonia

The chapter on Catalonia has its own introduction, providing an overview of the history and character of the region. The area covered is highlighted on the map of Spain shown on page 91. The chapter explores Catalonia's rich historical, cultural and natural heritage, from the monasteries of Montserrat and Poblet to Tarragona's casteller festivals, from the sandy beaches of the Costa Daurada to the snowy peaks of the Pyrenees.

5 Pictorial Map

This gives an illustrated overview of the whole region. All the sights covered in this chapter are numbered, and the network of major roads is marked. There are also useful tips on getting around the region by bus and train.

6 Detailed information on each sight

All the important cities, towns and other places to visit are described individually. They are listed in order following the numbering given on the Pictorial Map. Within each town or city there is detailed information on important buildings and other sights.

Stars indicate the best features and works of art.

The Visitors' Checklist provides a summary of the practical information you will need to plan your visit.

7 The top sights

These are given two or more full pages. Historic buildings are dissected to reveal their interiors. For larger historic sites, all the important buildings are labelled to help you locate those that most interest you.

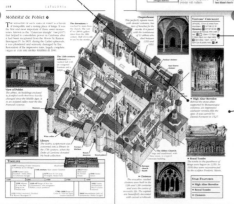

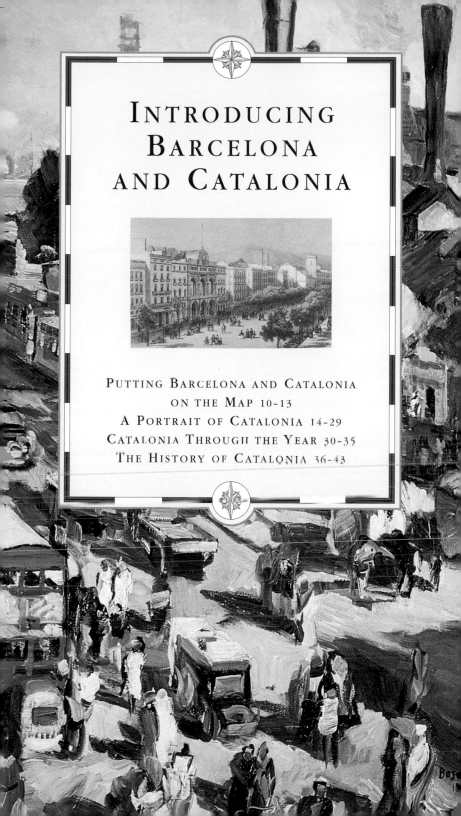

INTRODUCING
BARCELONA
AND CATALONIA

PUTTING BARCELONA AND CATALONIA
ON THE MAP 10-13
A PORTRAIT OF CATALONIA 14-29
CATALONIA THROUGH THE YEAR 30-35
THE HISTORY OF CATALONIA 36-43

Putting Barcelona and Catalonia on the Map

CATALONIA LIES in the northeastern corner of the Iberian Peninsula and occupies six per cent of Spain. Barcelona, its capital, lies almost exactly halfway along its coastline, which in turn stretches a quarter of the way down Spain's Mediterranean seaboard. Barcelona is the main bridging point to the Catalan-speaking Balearic Islands.

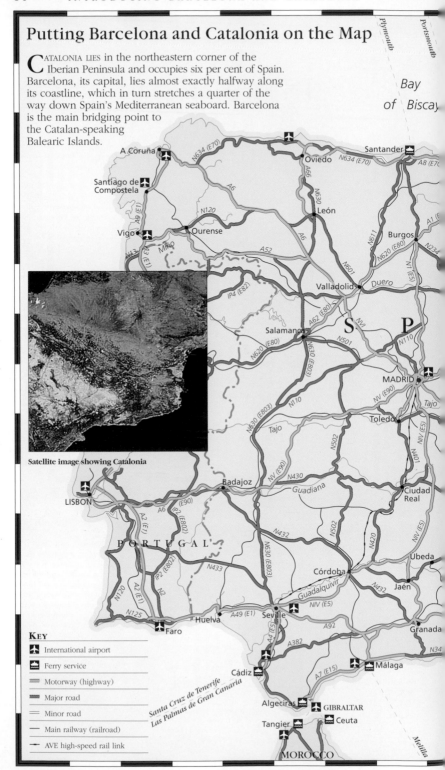

Satellite image showing Catalonia

KEY

- ✈ International airport
- ⛴ Ferry service
- ══ Motorway (highway)
- ▬ Major road
- ═ Minor road
- — Main railway (railroad)
- ⊷ AVE high-speed rail link

◁ *Paral·lel any 1930*, a portrait of one of Barcelona's main avenues in 1930 by Emili Bosch Roger (1894–1980)

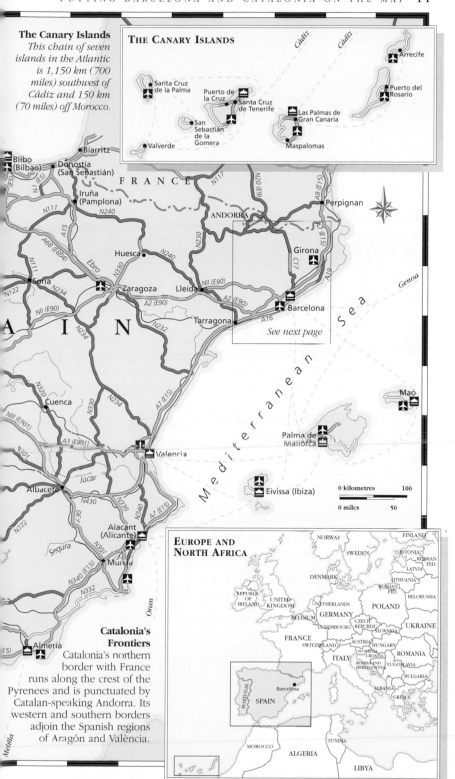

The Canary Islands
This chain of seven islands in the Atlantic is 1,150 km (700 miles) southwest of Cádiz and 150 km (70 miles) off Morocco.

THE CANARY ISLANDS

Santa Cruz de la Palma
Puerto de la Cruz
Santa Cruz de Tenerife
San Sebastián de la Gomera
Valverde
Las Palmas de Gran Canaria
Maspalomas
Arrecife
Puerto del Rosario

Cádiz
Cádiz

Bilbo (Bilbao)
Biarritz
Donostia (San Sebastián)
Iruña (Pamplona)
FRANCE
ANDORRA
Perpignan
Huesca
Girona
Soria
Zaragoza
Lleida
Barcelona
Tarragona
See next page
Cuenca
Maó
Palma de Mallorca
Valencia
Albacete
Eivissa (Ibiza)
Alacant (Alicante)
Murcia
Almería

Mediterranean Sea
Genoa

Ebro
Júcar
Segura
Oran
Melilla

0 kilometres 100
0 miles 50

EUROPE AND NORTH AFRICA

NORWAY
FINLAND
SWEDEN
ESTONIA
RUSSIAN FED
LATVIA
DENMARK
LITHUANIA
RUSSIAN FED.
REPUBLIC OF IRELAND
UNITED KINGDOM
NETHERLANDS
BELORUSSIA
GERMANY
POLAND
BELGIUM
LUXEMBOURG
CZECH REPUBLIC
UKRAINE
FRANCE
SLOVAKIA
SWITZERLAND
AUSTRIA
HUNGARY
SLOVENIA
ROMANIA
ITALY
CROATIA
BOSNIA AND HERZEGOVINA
YUGOSLAVIA
BULGARIA
PORTUGAL
SPAIN
Barcelona
ALBANIA
GREECE

MOROCCO
ALGERIA
TUNISIA
LIBYA

Catalonia's Frontiers
Catalonia's northern border with France runs along the crest of the Pyrenees and is punctuated by Catalan-speaking Andorra. Its western and southern borders adjoin the Spanish regions of Aragón and València.

Barcelona City Centre

SET BETWEEN THE MOUNTAINS AND THE SEA, which still play an integral part in city life, Barcelona is a rare city, a patchwork of distinctive districts telling the story of its growth from a medieval core to the 19th-century expansion and today's ultra-modern showpieces. The three main sightseeing areas described in this guide illustrate this startling diversity. The hill of Montjuïc, abutting the sea, forms the southwestern end of an arc of steep hills that almost completely encloses the city. It is a district of monumental buildings and open spaces. The Old Town has a superb Gothic heart with a myriad of narrow streets twisting among ancient houses. The densely populated Eixample, in contrast, is a district of immensely long, straight streets and superb Modernista architecture.

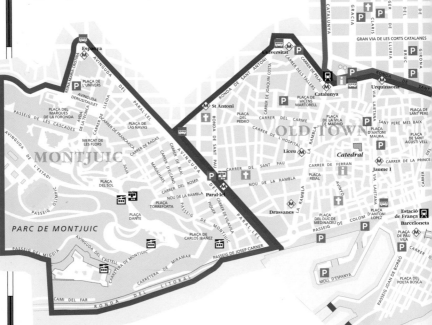

Montjuïc
There are wonderful views from the top of this large hill. Several of Barcelona's best museums are here, including the Archaeological Museum (see p80) which displays this Roman mosaic excavated in the city.

0 kilometres   1

0 miles   0.5

KEY

▣	Major sight
Ⓜ	Metro station
🚆	Train station
🚌	Bus stop
🚢	Boat boarding point
🚠	Cable car
🚟	Funicular
🚓	Police station
P	Parking
ℹ	Tourist information
✝	Church

Eixample
This area covers the most interesting part of the city's 19th-century expansion. Walks along its streets will reveal countless details of the Modernista style, such as this ornate doorway of Casa Comalat (see p48) in Avinguda Diagonal.

Old Town
This area includes all the oldest districts of Barcelona and its port, the 18th-century fishing "village" of Barceloneta and the new waterside developments. This new swing bridge is in the Old Port (see p64).

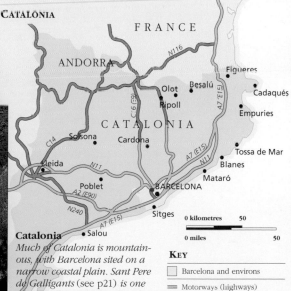

CATALONIA

FRANCE

ANDORRA

N116

Figueres

Olot   Besalú

Cadaqués

Ripoll

Empuries

CATALONIA

C14   Solsona   Cardona

Tossa de Mar

Lleida   N11

Blanes

Poblet   A2 (E90)

Mataró

BARCELONA

N240   A7 (E15)

Sitges

0 kilometres   50

0 miles   50

Salou

KEY

   Barcelona and environs

   Motorways (highways)

   Other major roads

Catalonia
Much of Catalonia is mountainous, with Barcelona sited on a narrow coastal plain. Sant Pere de Galligants (see p21) is one of many Romanesque churches.

A PORTRAIT OF CATALONIA

BARCELONA IS ONE OF THE GREAT *Mediterranean cities. Few places are so redolent with history, few so boldly modern. Animated and inspired, it is a city that sparkles as much at night-time as in the full light of day. It is famous for its main avenue, La Rambla, for its bars, its museums and its enthusiasm for life.*

Barcelona is the capital of the autonomous region of Catalonia, the most northeasterly corner of Spain, bordering France. The region is divided into four provinces, named after their provincial capitals: Barcelona, Girona, Lleida and Tarragona.

The city of Barcelona lies between two rivers, the Llobregat and the Besòs, and is backed by the Collserola hills which rise to a 512-m (1,680-ft) peak at the Tibidabo amusement park. The city grew up as the industrial sweatshop of Spain, though the shunting yards and seaside warehouses have now gone. Around four million people live in Barcelona and its suburbs – about half the population of Catalonia. It is Spain's second city after its old rival, Madrid.

La dama del paraigua

POLITICS AND SOCIETY

Catalonia is governed by the Generalitat, housed in the Palau de la Generalitat in the heart of the Old Town and on the site of the Roman forum. The region's parliament, in the Parc de la Ciutadella, shares a building with the Museu d'Art Modern. The city of Barcelona has a separate administration, and its town hall, the Casa de la Ciutat, faces the Generalitat across the Plaça de Sant Jaume. Catalonia is developing its own police force, which has now taken over from Spain's national police in most of Catalonia.

Catalans are conservative and, as in many other countries, people in rural areas are more conservative than those in the cities. For the more than 20 years

Strollers and shoppers on La Rambla enjoying Barcelona's plentiful winter sunshine

◁ Stunning floral mosaic pillars at the Palau de la Música Catalana in Barcelona

St George's Day in April – the day for giving books

Catalans are not burdened with self doubt. The vigour with which they have rebuilt parts of their capital since the early 1980s shows flair and a firm hand. Places of great sentimental value, such as Barceloneta's beach-side restaurant shacks and the Cafè Zurich, a famous rendezvous for writers, artists and intellectuals at the top of La Rambla, were torn down. Stunning new buildings such as the Museu d'Art Contemporani were put up in the middle of the Old Town, but restoration work on old buildings is also carried out without hesitation.

since Franco's death, the Generalitat has been run by the conservative Convergència i Unió under the charismatic presidency of Jordi Pujol. During the same period the city council has been run by a socialist party.

Catalans, who have no taste for bull-fighting and whose sedate national dance, the *sardana*, is unruffled by passion, are a serious, hardworking people. Some would rather be associated with northern Europeans than with other Spaniards, whom they regard as indolent. Part of their complaint against Madrid has been that, as one of the richest regions of Spain, they put more into the national coffers than they take out.

Two emotions are said to guide Catalans: *seny*, which means solid common sense, and *rauxa*, a creative chaos. A bourgeois, conservative element of Barcelona society can be seen at concerts and in pastry shops, but a certain surreal air is often evident, on La Rambla, for instance, where sometimes it seems that anything goes. The two elements are mixed in each person, and even the most staid may have the occasional *cop de rauxa*, or moment of chaotic ecstasy. Such outbursts are used to explain the more incendiary moments of Catalonia's history.

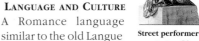

Street performer on La Rambla

LANGUAGE AND CULTURE

A Romance language similar to the old Langue d'Oc, or Provençal, once used in France, Catalan is Catalonia's official language, spoken by some eight million people. It has always been a living language and it continued to be spoken in the home even when it was banned by Franco. Catalans do not think it rude to talk to each other in Catalan in front of

Poster for a Pedro Almodóvar film

Beach at Tossa de Mar on the Costa Brava

Catalans read more books than other Spaniards. New Catalan writing has burgeoned since the 1970s and there are many literary prizes, but few Catalan writers of any era have been translated into English.

WORK AND LEISURE

Catalans stay true to their traditions and their families. Sunday lunch is a time to get together, although even during the week, most people who can do so return home for lunch. This creates a rush hour four times a day, with a lull in the early afternoon. Shops close around 8pm, and between 6pm and 8pm the streets are crowded. Dinner or entertainment starts around 10pm, but there is increasing pressure for business hours to conform with the rest of Europe.

Allegiance to the local football team, Barça, is a matter of national pride for its supporters. Meals out, concerts and the cinema are popular activities. The week begins quietly but, as the weekend approaches, streets fill and visitors leaving La Rambla at midnight to go to bed may feel they are leaving a good party too soon.

somcone who speaks only Spanish. All public signs and official documents in Catalonia are in Spanish and Catalan.

If *rauxa* is responsible for the creative spirit as claimed, then Catalonia has been blessed with an abundance. Modernisme, led by Antoni Gaudí, is the region's gift to world architecture. Painters Joan Miró, Salvador Dalí and Antoni Tàpies were born here, while Pablo Picasso spent his formative years in Barcelona. Designs by Javier Mariscal, creator of the 1992 Olympic motifs and Cobi, the mascot, furniture by Oliver Tusquets and fashion by Toni Miró help make Barcelona a city of great style. Bigas Luna, locally-born director of *Jamón Jamón*, and Pedro Almodóvar, whose film *All About My Mother* was shot in Barcelona have raised the area's profile in the cinema.

Montserrat Caballé

Over the last 150 years, some outstanding musicians have emerged from Catalonia. The composers Isaac Albéniz (1860–1909), Enric Granados (1867–1916) and Frederic Mompou (1893–1987) brought music imbued with a true Iberian idiom into the classical mainstream. Pau Casals (1876–1973) was considered one of the greatest of all cellists, and Montserrat Caballé and Josep Carreras can fill opera houses anywhere in the world.

Demonstration for Catalan independence

Flowers of the Matollar

Yellow bee orchid

THE MATOLLAR is the distinctive landscape of Spain's eastern Mediterranean coast. This scrubland rich in wild flowers is the result of centuries of woodland clearance, during which the native holm oak was felled for timber and to provide land for grazing and cultivation. Many colourful plants have adapted to the extremes of climate here. Most flower in spring, when hillsides are daubed with yellow broom and pink and white cistuses, and the air is perfumed by aromatic herbs such as rosemary, lavender and thyme. Buzzing insects feed on the abundance of nectar and pollen.

Spanish broom *is a small bush with yellow flowers on slender branches. The black seed pods split when dry, scattering the seeds on the ground.*

The century plant's flower stalk can reach 10 m (32 ft).

Jerusalem sage, *an attractive shrub which is often grown in gardens, has tall stems surrounded by bunches of showy yellow flowers. Its leaves are greyish-white and woolly.*

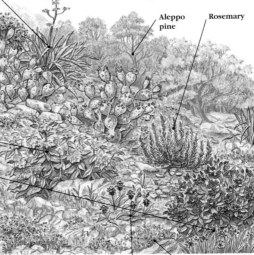

Aleppo pine   **Rosemary**

Rose garlic *has round clusters of violet or pink flowers at the end of a single stalk. It survives the summer as the bulb familiar to all cooks.*

FOREIGN INVADERS

Prickly pear in bloom

Several plants from the New World have managed to colonize the bare ground of the *matollar*. The prickly pear, thought to have been brought back by Christopher Columbus, produces a delicious fruit which can be picked only with thickly gloved hands.
The rapidly growing century plant, a native of Mexico which has tough, spiny leaves, sends up a tall flower shoot only when it is 10–15 years old, after which it dies.

Flowering shoots of the century plant

Common thyme *is a low-growing aromatic herb which is widely cultivated for use in the kitchen.*

The mirror orchid, *a small plant which grows on grassy sites, is easily distinguished from other orchids by the brilliant metallic blue patch inside the lip, fringed by brown hairs.*

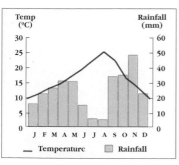

Temp (°C) / Rainfall (mm)

J F M A M J J A S O N D

— Temperature ■ Rainfall

CLIMATE CHART

Most plants found in the *matollar* come into bloom in the warm, moist spring. The plants protect themselves from losing water during the dry summer heat with thick leaves or waxy secretions, or by storing moisture in bulbs or tubers.

WILDLIFE OF THE MATOLLAR

The animals which live in the *matollar* are most often seen early in the morning, before the temperature is high. Countless insects fly from flower to flower, providing a source of food for birds. Smaller mammals, such as mice and voles, are active only at night when it is cooler and there are few predators around.

Holm oaks are very common in eastern Spain. The leaves are tough and rubbery to prevent water loss.

The strawberry tree is an evergreen shrub with glossy serrated leaves. Its inedible strawberry-like fruit turns red when ripe.

Ladder snakes *feed on small mammals, birds and insects. The young are identified by a black pattern like the rungs of a ladder, but adults are marked with two simple stripes.*

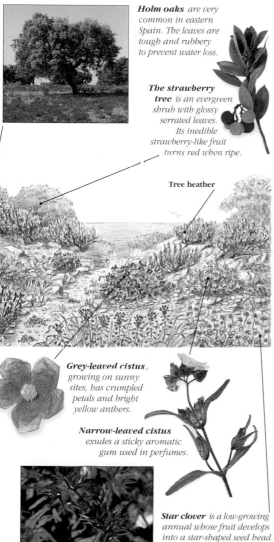

Tree heather

Scorpions *hide under rocks or wood by day. When disturbed, the tail is curled quickly over the body in a threatening gesture. The sting, lethal to small animals, can cause some irritation to humans.*

*The **Dartford warbler**, a skulking bird which has a dark plumage and a cocked tail, sings melodiously during its mating display. Males are more vividly coloured than females.*

Grey-leaved cistus, *growing on sunny sites, has crumpled petals and bright yellow anthers.*

Narrow-leaved cistus *exudes a sticky aromatic gum used in perfumes.*

*The **swallow-tail butterfly** is one of the most conspicuous of the great many insects living in the matollar. Bees, ants and grasshoppers are also extremely common.*

Star clover *is a low-growing annual whose fruit develops into a star-shaped seed head. Its flowers are often pale pink.*

Romanesque Art and Architecture

CATALONIA HAS AN EXCEPTIONAL collection of medieval buildings constructed between the 11th and 13th centuries in a distinctive local Romanesque style. There are more than 2,000 examples, most of them churches. Those in the Pyrenees, which have largely escaped both attack and modernization, have survived particularly well. Churches had lofty bell towers, barrel-vaulted naves, rounded arches and imaginative sculpture, as well as remarkable wall paintings. Some frescoes and furniture have come to rest in the Museu Nacional d'Art de Catalunya *(see p80)* in Barcelona, which has the largest Romanesque collection in the world.

Sant Jaume de Frontanyà (see p96) *is a former Augustinian canonry with typical 11th-century features, such as the Lombard bands below the roofs of the three apses. The large octagonal central lantern is, however, unusual.*

• Vielha

Pont de Suert •

• Sort

• Andorra la Vella

Puigcerdà •

• La Seu d'Urgell

Berga •

Sant Climent de Taüll, *an exemplary church in the Vall de Boí* (see p95), *was consecrated in 1123. Its frescoes, including a Christ in Majesty* (see p80), *are replicas, but the originals, which are now in Barcelona, are among the best in Catalonia.*

0 kilometres   30

0 miles   15

MONESTIR DE SANTA MARIA DE RIPOLL

The saints

The story of Solomon

The Old Testament

David and his musicians

The story of Moses

Christ with historical figures

The visions of Daniel

Plinth with patterns

The portal of the church of the former Benedictine monastery at Ripoll is known as "The Ripoll Bible" for its allegorical carvings. Although the church was founded in 879 and rebuilt under Abbot Oliva in 1032, the portal was added only in the late 12th century. In this fine piece of Romanesque decoration Christ sits above the doorway amid the beasts symbolizing the Apostles, and the monthly agricultural occupations are represented on the doorway pillars. There are seven biblical friezes running the length of the wall. The top frieze *(see p96)* over the tympanum represents the old men of the Apocalypse; the others are described in the captions above.

Sant Pere de Camprodon (see p97), *consecrated in 1169, is a monastery church in mature Romanesque style with five square apses. The slightly pointed barrel vault over the nave hints at the Gothic style to come.*

AREA OF MAJOR ROMANESQUE INTEREST

Sant Cristòfol de Beget (see p97) *is a beautiful church in a picturesque hamlet hidden deep in a valley. It has a uniquely preserved interior which includes a Romanesque baptismal font and this famous 12th-century crucifix – the* Majestat.

Sant Pere de Rodes*, situated at 600 m (1,968 ft) above sea level, was a Benedictine monastery. In its church's nave are the pillars of a Roman temple once on this site. Restoration work is in progress.*

Ripoll

Figueres

Roses

Olot

Girona

Vic

Sant Feliu de Guíxols

Sant Pere de Besalú (see p97) *is the 12th-century church of an earlier Benedictine monastery. Stone lions guard this window over the portal. Inside, the ambulatory has finely carved capitals.*

The Museu Episcopal de Vic (see p106) *adjacent to the cathedral has an exquisite collection of Romanesque art. It includes this richly coloured and moving portrayal of the Visitation which was originally an altar decoration in Lluçà monastery.*

Sant Pere de Galligants (see p98), *a former Benedictine abbey, captures the very essence of Romanesque style. It has an 11th-century portal with a rose window, three naves and an octagonal bell tower. The cloister capitals are carved with biblical scenes. It now houses Girona's archaeology museum.*

Gaudí and Modernisme

Chimney, Casa Vicens

TOWARDS THE END of the 19th century a new style of art and architecture, Modernisme, a variant of Art Nouveau, was born in Barcelona. It became a means of expression for Catalan nationalism and counted Josep Puig i Cadafalch, Lluís Domènech i Montaner and, above all, Antoni Gaudí i Cornet *(see p72)* among its major exponents. Barcelona's Eixample district *(see pp66–75)* is full of the highly original buildings that they created for their wealthy clients.

All aspects of decoration *in a Modernista building, even interior design, were planned by the architect. This door and its tiled surround are in Gaudí's 1906 Casa Batlló (see p72).*

A dramatic cupola *covers the central salon, which rises through three floors. It is pierced by small round holes, inspired by Islamic architecture, giving the illusion of stars.*

Upper galleries are richly decorated with carved wood and cofferwork.

The spiral carriage ramp *is an early sign of Gaudí's predilection for curved lines. He would later exploit this to the full in the wavy façade of his masterpiece, the Casa Milà (see p73).*

THE EVOLUTION OF MODERNISME

Detail of Sagrada Família

1859 Civil engineer Ildefons Cerdà i Sunyer submits proposals for expansion of Barcelona

1878 Gaudí graduates as an architect

1883 Gaudí takes over design of Neo-Gothic Sagrada Família *(see pp74–5)*

1888 Barcelona Universal Exhibition gives impetus to Modernisme

1900 Josep Puig i Cadafalch builds Casa Amatller *(see p72)*

1903 Lluís Domènech i Montaner builds Hospital de la Santa Creu i de Sant Pau *(see p73)*

Hospital detail

1910 Casa Milà completed

1905 Domènech i Montaner builds Casa Lleó Morera *(see p72)*. Puig i Cadafalch builds Casa Terrades *(see p73)*

1910 Casa Milà completed

1926 Gaudí dies

1850	1865	1880	1895	1910	1925

Bizarrely decorated chimneys became one of the trademarks of Gaudí's later work. They reach a fantastic extreme on the gleaming, hump-backed roof of the Casa Batlló.

Elaborate wrought iron lamps light the grand hall.

Ceramic tiles decorate the chimneys.

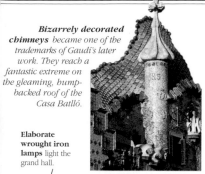

GAUDÍ'S MATERIALS

Gaudí designed, or collaborated on designs, for almost every known media. He combined bare, undecorated materials – wood, rough-hewn stone, rubble and brickwork – with meticulous craftwork in wrought iron and stained glass. Mosaics of ceramic tiles were used to cover his fluid, uneven forms.

Stained-glass window in the Sagrada Família

Mosaic of ceramic tiles, Parc Güell (see p88)

Detail of iron gate, Casa Vicens (see p48)

Tiles on El Capricho in Comillas, Cantabria

Parabolic arches, used extensively by Gaudí, beginning in the Palau Güell, show his interest in Gothic architecture. These arches form a corridor in his 1890 Col·legi de les Teresianes, a convent school in the west of Barcelona.

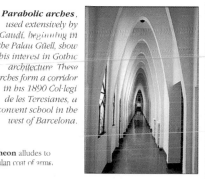

Escutcheon alludes to the Catalan coat of arms.

PALAU GÜELL

Gaudí's first major building in the centre of the city *(see p59)* established his international reputation for outstanding, original architecture. Built in 1889 for his life-long patron, the industrialist Eusebi Güell, the mansion stands on a small plot of land in a narrow street, making the façade difficult to see. Inside, Gaudí creates a sense of space by using carved screens, recesses and galleries. Furniture by him is also on view.

Organic forms inspired the wrought iron around the gates to the palace. Gaudí's later work teems with wildlife, such as this dragon, covered with brightly coloured tiles, which guards the steps in the Parc Güell.

Catalan Painting

CATALONIA HAS A FINE, if uneven, painterly tradition. It began where Spanish medieval painting was born – in the Pyrenees, where Romanesque churches were brightened by bold frescoes full of imagination (see pp20–21). The subsequent Gothic period, which represented Catalonia at the height of its powers, was followed by a long period of lesser artistic achievement until the wealth of the 19th century revived the creative spirit. This fostered some of Europe's great 20th-century painters, all of whom, as Catalans, felt a close affinity to the spirit of Catalonia's incomparable Romanesque art.

of their works can be seen at the Museu Nacional d'Art de Catalunya alongside Catalonia's only two distinguished artists of the period – Francesc Pla and Antoni Viladomat.

Procession outside Santa Maria del Mar (c.1898) by Ramon Casas

St George and the Princess (late 15th century) by Jaume Huguet

GOTHIC

ONE OF THE first-named artists in Catalonia was Ferrer Bassa (1285–1348), court painter to Jaume II. Bassa's exquisite decoration in the chapel of the Monastery of Pedralbes (see p87) constitutes the first-known example of oil-painted murals, a style undoubtedly influenced by contemporary Italian painting.

In sculpture, Catalan Gothic begins with the work of Mestre Bartomeu (1250–1300), whose extraordinary, Oriental-looking *Calvary* is in the fine Gothic collection of Girona's Museu d'Art (see p99).

There are also Gothic collections in Vic and Solsona (see p106) and particularly Barcelona, where the Museu Nacional d'Art de Catalunya (see p80) has the most impressive. Important works include those by Lluís Borrassà (1365–

1425), who painted Tarragona cathedral's altarpiece, and Lluís Dalmau (d. 1463), who visited Bruges and studied under Jan van Eyck. A feature of Catalan Gothic is *esgrafiat*, a process of gilding haloes, garments and backgrounds, which was favoured by one of the greatest Catalan Gothic artists, Jaume Huguet (1415–92). His *St George and the Princess* seems to capture the full majesty of a cultured and prosperous nation.

RENAISSANCE TO NEO-CLASSICAL

ARTISTICALLY, Catalonia languished from the 16th to the 18th century, a period dominated by great masters from elsewhere in Spain: El Greco in Toledo, Murillo and Zurbarán in Seville, Ribera in Valencia, and Velázquez and later Goya in Madrid. A few

THE 19TH CENTURY

BARCELONA'S ART school opened above La Llotja (see p60) in 1849 and new patrons of the arts appeared with wealth generated by the industrial revolution. Industry had, however, already begun to train its own artists. In 1783 a school was founded in Olot (see p97) to train designers for local textile firms. An Olot School of artists developed; its main figures were Josep Berga i Boix (1837–1914) and Joaquim Vayreda i Vila (1843–94), who also founded the Art Cristià (Christian Art) workshops which today still produce church statuary.

The greens and browns of the Olot landscape artists were countered by the pale

The Gardens at Aranjuez (1907) by Santiago Rusiñol

Waiting for Soup (1899) by Isidre Nonell

blues and pinks of the Sitges Luminists – Arcadi Mas i Fontdevila (1852–1943) and Joan Roig i Soler (1852–1909). They were influenced by Marià Fortuny, who was born in Reus in 1838 and had lived in Rome and Paris. He was commissioned by Barcelona's city council to paint a vast canvas of the Spanish victory at Tetuan, Spanish Morocco, in which 500 Catalan volunteers had taken part. It is now in the Museu d'Art Modern *(see p63)*.

In 1892, 18 years after the first Impressionist exhibition in Paris, Mas i Fontdevila staged an exhibition in Sitges bringing together the Olot School and the Luminists. It was seen as the first Modernista event and featured two other artists: Santiago Rusiñol (1861–1931) and Ramon Casas (1866–1932), the towering figures of Modernista painting. Rusiñol, the son of a textile magnate, bought a house in Sitges, Cau Ferrat *(see p110)*, which became a Modernista haunt. Casas, the first man in Barcelona to own a car, drew all the famous people of the day *(see p63)* and also painted large, powerful canvases such as *The Charge* and *Vile Garroting*. Rusiñol and Casas were founding members of Els Quatre Gats café *(see p63)*, modelled on Le Chat Noir in Paris.

The Cathedral of the Poor (1897) by Joaquim Mir

THE 20TH CENTURY

ALTHOUGH PABLO RUIZ PICASSO (1881–1973) lived in Barcelona for only eight years *(see p60)*, they were extremely formative. His early work was strongly influenced by the city and its surroundings, as can be seen in the Museu Picasso *(see p61)*, as well as by the leading Catalan artists – landscape painter Isidre Nonell (1873–1911), Joaquim Mir (1873–1940), and Rusiñol and Casas. He shared their view that Paris was essential to an artistic life and soon joined its Catalan fraternity. Despite a self-imposed exile during the Franco years, he kept in touch with Catalonia all his life.

Joan Miró (1893–1983) also attended the art school. Thrown out for poor draughtsmanship, he went on to become one of the 20th-century's most original talents, remarkable for his playful abstracts.

A sense of play was also never far from Salvador Dalí *(see p99)*, whom Miró encouraged in the way that he himself had been encouraged by Picasso. Dalí joined them in Paris, where Miró introduced him to the Surrealists. Unlike his mentors, Dalí remained in Catalonia after the Civil War, and his house in Port Lligat *(see p102)* is in many ways his finest creation.

Also to remain was Josep-Maria Sert (1876–1945). He was a more traditional painter, best remembered for vast murals in Barcelona's Casa de la Ciutat *(see p55)*, and in Rockefeller Center and the dining room of the Waldorf Astoria in New York. His startling work in Vic cathedral *(see p106)* was burnt out in the Civil War, but he was able to repaint it before he died.

Today, Catalonia's best-known living painter is Antoni Tàpies. A modest, uncompromising man, he is, like many before him, deeply rooted in his own culture. Though an abstract painter, he often uses the colours of the Catalan flag and admits to an influence of Romanesque art. Like Picasso and Miró, he has his own museum *(see p72)*. Other living Catalan artists' work can be seen at Barcelona's Museu d'Art Contemporani *(see p58)*.

Lithograph (1948) in Catalan flag colours by Antoni Tàpies

The Food of Catalonia

CATALONIA'S distinctive cuisine was first described in the *Llibre de Sent Sovè*, written in the early 14th century. It incorporates *mar i muntanya* (sea and mountain) – meats, sausages and game from inland blended with seafood and fish from the coast – leading to combinations such as chicken with lobster. Saffron, brought by the Arabs, is used in paella, and chocolate, from America, in savoury and sweet recipes. Classic dishes are based on sauces: *allioli* (garlic mayonnaise), *picada* (garlic, nuts, toasted bread, parsley, spices), *romesco* (toasted nuts, garlic, tomatoes, nyora peppers, bread), *samfaina* (onion, peppers, tomatoes, garlic, courgettes/zucchini, aubergines/eggplant), and *sofregit* (onion, garlic, tomatoes, peppers).

Nyora peppers

Amanida catalana *is a salad that combines vegetables with cured meat or cheese, or some kind of fish or seafood.*

Parsley · Squid · Tomato · Mussels · Large prawn · Monkfish

Graellada de marisc *consists of an assortment of grilled shellfish served with* allioli *(garlic mayonnaise).*

Arròs negre *(black rice) is Catalonia's most famous rice dish – a truly inspirational contribution to rice cooking. Originating on the Costa Brava, it combines rice, squid, monkfish, shellfish, onion, garlic, tomatoes, fish stock, olive oil and the all-important squid ink which gives it a wonderful fullness of taste and depth of colour.*

Avellanes *(hazelnuts) are a major Catalan crop, with tarragonins claiming that those grown in their province (Tarragona) are the best. They feature in many cakes and sweets but, most notably, in combination with almonds in the famous* romesco *and* picada *sauces.*

Suquet, *one of Catalonia's famous fish and seafood stews, is made with saffron, wine, tomatoes and potatoes.*

Canelons a la barcelonesa *are a type of cannelloni stuffed with chicken livers and pork, and adored by* barcelonins.

Paella, *traditionally cooked on an open fire with rice from the Ebre Delta, is made with seafood on the coast and game inland.*

Fideus a la cassola *is a dish of* fideus *(a kind of noodle) with red peppers, pork chops or pork fillet and sausages.*

Botifarra amb mongetes *is a traditional Catalan dish of grilled black sausage with haricot (white) beans.*

Esqueixada *is another strongly flavoured and much loved Catalan dish. It is a salad of salt cod, onion and peppers.*

Llagosta i pollastre *is a typical Catalan combination of lobster with chicken in a tomato and hazelnut sauce.*

Pollastre rostit amb samfaina *combines roast chicken with samfaina, one of the classic Catalan vegetable medleys.*

Crema catalana *is a rich egg custard with a golden brown layer of caramelized sugar on top. It is served very cold.*

Coca de Sant Joan *is a yeasty cake topped with candied fruits and pine nuts always served on St John's night* (see p31)

Pear

Apple

Cherry

Orange

Pumpkin

Fruites confitades *(candied fruits) are a popular way of preserving the abundant produce of the region and are much used as cake toppings as well as sweets.*

Ametlles garrapinyades

Torró d'Agramunt

Nut sweets*, such as* ametlles garrapinyades *(almonds coated in crunchy sugar) were introduced to Spain by the Moors.* Torró (turrón) *comes in two main varieties: one made from a soft paste of ground almonds; the other hard and studded with whole nuts such as the hazelnut torró from Agramunt in Lleida province.*

Botifarra blanca

Botifarra negra

Xoriço

Fuet

SAUSAGES

Catalan sausages, *embotits*, especially those from the inland town of Vic, are renowned. The white, cooked *botifarra* contains pork, tripe and pine nuts, while the black variety uses blood, pork belly and spices. *Bulls* (from *bullit* – boiled) consist of various meats stuffed into pigs' intestines. Among the cured sausages are the fine-textured *llonganisseta*, and the long, dry *fuet*. *Pernil* is air-cured ham from a leg of pork. *Salsitxa* is thin, raw sausage. Coarser, scarlet *xoriço* (chorizo) is spiced with paprika and can be sliced and eaten with bread, or cooked in stews.

Cava Country

Cordoníu's world-famous *cava* label

Cava is one of Catalonia's most appreciated exports. This relatively inexpensive sparkling wine is made in the same way as French champagne, undergoing a second fermentation in the bottle in which it is sold. It was made commercially from the mid-19th century and, in 1872, full-scale production was begun by Josep Raventós, head of Codorníu. This famous winery is still run by his descendants in Sant Sadurní d'Anoia, *cava* capital of the Penedès wine-producing region. Today *cava* continues to be made using local grape varieties – Macabeo, Xarel·lo and Parellada – and some pleasant pink *cava* is also produced. The literal meaning of *cava* is simply "cellar".

Codorníu, the first wine to be made using the méthode champenoise, *brought* cava *international renown as one of the great sparkling wines.*

Freixenet was established by the Sala family in 1914 and is now one of the leading cava *brands. Their estate is in Sant Sadurní d'Anoia, heart of cava country, and Freixenet's distinctive black bottle is recognized throughout the world.*

Raïmat, developed by the Raventós family using the Chardonnay grape, is considered by many to be the ultimate cava. *Wrested from wasteland, the 3,000-hectare (7,410-acre) Raïmat estate, 14 km (9 miles) west of Lleida, has its own railway station and workers' village and has been declared a "model agricultural estate" by the Spanish government.*

The Other Wines of Catalonia

Wine *(vi)* in Catalonia is *negre* (red), *rosat* (pink) or *blanc* (white). *Garnatxa* is a dessert wine named after the grape it comes from; *ranci* is a matured white wine. A tradition, now only practised at local *festes* or old-style bars, is to pour wine into the mouth from a *porró* (long-spouted wine jug). There are seven official DO *(Denominació de Origen)* regions:

Empordà-Costa Brava: light wines from the northeast. They include *vi de l'any*, drunk in the year it is produced. *Cava* is made in Peralada.
Alella: a tiny region, just north of Barcelona, with good light whites.
Penedès: great reds as well as some whites, with names such as Torres and Codorníu. Visit the wine museum in Vilafranca del Penedès *(see p107)*.
Conca de Barberà: small quantities of both reds and whites.
Costers del Segre: includes the delicious reds from the Raïmat estate.
Priorat: characterful reds and good whites (Falset) from a pretty region of small villages west of Tarragona.

A *porró* for drinking wine

Tarragona and Terra Alta: traditionally hefty wines, but getting lighter.

The Art Nouveau *winery in Sant Sadurní d'Anoia is Codorníu's Modernista showpiece, designed by Josep Puig i Cadafalch in 1906. There are 26 km (16 miles) of cellars on five floors and visitors are taken round on a small train.*

SPAIN

Madrid

Gold medals were awarded to Codorníu for its *cava* as early as 1888. By 1897 it was being served at state functions instead of champagne.

KEY

☐ Main *cava* districts

0 kilometres   20

0 miles   20

Manresa

DÈS

Igualada

Terrassa

Sabadell

Masquefa ⑥

BARCELONA

② ①
③ Sant Sadurní
d'Anoia

Montblanc ④

Valls   Vilafranca del Penedès

El Vendrell   Castelldefels

Vilanova
i la Geltrú

Tarragona

BEST PRODUCERS

Codorníu
  Sant Sadurní d'Anoia ①
Freixenet
  Sant Sadurní d'Anoia ②
Gramona
  Sant Sadurní d'Anoia ③
Mascaró
  Vilafranca del Penedès ④
Raïmat
  Costers del Segre ⑤
Raventós Rosell
  Masquefa ⑥

CAVA TIPS

What to buy
As with champagne, the drier the wine, the higher the price. The driest *cavas* are *brut de brut* and *brut nature*. *Brut* and *sec* are slightly less dry. Sweet *semiseco* and *dulce* are best with desserts. Although inexpensive compared with the French equivalent, costs do vary, with small, specialist producers commanding high prices.

Visiting a winery
The main *cava* producers are open to the public during office hours (but many close in August). Sant Sadurní d'Anoia is 45 minutes by train from Barcelona's Sants station and the most impressive cellars to visit here are Freixenet's and Codorníu's. Vilafranca del Penedès tourist office (*see p107*) has details of all *cava* winery visits.

A rewarding tour *can be had by visiting the Freixenet cellars. The company sells more bottles of cava each year than the French sell champagne.*

CATALONIA THROUGH THE YEAR

EACH *barri* (district) in Barcelona and every town and village in Catalonia has a saint's day to be celebrated in an annual *festa major.* The *sardana (see p111)* is danced and, on the Costa Brava, *havaneres* (habaneras) are sung. Food is central to any event, and open-air feasts and special pastries and cakes feature strongly. Many towns, including Barcelona, have

Men give women a red rose on Sant Jordi's Day

parades of giants *(gegants)*, bigheads *(capgrosses)* and dwarfs *(nans)* – papier-mâché caricatures of people once linked with local trade guilds. Demons and dragons provide drama. Catalans love pyrotechnics, and the fires at the midsummer *Revetlla de Sant Joan* are a lavish incendiary event. Many celebrations often start on the eve of the feast day proper.

Book stalls set up in Barcelona on Sant Jordi's Day, *el dia del llibre*

SPRING

ALMOND BLOSSOM gives way to cherry and apple as the earth warms and the melting snows swell the rivers. The fishing season for trout and other freshwater fish starts in late March. At Easter, families get together, often going out of town to visit relatives, or to picnic and search for wild asparagus. May is the best month in which to see wild flowers, which are particularly spectacular in the Pyrenees.

MARCH

Sant Medir *(3 Mar)*. In Barcelona processions distribute sweets in the district of Gràcia, and in Sants a week later.
Sant Josep *(19 Mar)*. Many Catalans are called Josep (often shortened to Pepe), and this is a local holiday. People celebrate their "name day" – the day of the saint they are named after – more than they celebrate their birthday.

Terrassa Jazz Festival *(whole of Mar)*. Concerts by musicians from all over the world. Free outdoor concerts at weekends.

APRIL

Setmana Santa (Holy Week) is the week before Easter and is filled with events.
Diumenge de Rams (Palm Sunday). Palm leaves are blessed in church, notably at the Sagrada Família in Barcelona. Processions of Roman soldiers turn out in Girona, and *via crucis* (passion plays) are put on in several places, notably the spa town of Sant Hilari Sacalm, Girona province.
Dijous Sant (Maundy Thursday), Verges, Girona province. Men dressed as skeletons perform a death dance *(dansa de la mort)* thought to date back to times of plague in the 1300s.
Pasqua (Easter). On Good Friday *(Divendres Sant)* crucifixes are carried through the streets following the Stations of the Cross. On Easter Monday

(Dilluns de Pasqua) godparents buy their godchildren *mona* (egg cake), and bakers compete to make the most elaborate confections.
Sant Jordi *(23 Apr)*. Feast of St George, patron saint of Catalonia, and a day devoted to the memory of Cervantes *(see p39)*, who died on this day in 1616. Men and boys give single red roses to their mothers, wives and girlfriends, who give them books in return. The festival is also known as *el dia del llibre* (book day).

MAY

Fira de Sant Ponç *(11 May)*. Ancient celebration around the Carrer de l'Hospital in Barcelona, once the site of the city hospital. Aromatic and medicinal herbs and honey are sold.
Corpus Christi *(May/Jun)*. Flowers are laid in the streets of Sitges, and in Berga, Barcelona province, a monster dragon (la Patum) dances through the town's streets.

The feast of Corpus Christi, when carpets of flowers cover the streets

AVERAGE DAILY HOURS OF SUNSHINE

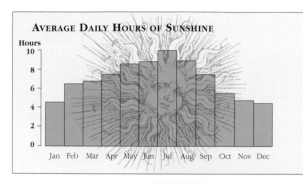

Sunshine Chart
Barcelona is a sunny city, enjoying clear blue skies for a large part of the year and often up to ten hours' sunshine a day in summer. In winter, even though it can be cold in the shade, the sun is high enough to give it warming power and it can be pleasant to sit outdoors on a sheltered, sunny terrace or patio.

SUMMER

THE MAJORITY OF Barcelona's inhabitants live in apartments, so they like to head out of town at weekends, either to the coast or the mountains. Consequently, motorways (highways) on Friday afternoons and Sunday evenings are best avoided. School holidays are long, starting in early June when the sea is warm enough for swimming. Crowds throng the marinas, the aroma of barbecued mussels fills the air, and a plethora of summer entertainment provides limitless options. Many businesses in Barcelona close in August.

Holidaymakers at Platja d'Aro, a popular Costa Brava resort

JUNE

Festival del Grec *(Jun–Jul)*. In this summer arts festival, there are national and international performances throughout Barcelona; the main venues are the Teatre Grec, Mercat de les Flors and Poble Espanyol.
Revetlla de Sant Joan *(24 Jun)*. St John's (Midsummer's) Eve is celebrated with fireworks, especially on Montjuïc in Barcelona. Bonfires are lit throughout Catalonia and lighted torches are brought down from the top of Mont Canigó, just over the border in France. *Cava* – a sparkling white wine *(see pp28–9)* – is drunk with a special *coca* (cake) sprinkled with pine nuts and crystallized fruit *(see p27)*.
Castellers *(24 Jun)*. In Valls, Tarragona, a province famous for its *casteller* festivals, teams of men stand on each other's shoulders hoping to take the prize for building the highest human tower *(see p107)*.

Concert season *(Jun/Jul)*. Classical music concerts, held at different parks in Barcelona, are organized by the Institut Municipal de Parcs i Jardins.

JULY

Cantada d'havaneres *(first Sun in Jul)*. Drinking *cremat* (coffee and rum), musicians and singers belt out *havaneres* in towns along the coast, most famously at Calella de Palafrugell on the Costa Brava.

A team of *castellers* in action

Virgen del Carmen *(16 Jul)*. A maritime festival that takes place around Barcelona's port. As well as processions, there are bands playing *havaneres*.
Santa Cristina *(24 Jul)*. The biggest festival of Lloret de Mar, Costa Brava, when a statue of the Virgin is brought ashore by a decorated flotilla.

AUGUST

Festa major de Gràcia *(one week beginning around 15 Aug)*. Each district of Barcelona hosts its own *festa* in which streets try to outdo each other in the inventiveness of their decorations. The *festa* in the old district of Gràcia is the biggest and most spectacular and incorporates concerts, balls, music, competitions and street games.
Festa major de Sants *(around 24 Aug)*. The big annual *festa* in the Sants district of Barcelona.
Festa major de Vilafranca del Penedès *(mid-Aug)*. This town's annual festival is one of the best places to see *casteller* (human tower) competitions *(see p107)*.

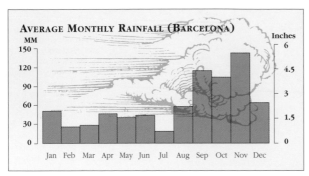

AVERAGE MONTHLY RAINFALL (BARCELONA)

MM

150
120
90
60
30
0

Inches

6
4.5
3
1.5
0

Jan Feb Mar Apr May Jun Jul Aug Sep Oct Nov Dec

Rainfall Chart
Barcelona experiences modest rainfall year round – just sufficient to maintain the city's green spaces. However, rain tends to fall in sudden, but short-lived, torrential downpours and heavy thunder storms are a feature of the summer months. Grey, drizzly weather lasting for days on end is very rare.

AUTUMN

T HE GRAPE HARVEST (*verema*) is a highlight of the autumn, just before the vines turn red and gold. It is the season for seeking out mushrooms which swell the market stalls. From October hunters set off to bag red-legged partridge, migrating ducks and wild boar. Hardier people can be seen swimming in the sea right up until November.

SEPTEMBER

Diada de Catalunya *(11 Sep).* Catalonia's national day marks Barcelona's fall to Felipe V in 1714 *(see p41)* when the region lost its autonomy. Political demonstrations convey strong separatist sentiment. *Sardana (see p111)* bands and people singing *Els segadors (see p40)* can be heard and Catalan flags are everywhere.
La Mercè *(24 Sep).* This annual festival in Barcelona honours *Nostra Senyora de la Mercè* (Our Lady of Mercy) in a week of concerts, masses and dances. Look out for the

Cattle descending from the Pyrenees at the end of the summer

carrefoc – a parade of fire-breathing dragons, giants and monsters; and the *piro musical* – fireworks set to music.
Sant Miquel *(29 Sep).* Celebrations for Barceloneta's patron saint recall Napoleon's occupation of Spain *(see p41).* Bum Bum, a Napoleonic general, parades through the streets to salvoes of gunfire. There is dancing on the beach.

OCTOBER

Festes de Sarrià i de Les Corts *(first Sun in Oct).* Each of these Barcelona districts has a festival for its patron saint.
Dia de la Hispanitat *(12 Oct)* National holiday to mark the discovery of America in 1492 *(see p40),* but most Catalans do not celebrate this anniversary.

NOVEMBER

Tots Sants (All Saints' Day) *(1 Nov).* Roast chestnuts and sweet potatoes are eaten and the next day – *Dia dels difunts* (All Souls' Day) – people visit the graves of their relatives.

Harvesting grapes in autumn with high hopes for a successful crop

PUBLIC HOLIDAYS

Any Nou *(New Year's Day)* 1 Jan
Reis Mags *(Epiphany)* 6 Jan
Sant Josep 19 Mar
Divendres Sant *(Good Friday)* Mar/Apr
Dilluns de Pasqua *(Easter Monday)* Mar/Apr
Festa del Treball *(Labour Day)* 1 May
Sant Joan *(Saint John's Day)* 24 Jun
Assumpció *(Assumption Day)* 15 Aug
Diada de Catalunya *(National Day)* 11 Sep
La Mercè 24 Sep
Dia de la Hispanitat *(Day of the Spanish-speaking nations)* 12 Oct
Tots Sants *(All Saints' Day)* 1 Nov
Dia de la Constitució *(Constitution Day)* 6 Dec
Immaculada Concepció *(Immaculate Conception)* 8 Dec
Nadal *(Christmas)* 25 Dec
Sant Esteve 26 Dec

AVERAGE DAILY TEMPERATURE (BARCELONA)

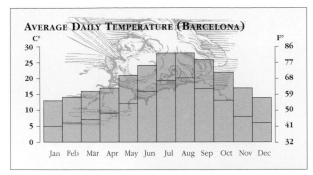

Temperature Chart
This chart shows the average minimum and maximum daily temperatures recorded in Barcelona. The sunshine in winter can be deceptive, as daytime temperatures can occasionally dip to near freezing. Summer days are consistently hot. Hats and a high-factor sun screen are essential.

WINTER

S KI RESORTS in the Pyrenees are a popular destination at weekends. Though days can be sunny and lunches still taken alfresco, the weather is unpredictable and the nights can be chilly. Christmas is a particularly delightful time to be in Barcelona, when the city vibrates with the spirit of celebration and sharing. Crafts and decorations are on sale in the Feria de Santa Llúcia in front of the Cathedral.

A ski resort in the Pyrenees, a popular destination for weekenders

DECEMBER

Nadal and **Sant Esteve** *(25 & 26 Dec)*. Christmas is a time for people to come together. Traditional Christmas lunch consists of an *escudella* (meat stew) followed by turkey stuffed with apples, apricots, prunes, pine nuts and raisins.
Revellón *(31 Dec)*. All over Spain on New Year's Eve it has become a custom for people to eat a grape between

each chime of the midnight bell. To manage the feat brings good luck all year.

JANUARY

Reis Mags *(6 Jan)*. On the eve of the Epiphany the three kings arrive in various guises throughout Catalonia giving sweets to children. The main cavalcade in Barcelona is down by the port.
Santa Eulàlia *(12 Jan)*. The feast of the ancient patron saint of Barcelona is celebrated in the old town. There is

dancing and many people dress up as giants.
Els Tres Tombs *(17 Jan)*. Horsemen in top hats and tails ride three times through the city to honour St Anthony, patron saint of animals.
Pelegrí de Tossa *(20 & 21 Jan)*, Tossa de Mar. A 40-km (25-mile) pilgrimage marking the end of the plague; this town's biggest annual event.

FEBRUARY

Carnestoltes (Carnival) *(Feb/ Mar)*. King Carnival presides over the pre-Lent celebrations, children wear fancy dress and every *barri* (district) in Barcelona puts on a party. Sausage omelettes are eaten on Shrove Tuesday *(Dijous gras)*, and on Ash Wednesday *(Dimecres de cendra)* a sardine is ceremoniously buried *(Enterrament de la sardina)*. There are big celebrations in Platja d'Aro on the Costa Brava and Vilanova on the Costa Daurada. Sitges is the place to go to see the full transvestite indulgence of the feast.
Rally Internacional de Cotxes d'Època *(first Sun in Lent)*. Veteran car rally that runs from Barcelona to Sitges.

The winter festival of Els Tres Tombs in Vilanova i la Geltrú

Procession of *gegants* (giants) during the September festival of La Mercè in Barcelona ▷

THE HISTORY OF CATALONIA

The Catalans have always been great seafarers, merchants and industrialists. Since they were united under the House of Barcelona, their nationhood has been threatened by marriages, alliances and conflicts with Madrid, and the road to their present status as a semi-autonomous region within Spain has been marked by times of power and wealth and troughs of weakness and despair.

Barcelona was not a natural site for human settlement. Its port was negligible and its heights, Montjuïc, had no water. The oldest evidence of man in Catalonia comes rather from other sites scattered across the region, notably the dolmens of the Alt (high) Empordà and passage graves of the Baix (low) Empordà and Alt Urgell.

In the first millennium BC the lands around Barcelona were settled by the agrarian Laeitani, while other parts of Catalonia were

Roman mosaic floor excavated in Barcelona depicting the Three Graces

simultaneously colonized by the Iberians. The latter were great builders in stone and remains of one of their settlements are still visible at Ullastret on the Costa Brava. Greek traders arrived on the coast around 550 BC, founding their first trading post at Empúries (*Emporion, see p102*) near Ullastret. It was the Carthaginians from New Carthage in southern Spain who put Barcelona on the map. They named the city after Hamil Barca, father of Hannibal who led his army of elephants from Catalonia over the Pyrenees and Alps to attack Rome.

In reprisal, the Romans arrived at Empúries and began the subjugation of the whole Iberian peninsula. They wiped out the Carthaginians as well as the Laeitani and established Tarraco (Tarragona, *see p110*) in the south of Catalonia as the imperial capital of Tarraconensis, one of the three administrative regions of the peninsula.

Roman Barcelona can be seen in the city gate beside the cathedral, while the 3rd-century walls that once encircled the town lie by the medieval Royal Palace (*see p54*). Foundations of the Roman city have been excavated in the basement of the Museu d'Història de la Ciutat (*see p55*), and pillars from the Temple of Augustus can be glimpsed inside the Centre Excursionista de Catalunya (*see p53*) behind the cathedral.

When the Roman empire collapsed, Visigoths based in Toulouse moved in to fill the vacuum. They had been vassals of Rome, practised Roman law, spoke a similar language and in 587 their Aryan king, Reccared, converted to the Christianity of Rome.

TIMELINE

2500 BC	1500 BC	500 BC	AD 500

500–200 BC Fortified Iberian settlements at Ullastret. Cyclopean walls of Tarragona

550 BC Greeks establish trading settlement at Empúries

1000–500 BC Indo-Europeans invade Ter and Llobregat valleys; Iberians settle Montjuïc

Visigothic Cross

2000–1500 BC Megalithic monuments built throughout Catalonia

Hannibal

230 BC Barcelona founded by Hamil Barca, father of Hannibal

218 BC Romans arrive at Empúries to subjugate Spain

AD 531 Visigoths established in Barcelona after fall of Rome

AD 258 Barcelona city walls built after a Frankish invasion

◁ **Troops fraternizing with local militia in the Baixada de la Llibreteria, Barcelona, during the 1833–9 Carlist War**

THE MOORS AND CHARLEMAGNE

The Visigoths established their capital at Toledo, just south of modern Madrid. When King Wirtzia died in 710, his son, Akhila, is said to have called on the Saracens from north Africa for help in claiming the throne. In 711, with astonishing speed, Muslim and Berber tribes began to drive up through the Iberian peninsula, reaching Barcelona in 717, then Poitiers in France in 732, where they were finally stopped by the Frankish leader, Charles Martel.

Page from a 15th-century manuscript of the *Llibre del Consolat de Mar*

The Muslims made their capital in Córdoba in southern Spain, while the Visigothic nobles found hiding places in the Pyrenees, from which they conducted sorties against the invaders. They were aided by Charles Martel's grandson, Charles the Great (Charlemagne). In 801 Barcelona was retaken by the Franks, only to be lost and taken again. The shortness of the Muslim occupation left Catalonia, unlike the rest of Spain, unmarked by the culture and language of Islam.

Ramon Berenguer I of Barcelona (1035–76)

THE COUNTS OF BARCELONA

Charlemagne created the Hispanic Marc, a buffer state along the Pyrenees, which he entrusted to local lords. The most powerful figure in the east was Guifré el Pelós (Wilfred the Hairy), who consolidated the counties of Barcelona, Cerdanya, Conflent, Osona Urgell and Girona and founded the monastery of Ripoll *(see p96)* – *el bressol de Catalunya* (the cradle of Catalonia). Guifré died in battle against the Moors in 897, but he had started a dynasty of Counts of Barcelona which was to last, unbroken, for 500 years.

Before the end of the 11th century, under Ramon Berenguer I, Catalonia had established the first constitutional government in Europe with a bill of rights, the *Usatges*. By the early 12th century, under Ramon Berenguer III, Catalonia's boundaries had pushed south past Tarragona. Catalan influence also spread north and east when he married Dolça of Provence, linking the two regions and, more lastingly, the principality of Barcelona was united with its neighbour Aragon in 1137 by the marriage of Ramon Berenguer IV and Petronila of Aragon. In 1196 the great monastery of Poblet *(see pp108–9)* in Tarragona province took the place of Ripoll as the pantheon of Catalan royalty.

TIMELINE

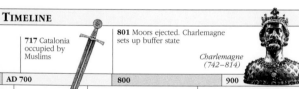

717 Catalonia occupied by Muslims

801 Moors ejected. Charlemagne sets up buffer state

Charlemagne (742–814)

1060 Constitution, *Usatges*, is drawn up around the time that the word Catalan is first recorded

AD 700	800	900	1000

711 North African Muslims invade Spanish mainland

Moorish sword

778 Charlemagne, leader of the Franks, begins campaign to drive Moors from Spain

878 Guifré el Pelós (Wilfred the Hairy), Count of Cerdanya-Urgell, consolidates eastern Pyrenees and gains virtual autonomy. He starts 500-year dynasty of Counts of Barcelona

1008–46 Abbot Oliva builds church at Ripoll and oversees Benedictine building including Vic and Monserrat

MARITIME EXPANSION

Under Jaume I the Conqueror (1213–76), Catalonia began a period of prosperity and expansion. By the end of the 13th century the Balearic islands and Sicily had been conquered; many of the ships used in the enterprise were built at the vast Drassanes shipyards in Barcelona *(see p65)*. Catalonia now ruled the seas and the *Llibre del Consolat de Mar* was a code of trading practice that held sway throughout the Mediterranean. Swashbuckling admirals included Roger de Llúria, who won a definitive victory over the French fleet in the Bay of Roses in 1285, and Roger de Flor, leader of a bunch of fierce Catalan and Aragonese mercenaries, the Almogàvers. These won battles for both the King of Sicily and the Byzantine emperor before Roger de Flor was murdered in 1305.

During Jaume I's long reign the *Corts* (parliament) was established, the city walls were rebuilt to enclose an area ten times larger than that enclosed by the old Roman walls, and noble houses arose down the new Carrer Montcada

(see pp 60–61). La Llotja (the stock exchange) was sited by what was then the main port, and the church of Santa Maria del Mar *(see p60)* was built by grateful merchants. Under Pere IV (1336–87) two great halls were built: the Royal Palace's Saló del Tinell and the Casa de la Ciutat's Saló de Cent *(see pp 54–5).*

Ex voto in the form of a 15th-century ship

Prosperity brought a flowering of Catalan literature. Jaume I wrote his own *Llibre dels Feits (Book of Deeds)*, and Pere el Gran's conquest of Sicily in 1282 was described in glowing terms in a chronicle of Catalan history written by Bernat Desclot around 1285. The great Catalan poet Ramon Lull (1232–1315), born in Mallorca, was the first to use a vernacular language in religious writing. From 1395 an annual poetry competition, the Jocs Florals, was held in the city, attracting the region's troubadours. In 1450, Joanot Martorell began writing his Catalan chivalric epic narrative *Tirant lo Blanc*, though he died in 1468, 22 years before it was published. Miguel de Cervantes, author of *Don Quijote*, described it as simply "the best book in the world".

Wall painting showing Jaume I during his campaign to conquer Mallorca

1137 Barcelona united to neighbouring Aragon by royal marriage

1258–72 *Consolat de Mar*, a code of trading practice, holds sway throughout the Mediterranean

1282 Pere el Gran takes Sicily. His exploits are recorded in Desclot's *Chronicles*

1347–8 Black death kills a quarter of the population

1359 Generalitat founded

1423 Conquest of Naples

1100   **1200**   **1300**   **1400**

1148 Frontier with Moors pushed back to Riu Ebre

1213–35 Jaume I (The Conqueror) takes Mallorca, Ibiza and Formentera

Jaume I (1213–76)

1324 Sardinia captured

1302–5 Catalan mercenaries under Admiral Roger de Flor aid Byzantium against the Turks

1287 Conquest of Mallorca under Alfons III

FERNANDO AND ISABEL OF CASTILE

Catholic Spain was united in 1479 when Fernando II of Catalonia-Aragon married Isabel of Castile, a region which by then had absorbed the rest of northern Spain. In 1492 they drove the last of the Moors from the peninsula, then, in a fever of righteousness, also drove out the Jews, who

Baptizing Jews during the era of the Catholic Monarchs

had large and commercially important populations in Barcelona *(see p54)* and Girona. This was the same year that Columbus had set foot in America, returning in triumph to Barcelona with six Carib Indians *(see p56)*. However, the city lost out when the monopoly on New World trade was given to Seville and Cádiz. Though it still had great moments, such as its involvement in the victory over the Turks at Lepanto in 1571 *(see p65)*, Barcelona went into a period of decline.

REVOLTS AND SIEGES

During the Thirty Years War with France (1618–59), Felipe IV forced Barcelona's *Corts* to raise an army to fight the French, towards whom the Catalans bore no grudge. A viceroy was imposed on the city and unruly Spanish troops were billeted throughout the region. In June 1640 the population arose, and harvesters *(segadors)* murdered the viceroy. The *Song of the Harvesters* is still sung at Catalan gatherings *(see p32)*. Barcelona then allied itself with France, but was besieged and defeated by Felipe. The peace of 1659 ceded Catalan lands north of the Pyrenees to France.

Wall tile for a Catalan trade guild

A second confrontation with Madrid arose during the War of the Spanish Succession when Europe's two dominant royal houses, the Habsburgs and Bourbons, both laid claim to the throne. Barcelona, with England as an ally, found itself on the losing side, supporting the Habsburgs. As a result, it was heavily

The great siege of Barcelona in 1714 during the War of the Spanish Succession

TIMELINE

1492 Columbus discovers Americas. Barcelona barred from trade with the New World. Jews expelled	**1494** Supreme Council of Aragon brings Catalonia under Castilian control	*The Spanish Inquisition, active from 1478*	**1619** Spanish capital established in Madrid	**1659** Treaty of the Pyrenees at end of Thirty Years War draws new border with France; Roussillon ceded to France	
AD 1450	**AD 1500**	**AD 1550**	**AD 1600**		**AD 1650**
1479 Fernando II of Catalonia-Aragon marries Isabel of Castile, uniting all the houses of Spain	**1490** *Tirant lo Blanc*, epic tale of chivalry by Martorell *(see p39)*, published in Catalan		**1571** Vast fleet sets sail from Barcelona to defeat the Ottomans at sea at Lepanto	**1640** Revolt of the harvesters *(segadors)* against Spanish exploitation of Catalan resources during Thirty Years War with France	

Women joining in the defence of Girona against the Napoleonic French in 1809

besieged by troops of the incoming Bourbon king, Felipe V. The city fell on 11 September 1714, today celebrated as National Day *(see p32)*. Felipe then proceeded to annul all of Catalonia's privileges. Its language was banned, its universities closed and Lleida's Gothic cathedral became a barracks. Felipe tore down the Ribera district of Barcelona and, in what is now Ciutadella Park *(see p62)*, built a citadel to keep an eye on the population.

With the lifting of trade restrictions with the Americas, Catalonia began to recover economically. Progress, however, was interrupted by the 1793–95 war with France and then by the 1808–14 Peninsular War (known in Spain as the War of Independence) when Napoleon put his brother Joseph on the Spanish throne. Barcelona fell in early 1808, but Girona withstood a seven-month siege. Monasteries, including Montserrat

(see pp104–5) were sacked and pillaged. They suffered further in 1835 under a republican government when many were seen as too rich and powerful and were dissolved. This was a politically vigorous time, when a minority of largely rural reactionaries fought a rearguard action against the liberal spirit of the century in the Carlist Wars.

THE CATALAN RENAIXENÇA

Barcelona was the first city in Spain to industrialize, mainly around cotton manufacture, from imported raw material from the Americas. It brought immigrant workers and a burgeoning population, and in 1854 the city burst out of its medieval walls *(see p67)*. Inland, industrial centres such as Terrassa and Sabadell flourished and *colònies industrials* (industrial workhouses) grew up along the rivers where mills were powered by water.

Just as the wealth of the 14th century inspired Catalonia's first flowering, so the wealth from industry inspired the *Renaixença*, a renaissance of Catalan culture. Its literary rallying points were Bonaventura Aribau's *Oda a la patria* and the poems of a young monk, Jacint Verdaguer, who won poetry prizes in the revived Jocs Florals *(see p39)*.

Well-to-do *barcelonins* selecting from a wide range of locally produced calico in the early 19th century

AD 1700	AD 1750	AD 1800	AD 1850

Felipe V (1700–24)

1714 Barcelona sacked by Felipe V, first Bourbon king. Catalan universities closed. Catalan language banned

1778 Catalonia allowed to trade with the Americas, bringing new wealth

1808–14 Peninsular War (War of Independence): Girona besieged, Barcelona occupied, Monastery of Montserrat sacked

1823–6 French occupy Catalonia

1833–9 First Carlist War

1835 Monasteries dissolved

1859 Revival of Jocs Florals poetry competition feeds Renaissance of Catalan culture.

1849 Spain's first railway built to link Barcelona and Mataró

1833 Aribau's *Oda a la patria* published

Poet Bonaventura Carles Aribau i Farriols

A hall of Spanish goods at the 1888 Universal Exhibition

CATALANISM AND MODERNISME

The *Renaixença* produced a new pride in Catalonia, and "Catalanism" was at the heart of the region's accelerating move towards autonomy, a move echoed in Galicia and the Basque Country. Interruptions by the Carlist Wars came to an end in 1876 and resulted in the restoration of the Bourbon monarchy.

The first home-rule party, the *Lliga de Catalunya*, was founded in 1887, and disputes with the central government continued. It was blamed for the loss of the American colonies, and therefore lucrative transatlantic trade, and for involving Spain in unnecessary conflict in Morocco. *La setmana tràgica* (tragic week) of 1909 saw the worst of the violent protests: 116 people died and 300 were injured.

Meanwhile, on a more cultural and artistic level and to show off its increasing wealth, Barcelona held in 1888 a

Universal Exhibition in the Parc de la Ciutadella where Felipe V's citadel had recently been torn down. The urban expansion *(eixample)* inland was carefully ordered under a plan by Ildefons Cerdà *(see p67)* and industrial barons employed imaginative architects to show off their wealth, most successfully Eusebi Güell and Antoni Gaudí *(see pp22–3)*. The destruction of the monasteries had left spaces for sumptuous buildings such as the Palau de la Música Catalana *(see p61)*, the Liceu opera house and La Boqueria market *(see p135)*.

Spain's non-involvement in World War I meant that Catalonia's Modernista architecture was unscathed. Barcelona's place as a showcase city was confirmed with the 1929 International

Antoni Gaudí, Modernisme's most creative architect

Exhibition on Montjuïc, many of whose buildings still remain.

CIVIL WAR

The *Mancomunitat*, a local council established in 1914, disappeared on the arrival in 1923 of the dictator Primo de Rivera, Barcelona's military governor. In 1931 Francesc Macià declared himself President of the Catalan Republic, which lasted three days. Three years later Lluís Companys was arrested and sentenced to 30 years' imprisonment for attempting to do the same.

Poster for 1929 Exhibition

TIMELINE

1872–6 Third and last Carlist War

1888 Universal Exhibition held in Parc de la Ciutadella, showing off the new Modernista style

Primo de Rivera (1870–1930)

1909 *Setmana tràgica*: violent protest against Moroccan Wars

AD 1875	AD 1900	AD 1925

Carlist soldiers

1893 Anarchist bombs in Liceu opera house kill 14

1901 *Lliga Regionalista*, new Catalan party, wins elections

1929 International Exhibition on Montjuïc

1931 Francesc Macià declares independence for Catalonia

Refugees on the march in 1939, fleeing towards the Pyrenees to seek asylum in France

Finally, on 16 July 1936, General Francisco Franco led an army revolt against the Republican government and the fledgling autonomous states. The government fled Madrid to Valencia, then Barcelona. City and coast were bombed by German aircraft, and shelled by Italian warships. When Barcelona fell three years later, thousands escaped to camps in France and thousands, including Companys, were executed in Franco's reprisals. Catalonia lost all it had gained, and its language was outlawed once more.

The *noche negra*, the dark night that followed Franco's victory, left Barcelona short of resources and largely neglected by Madrid. The 1960s, however, brought new economic opportunities, and between 1960 and 1975 two million Spaniards came to work in the city. The arrival of the first tourists to the coast during that time, to the Costa Brava and Costa Daurada, changed the face of Spain for ever.

LIFE AFTER FRANCO

Champagne flowed freely in Barcelona's streets on the news of Franco's death in 1975. Democracy and the monarchy, under the Bourbon Juan Carlos, were restored and Jordi Pujol of the conservative *Convergència i Unió* party was elected leader of the Generalitat, Catalonia's regional government. Catalonia has since won a large degree of autonomy, including tax-raising powers.

Barcelona's socialist mayor Pasqual Maragall, a town planner, steered through the radical shake-up of the city for the 1992 Olympic Games. In less than a decade, in what seems like a second *Renaixença*, Barcelona changed dramatically, with a bold new waterfront, inspired urban spaces, new access roads, and state-of-the-art museums and galleries.

Opening ceremony, 1992 Barcelona Olympic Games

1939 50,000 go into exile in France. Catalan President Companys executed		**1975** Franco dies. King Juan Carlos restores Bourbon line	
1947 Spain declared a monarchy with Franco as regent		**1979** Partial autonomy granted to Catalonia	**1992** Olympic Games held in Barcelona
AD 1950		**AD 1975**	**AD 2000**
1953 US bases welcomed	**1960s** Costa Brava leads package holiday boom	**1985** Medes Islands become Spain's first marine nature reserve	
1936–9 Spanish Civil War. Republican government retreats from Madrid to Valencia, then Barcelona		**1986** Spain enters European Union	

Cobi, the Olympic mascot

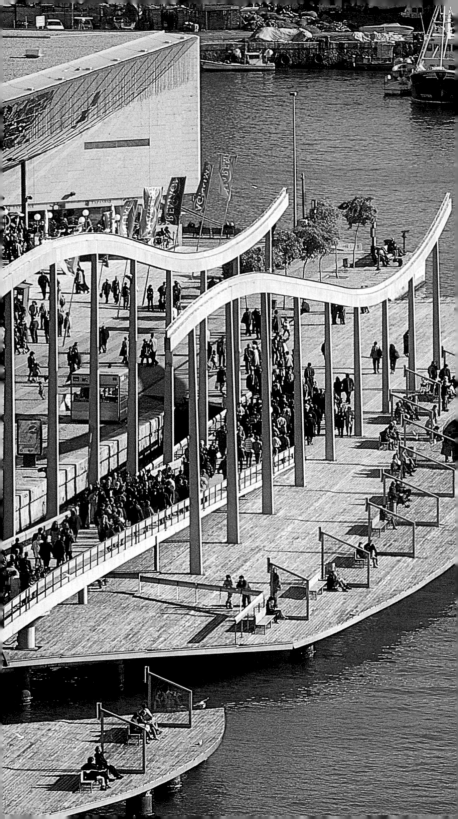

BARCELONA
AND CATALONIA

BARCELONA AT A GLANCE 46-49

OLD TOWN 50-65

EIXAMPLE 66-75

MONTJUÏC 76-83

FURTHER AFIELD 84-89

CATALONIA 90-111

Introducing Barcelona

Barcelona, one of the Mediterranean's busiest ports, is more than the capital of Catalonia. In culture, commerce and sports it not only rivals Madrid, but also considers itself on a par with the greatest European cities. The success of the 1992 Olympic Games, staged in the Parc de Montjuïc, confirmed this to the world. Although there are plenty of historical monuments in the Ciutat Vella (Old Town), Barcelona is best known for the scores of buildings in the Eixample left by the artistic explosion of Modernisme *(see pp22–3)* in the decades around 1900. Always open to outside influences because of its location on the coast, not too far from the French border, Barcelona continues to sizzle with creativity: its bars and the public parks speak more of bold contemporary design than of tradition.

Casa Milà (see p73) is the most avant-garde of all the works of Antoni Gaudí (see p72). Barcelona has more Art Nouveau buildings than any other city in the world.

Palau Nacional (see p80), on the hill of Montjuïc, dominates the monumental halls and the fountain-filled avenue built for the 1929 International Exhibition. It now houses the Museu Nacional d'Art de Catalunya, an exceptional collection of medieval art, rich in Romanesque frescoes.

MONTJUIC
(see pp76–83)

Montjuïc Castle (see p81) is a massive fortification dating from the 17th century. Sited on the crest of the hill of Montjuïc, it offers panoramic views of the city and port, and forms a sharp contrast to the ultra-modern sports halls built nearby for the 1992 Olympic Games.

Christopher Columbus surveys the waterfront from the top of a 60-m (200-ft) column (see p65) in the heart of the Port Vell (Old Port). From the top, visitors can look out over the new promenades and quays that have revitalized the area.

| 0 kilometres | 1 |
| 0 miles | 0.5 |

The Sagrada Família (see pp74–5), *Gaudí's unfinished masterpiece, begun in 1882, rises above the streets of the Eixample. Its polychrome ceramic mosaics and sculptural forms inspired by nature are typical of his work.*

EIXAMPLE
(see pp66–75)

Barcelona cathedral (see pp56–7) *is a magnificent 14th-century building in the heart of the Barri Gòtic (Gothic Quarter). It has 28 side chapels which encircle the nave and contain some splendid Baroque altarpieces. The keeping of white geese in the cloisters is a centuries-old tradition.*

OLD TOWN
(see pp50–65)

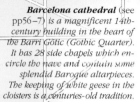

Parc de la Ciutadella (see p62), *between the Old Town and the Vila Olímpica, has something for everyone. The gardens full of statuary offer relaxation, the boating lake and the zoo are fun, while the three museums within its gates cover art, geology and zoology.*

La Rambla (see pp58–9) *is the most famous street in Spain, alive at all hours of the day and night. A stroll down its length to the seafront, taking in its palatial buildings, shops, cafés and street vendors, makes a perfect introduction to Barcelona life.*

La Ruta del Modernisme

THE 50 EXAMPLES of Modernista architecture in Barcelona, mapped here, lie along a route designed by the city's tourist office. A *Multi-ticket*, available from Casa Amatller *(see p72)*, allows you to plan your own itinerary as time allows and is the best way to see them. The Casa Lleó Morera, Palau Güell and Palau de la Música Catalana all have guided tours, and there is free entry to the selected museums. Many of the other premises are shops, cafés and hotels in private hands, and often, tantalizingly, the interiors are not open to the public. The best-known sites are described in detail elsewhere in this book.

Casa Vicens

This bright, angular, turreted building by Antoni Gaudí, with ceramic mosaics and patterned brickwork, shows Moorish influence. The iron gate and fencing are hallmarks of his work ㊽

Palau Baró de Quadras

Built in 1906, this handsome house is by Josep Puig i Cadafalch. The intricate, sculptured frieze above the first floor windows has close affinities to Spanish early Renaissance Plateresque style ㊶

Casa Lleó Morera

The first-floor dining room of this house is one of Barcelona's most stunning interiors. The stained-glass windows are by Lluís Rigalt and the eight ceramic mosaic wall panels, depicting idyllic country scenes, are by Gaspar Homar ⑲

Antiga Casa Figueres

The mosaic, stained-glass and wrought iron decoration of this, the most famous of the city's Modernista stores, was carried out in 1902 by Antoni Ros i Güell. It is today the elegant Pastisseria Escribà ⑦

KEY

- - - Walking route

—24— Bus route

— Metro route

0 metres   500

0 yards   500

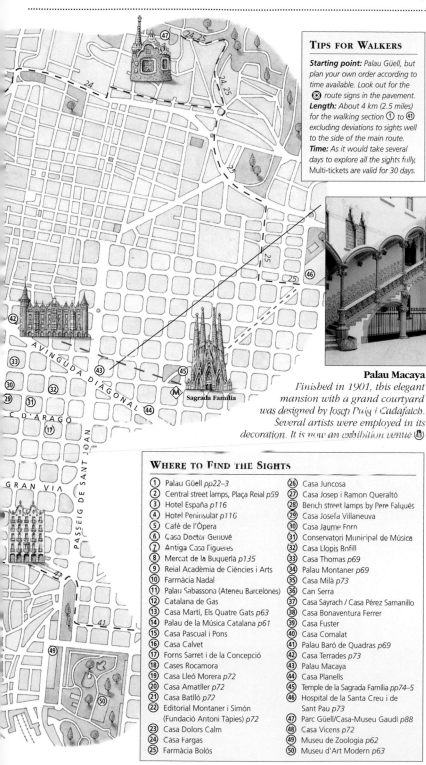

TIPS FOR WALKERS

Starting point: Palau Güell, but plan your own order according to time available. Look out for the ⊗ route signs in the pavement.
Length: About 4 km (2.5 miles) for the walking section ① to ④ excluding deviations to sights well to the side of the main route.
Time: As it would take several days to explore all the sights fully, Multi-tickets are valid for 30 days.

Palau Macaya
Finished in 1901, this elegant mansion with a grand courtyard was designed by Josep Puig i Cadafalch. Several artists were employed in its decoration. It is now an exhibition venue ④

WHERE TO FIND THE SIGHTS

① Palau Güell pp22–3
② Central street lamps, Plaça Reial p59
③ Hotel España p116
④ Hotel Peninsular p116
⑤ Cafè de l'Òpera
⑥ Casa Doctor Genové
⑦ Antiga Casa Figueres
⑧ Mercat de la Boqueria p135
⑨ Reial Acadèmia de Ciències i Arts
⑩ Farmàcia Nadal
⑪ Palau Sabassona (Ateneu Barcelonès)
⑫ Catalana de Gas
⑬ Casa Martí, Els Quatre Gats p63
⑭ Palau de la Música Catalana p61
⑮ Casa Pascual i Pons
⑯ Casa Calvet
⑰ Forns Sarret i de la Concepció
⑱ Cases Rocamora
⑲ Casa Lleó Morera p72
⑳ Casa Amatller p72
㉑ Casa Batlló p72
㉒ Editorial Montaner i Simón (Fundació Antoni Tàpies) p72
㉓ Casa Dolors Calm
㉔ Casa Fargas
㉕ Farmàcia Bolós
㉖ Casa Juncosa
㉗ Casa Josep i Ramon Queraltó
㉘ Bench street lamps by Pere Falqués
㉙ Casa Josefa Villanueva
㉚ Casa Jaume Forn
㉛ Conservatori Municipal de Música
㉜ Casa Llopis Bofill
㉝ Casa Thomas p69
㉞ Palau Montaner p69
㉟ Casa Milà p73
㊱ Can Serra
㊲ Casa Sayrach / Casa Pérez Samanillo
㊳ Casa Bonaventura Ferrer
㊴ Casa Fuster
㊵ Casa Comalat
㊶ Palau Baró de Quadras p69
㊷ Casa Terrades p73
㊸ Palau Macaya
㊹ Casa Planells
㊺ Temple de la Sagrada Família pp74–5
㊻ Hospital de la Santa Creu i de Sant Pau p73
㊼ Parc Güell/Casa-Museu Gaudí p88
㊽ Casa Vicens p72
㊾ Museu de Zoologia p62
㊿ Museu d'Art Modern p63

OLD TOWN

THE OLD TOWN, traversed by the city's most famous avenue, La Rambla, is one of the most extensive and harmonious medieval city centres in Europe. The Barri Gòtic (Gothic Quarter) contains the cathedral and ancient royal palace. Adjoining it is La Ribera, full of 14th-century mansions, one of which is occupied by the Museu Picasso. This area is bounded by the pleasant Parc de la Ciutadella, which contains the Museu d'Art Modern and the zoo. The revitalized seafront is a stimulating mix of old and new. Trendy shops and restaurants and a fashionable marina contrast with the historic shipyards, while reclaimed beaches flank the new Olympic Port.

SIGHTS AT A GLANCE

Museums and Galleries
Museu d'Art Contemporani **9**
Museu d'Art Modern **21**
Museu Frederic Marès **2**
Museu de Geologia **19**
Museu d'Història de la
 Ciutat **4**
Museu Marítim and
 Drassanes **28**
Museu Picasso **14**
Museu de Zoologia **18**

Harbour Sights
Golondrinas **27**
Port Olímpic **23**
Port Vell **25**

Streets and Districts
Barceloneta **24**
Carrer Montcada **13**
La Rambla **10**

El Raval **8**

Churches
Basílica de Santa Maria
 del Mar **12**
Cathedral (pp56–7) **7**

Historic Buildings
Casa de l'Ardiaca **1**
Casa de la Ciutat **5**
La Llotja **11**
Palau de la Generalitat **6**
Palau de la Música Catalana **15**
Palau Reial Major **3**

Monuments
Arc del Triomf **16**
Homenatge a Picasso **20**
Monument a Colom **26**

Parks and Gardens
Parc de la Ciutadella **17**
Parc Zoològic **22**

GETTING THERE
The area is well served by Metro lines 1, 3 and 4; Jaume I station is in the heart of the Barri Gòtic. Many buses pass through the Plaça de Catalunya on the edge of the Barri Gòtic.

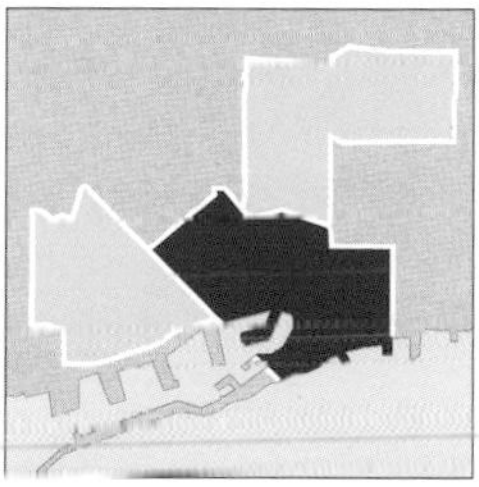

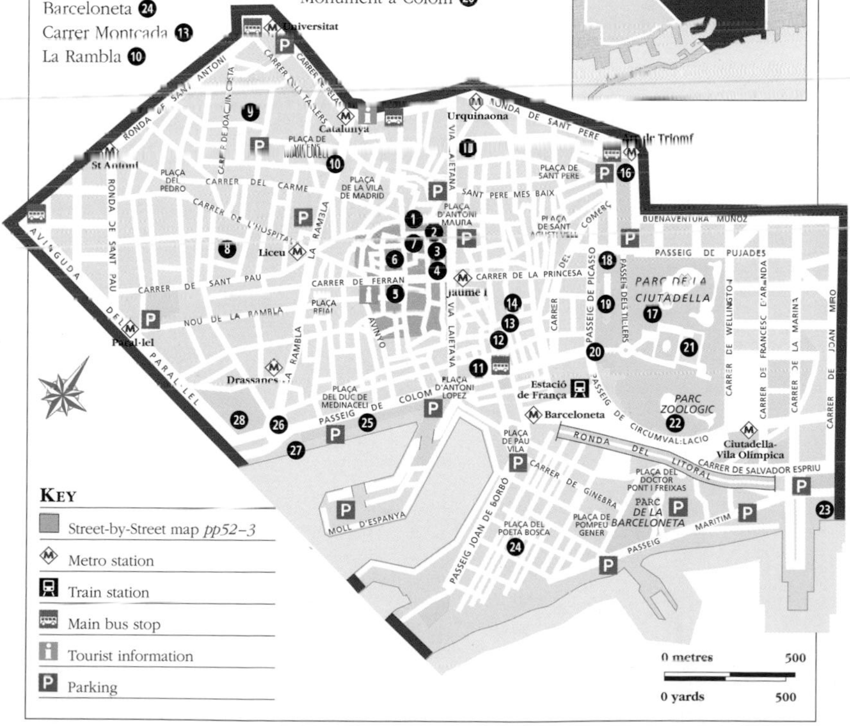

KEY

▢	Street-by-Street map *pp52–3*
Ⓜ	Metro station
🚉	Train station
🚌	Main bus stop
ℹ	Tourist information
🅿	Parking

0 metres 500

0 yards 500

◁ **Els Quatre Gats café in one of the narrow streets of Barcelona's Barri Gòtic**

Street-by-Street: Barri Gòtic

Wax candle,
Cereria
Subirà

THE BARRI GOTIC (Gothic Quarter) is the true heart of Barcelona. The oldest part of the city, it was the site chosen by the Romans in the reign of Augustus (27 BC–AD 14) on which to found a new *colonia* (town), and has been the location of the city's administrative buildings ever since. The Roman forum was on the Plaça de Sant Jaume, where now stand the medieval Palau de la Generalitat, the seat of Catalonia's government, and the Casa de la Ciutat, the city's town hall. Close by are the Gothic cathedral and royal palace, where Columbus was received by Fernando and Isabel on his return from the New World in 1492 *(see p40).*

Casa de l'Ardiaca
Built on the Roman city wall, the Gothic-Renaissance archdeacon's residence now houses Barcelona's historical archives ❶

To Plaça de Catalunya

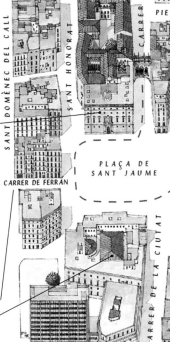

★ **Cathedral**
The façade and spire are 19th-century additions to the original Gothic building. Among the artistic treasures inside are medieval Catalan paintings ❼

Palau de la Generalitat
Catalonia's seat of government has superb Gothic features, such as the chapel and a stair-case to an open-air, arcaded gallery ❻

To La Rambla

Casa de la Ciutat
Barcelona's town hall was built in the 14th and 15th centuries. The façade is a Neo-Classical addition. In the entrance hall stands Three Gypsy Boys *by Joan Rebull (1899–1981), a 1976 copy of a sculpture he originally created in 1946* ❺

KEY

  Suggested route

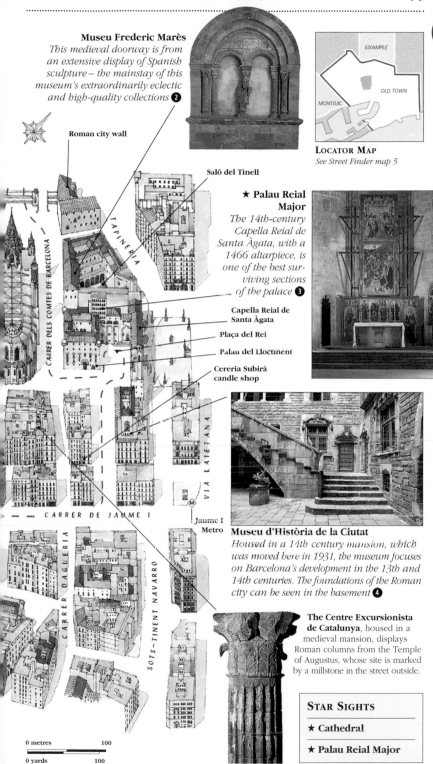

Museu Frederic Marès
This medieval doorway is from an extensive display of Spanish sculpture – the mainstay of this museum's extraordinarily eclectic and high-quality collections ②

LOCATOR MAP
See Street Finder map 5

Roman city wall

Saló del Tinell

★ **Palau Reial Major**
The 14th-century Capella Reial de Santa Àgata, with a 1466 altarpiece, is one of the best surviving sections of the palace ③

Capella Reial de Santa Àgata

Plaça del Rei

Palau del Lloctinent

Cereria Subirà candle shop

TAPINERIA

CARRER DELS COMTES DE BARCELONA

VIA LAIETANA

CARRER DE JAUME I

Jaume I Metro

CARRER DAGUERIA

SOTS–TINENT NAVARRO

Museu d'Història de la Ciutat
Housed in a 14th century mansion, which was moved here in 1931, the museum focuses on Barcelona's development in the 13th and 14th centuries. The foundations of the Roman city can be seen in the basement ④

The Centre Excursionista de Catalunya, housed in a medieval mansion, displays Roman columns from the Temple of Augustus, whose site is marked by a millstone in the street outside.

STAR SIGHTS

★ **Cathedral**

★ **Palau Reial Major**

0 metres 100
0 yards 100

Decorated marble mailbox, Casa de l'Ardiaca

Casa de l'Ardiaca ❶

Carrer de Santa Llúcia 1. **Map** 5 B2.
[93 318 11 95. ♠ *Jaume I.*
○ *9am–9pm Mon–Fri, 9am–1pm
Sat.* ● *public hols.*
W www.bcn.es/arxiu/arxiuhistoric

STANDING BESIDE what was
originally the Bishop's
Gate in the Roman wall is
the Archdeacon's House.
It was built in the 12th
century, but its present
form dates from around
1500 when it was remodel-
led, including the addition
of a colonnade. In 1870
this was extended to
form the Flamboyant
Gothic patio around a
fountain. The Modernista
architect Domènech i Montaner
(1850–1923) added the fanciful
marble mailbox, carved with
three swallows and a tortoise,
beside the Renaissance portal.
Upstairs is the Arxiu Històric
de la Ciutat (City Archives).

Museu Frederic Marès ❷

Plaça de Sant Iu 5. **Map** 5 B2.
[93 310 58 00. ♠ *Jaume I.*
○ *10am– 5pm Tue & Thu, 10am–7pm
Wed, Fri & Sat, 10am–3pm Sun.*
● *1 Jan, Good Fri, 1 May, 25 & 26
Dec.* 🎟 *(free Wed pm & 1st Sun of
every month).* ♿ 🎫 *by appointment.*

THE SCULPTOR Frederic Marès
i Deulovol (1893–1991) was
also a traveller and collector,
and this museum is a monument to his eclectic taste. As
part of the Royal Palace, it was
occupied by 13th-century
bishops, 14th-century counts
of Barcelona, 15th-century

judges and 18th-century nuns,
who lived here until they were
expelled in 1936. Marès, who
had a small apartment
in the building, opened
this museum in 1948.
It is one of the most
fascinating in the
city, and has an out-
standing collection
of Romanesque
and Gothic
religious art. In the
crypt there are
stone sculptures
and two complete
Romanesque
portals. Exhibits
on the three floors
above range from
clocks, crucifixes
and costumes to
antique cameras, pipes,
tobacco jars and postcards.
There is also an amusement
room full of children's toys.

Virgin, Museu
Frederic Marès

Palau Reial Major ❸

Plaça del Rei. **Map** 5 B2. **[** 93 315
11 11. ♠ *Jaume I.* ○ *Jun–Sep:
10am–8pm Tue–Sat, 10am–2pm Sun;
Oct–May: 4–8pm Tue–Sat, 10am–
2pm Sun.* ● *1 Jan, 25 & 26 Dec.* 🎟
🎫 *by appointment.*

THE ROYAL PALACE was the
residence of the count-
kings of Barcelona from its
foundation in the 13th century.
The complex includes the 14th-
century Gothic Saló del Tinell,
a vast room with arches span-
ning 17 m (56 ft). This is where
Isabel and Fernando *(see p40)*
received Columbus after his
triumphal return from America.
It is also where the Holy Inquisition sat, believing the walls
would move if lies were told.
On the right, built into the
Roman city wall, is the royal
chapel, the Capella de Santa

Gothic nave of the Capella de
Santa Àgata, Palau Reial

BARCELONA'S EARLY JEWISH COMMUNITY

Hebrew tablet

From the 11th to the 13th centuries Jews
dominated Barcelona's commerce and
culture, providing doctors and founding
the first seat of learning. But in 1243, 354
years after they were first documented in
the city, violent anti-Semitism led to the
Jews being consigned to a ghetto, El Call.
Ostensibly to provide protection, the
ghetto had only one entrance, which led
into the Plaça de Sant Jaume. Jews were
heavily taxed by the monarch, who viewed
them as "royal serfs"; but in return they also received
privileges, as they handled most of Catalonia's lucrative trade
with North Africa. However, official and popular persecution
finally led to the disappearance of the ghetto in 1401, 91
years before Judaism was fully outlawed in Spain *(see p40)*.
Originally there were three synagogues, the main one being
in Carrer Sant Domènec del Call, but only the foundations
are left. A 14th-century Hebrew tablet is embedded in the wall
at No. 1 Carrer de Marlet, which reads: "Holy Foundation
of Rabbi Samuel Hassardi, for whom life never ends".

Àgata, with a painted wood ceiling and an altarpiece (1466) by Jaume Huguet *(see p24)*. Its bell tower is formed by part of a watchtower on the Roman wall. Stairs through a small door on the right of the altar lead to the 16th-century tower of Martí the Humanist (who reigned from 1396–1410), the last ruler of the 500-year dynasty of the count-kings of Barcelona. From the top of the tower there are fine views.

Museu d'Història de la Ciutat ❹

Plaça del Rei. **Map** 5 B2. 93 315 11 11. Jaume I. 10am–2pm & 4–8pm Tue–Sat, 10am–2pm Sun. 1 Jan, 25 & 26 Dec.

THE CITY MUSEUM occupies the Casa Clariana-Padellàs, a Gothic building that, in 1931, was brought stone by stone to its present location from its original site in Carrer dels Mercaders. During the excavation of its new site, the remains of Roman water and drainage systems, baths, mosaic floors and a road were found. These can be seen in the basement that extends beneath the Plaça de l'Àngel. A short stretch of the Roman city wall is accessible from the upper floors, which are devoted to Barcelona's post-Roman development.

Casa de la Ciutat ❺

Plaça de Sant Jaume 1. **Map** 5 A2. 93 402 70 00. Jaume I or Liceu. 10am–2pm Sun (12 Feb & 23 Apr: 10am–8pm), or by appointment (93 402 73 62).

THE MAGNIFICENT 14th-century city hall *(ajuntament)* faces the Palau de la Generalitat. Flanking the entrance are statues of Jaume I *(see p39)*, who granted the city rights to elect councillors in 1249, and Joan Fiveller, who levied taxes on court members in the 1500s. Inside is the huge council chamber, the 14th-century Saló de Cent, built for the city's 100 councillors. The Saló de les Cròniques was commissioned for the 1929 International Exhibition and decorated by Josep-Maria Sert *(see p25)* with murals of great events in Catalan history.

Palau de la Generalitat ❻

Plaça de Sant Jaume 4. **Map** 5 A2. 93 402 46 00. Jaume I. 23 Apr (St Jordi's Day) 2nd & 4th Sun of every month. www.gencat.es

SINCE 1403 the Generalitat has been the seat of the Catalonian Government. Above the entrance, in its Renaissance

The Italianate façade of the Palau de la Generalitat

façade, is a statue of Sant Jordi (St George) – the patron saint of Catalonia – and the Dragon. The late Catalan-Gothic courtyard is by Marc Safont (1416).

Among the fine interiors are the Gothic chapel of Sant Jordi, also by Safont, and Pere Blai's Italianate Saló de Sant Jordi. The building is open to the public only on the saint's feast day. At the back, one floor above street level, lies the *Pati dels Tarongers*, the Orange Tree Patio, by Pau Mateu, which has a bell tower built by Pere Ferrer in 1568.

The Catalan president has offices here as well as in the Casa dels Canonges. The two buildings are connected across Carrer del Bisbe by a bridge built in 1928 and modelled on the Bridge of Sighs in Venice.

The magnificent council chamber, the Saló de Cent, in the Casa de la Ciutat

Barcelona Cathedral ❼

THIS COMPACT GOTHIC CATHEDRAL, with a Romanesque chapel (the Capella de Santa Llúcia) and beautiful cloister, was begun in 1298 under Jaume II, on the foundations of a Roman temple and Moorish mosque. It was not finished until the early 20th century, when the central spire was completed. A white marble choir screen, sculpted in the 16th century, depicts the martyrdom of St Eulàlia, the city's patron. Next to the font, a plaque records the baptism of six native Caribbeans, brought back from the Americas by Columbus in 1493.

Statue of St Eulàlia

The twin octagonal bell towers date from 1386–93. The bells were installed in this tower in 1545.

The main façade was not completed until 1889, and the central spire until 1913. It was based on the original 1408 plans of the French architect Charles Galters.

Nave Interior
The Catalan-style Gothic interior has a single wide nave with 28 side chapels. These are set between the columns supporting the vaulted ceiling, which rises to 26 m (85 ft).

★ Choir Stalls
The top tier of the beautifully carved 15th-century stalls contains painted coats of arms (1518) of several European kings.

Capella del Santíssim Sagrament
This small chapel houses the 16th-century Christ of Lepanto crucifix.

Capella de Sant Benet
This chapel, dedicated to the founder of the Benedictine Order and patron saint of Europe, houses a magnificent altarpiece showing The Transfiguration *by Bernat Martorell (1452).*

VISITORS' CHECKLIST

Plaça de la Seu. **Map** 5 A2. 🛈
93 315 15 54. 🚇 *Jaume I.* 🚌
17, 19, 45. ◻ *8am–1:30pm, 4–7:30pm Mon–Fri (Sat & Sun until 7pm).* 🎟 ♿ **Sacristy Museum** ◻ *11am–1pm daily.* 🎟 **Choir** ◻ *9am–1pm, 4–7pm Mon–Fri, 9am–1pm Sat.* 🎟 ✝ *9am, 10am, 11am, noon, 7pm daily.*

★ **Crypt**
In the crypt, beneath the main altar, is the alabaster sarcophagus (1339) of St Eulàlia, martyred for her beliefs by the Romans during the 4th century AD.

★ **Cloisters**
The fountain, set in a corner of the Gothic cloisters and decorated with a statue of St George, provided fresh water.

Porta de Santa Eulàlia, entrance to cloisters

The Sacristy Museum has a small treasury. Pieces include an 11th-century font, tapestries and liturgical artifacts.

Capella de Santa Llúcia

STAR FEATURES

★ **Choir Stalls**

★ **Crypt**

★ **Cloisters**

TIMELINE

400	700	1000	1300	1600	1900
	559 Basilica dedicated to St Eulàlia and Holy Cross	**1339** St Eulàlia's relics transferred to alabaster sarcophagus		**1913** Central spire completed	
	877 St Eulàlia's remains brought here from Santa Maria del Mar	**1046–58** Romanesque cathedral built under Ramon Berenguer I		**1889** Main façade completed, based on plans dating from 1408 by architect Charles Galters	
4th century Original Roman (paleo-Christian) basilica built	**985** Building destroyed by the Moors	**1257–68** Romanesque Capella de Santa Llúcia built	**1493** Indians brought back from the Americas are baptized		
		1298 Gothic cathedral begun under Jaume II		*Plaque of the Caribbeans' baptism*	

El Raval ⑧

Map 2 F3. ⓜ *Catalunya, Liceu.*

THE DISTRICT of El Raval lies to the right of La Rambla, if you are heading towards the sea, and includes the old red-light area near the port – once known as the Barri Xinès (Chinese quarter).

From the 14th century, the city hospital was in Carrer de l'Hospital, which still has several herbal and medicinal shops. It was here that Gaudí *(see p72)* was brought after being fatally hit by a tram in 1926, just before the hospital closed. The buildings, with quiet courtyards, now house the Biblioteca de Catalunya (Catalonian Library), but the elegant former dissecting room has been fully restored.

Towards the port in Carrer Nou de la Rambla is Gaudí's Palau Güell *(see p23)*. At the end of the street is the city's most complete Romanesque church, the 12th-century Sant Pau del Camp, where resident Franciscan monks still sing a plainsong mass.

Museu d'Art Contemporani ⑨

Plaça dels Angels 1. **Map** 2 F2.
🄴 *93 412 08 10.* ⓜ *Universitat, Catalunya.* ◯ *11am–7:30pm Mon & Wed–Fri, 10am–8pm Sat, 10am–3pm Sun & public hols.* ● *1 Jan, 25 Dec.* 🄰 🄰 🄴 *6pm Wed & Sat, noon Sun.* Ⓦ *www.macba.es*

THIS DRAMATIC, white, glass-fronted building in the heart of El Raval was designed by the American architect Richard Meier and completed in 1995. Its light, airy galleries on three floors display paintings, installation art and other modern works. Much of the space is devoted to changing exhibitions, but there is a growing permanent collection of works from the 1950s onwards. The focus is on Catalan art and the foreign trends and artists that have influenced it.

Next door, an 18th-century hospice, the Casa de la Caritat, is now a centre for contemporary culture, with imaginative temporary exhibitions.

La Rambla ⑩

THE HISTORIC AVENUE of La Rambla, leading to the sea, is busy around the clock, especially in the evenings and at weekends. Newsstands, caged bird and flower stalls, tarot readers, musicians and mime artists throng the wide, tree-shaded central walkway. Among its famous buildings are the Liceu Opera House, the huge Boqueria food market and some grand mansions.

Exploring La Rambla

The name of this long avenue, also known as Les Rambles, comes from the Arabic *ramla*, meaning the dried-up bed of a seasonal river. The 13th-century city wall followed the left bank of such a river that flowed from the Collserola hills to the sea. Convents, monasteries and the university were built on the other bank in the 16th century. As time passed, the riverbed was filled in and those buildings demolished, but they are remembered in the names of the five consecutive Rambles that make up the great avenue between the Port Vell and Plaça de Catalunya.

Palau Güell C/ Nou de la Rambla 3–5.
Map 2 F3. 🄴 *93 317 39 74.*
ⓜ *Liceu.* ◯ *Mar–Sep: 10am–8pm Mon–Sat; Oct–Feb: 10am–5pm Mon–Sat.* ● *public hols.* 🄰 🄰
Museu de Cera Pg de la Banca 7.
Map 2 F4. 🄴 *93 317 26 49.*
ⓜ *Drassanes.* ◯ *Jul–Sep: 10am–10pm daily; Oct–Jun: 10am–1:30pm & 4–7:30pm Mon–Fri, 11am–2pm & 4:30–8:30pm Sat, Sun & public hols.* 🄰 🄰

The monument to Columbus at the bottom of the tree-lined Rambla

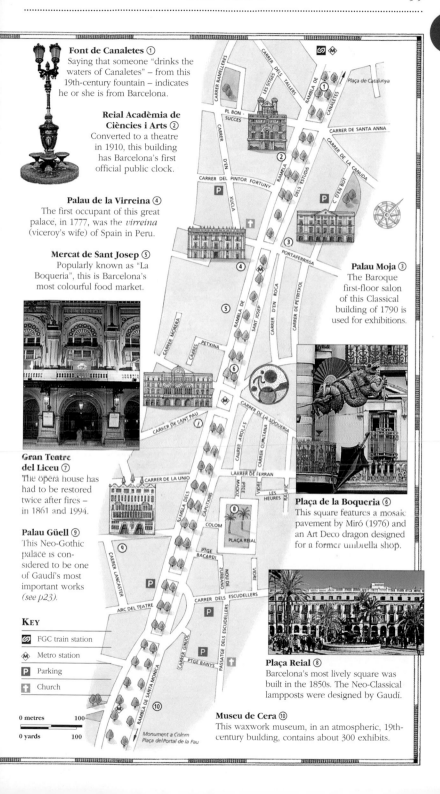

Font de Canaletes ①
Saying that someone "drinks the waters of Canaletes" – from this 19th-century fountain – indicates he or she is from Barcelona.

Reial Acadèmia de Ciències i Arts ②
Converted to a theatre in 1910, this building has Barcelona's first official public clock.

Palau de la Virreina ④
The first occupant of this great palace, in 1777, was the *virreina* (viceroy's wife) of Spain in Peru.

Mercat de Sant Josep ⑤
Popularly known as "La Boqueria", this is Barcelona's most colourful food market.

Gran Teatre del Liceu ⑦
The opera house has had to be restored twice after fires – in 1861 and 1994.

Palau Güell ⑨
This Neo-Gothic palace is considered to be one of Gaudí's most important works *(see p23)*.

Palau Moja ③
The Baroque first-floor salon of this Classical building of 1790 is used for exhibitions.

Plaça de la Boqueria ⑥
This square features a mosaic pavement by Miró (1976) and an Art Deco dragon designed for a former umbrella shop.

Plaça Reial ⑧
Barcelona's most lively square was built in the 1850s. The Neo-Classical lampposts were designed by Gaudí.

Museu de Cera ⑩
This waxwork museum, in an atmospheric, 19th-century building, contains about 300 exhibits.

KEY

〰	FGC train station
Ⓜ	Metro station
🅿	Parking
✝	Church

0 metres   100
0 yards   100

Statue of Poseidon in the courtyard of La Llotja

La Llotja ⓫

Carrer del Consolat de Mar 2. **Map** 5 B3. ⓴ *Jaume I.* ◐ *for renovation.* 🖼

L*A LLOTJA* (meaning commodity exchange) was built in the 1380s as the headquarters of the Consolat de Mar, the guild of Catalan sea-traders *(see p39)*. It was remodelled in Neo-Classical style in 1771 and housed the city's stock exchange until 1994, the original Gothic hall acting as the main trading room. It can still be glimpsed through the large ground-floor windows.

The upper floors housed the Barcelona School of Fine Arts from 1849 to 1970, attended by the young Picasso and Joan Miró *(see p25)*. La Llotja is now occupied by a public library and local government offices.

Basílica de Santa Maria del Mar ⓬

Pl Sta Maria 1. **Map** 5 B3. 📞 *93 310 23 90.* ⓴ *Jaume I.* ◐ *9am–1:30pm & 4:30–8pm daily (10am Sun).*

T*HIS BEAUTIFUL* building, the city's favourite church with superb acoustics for concerts, is the only example of a church entirely in the Catalan Gothic style. It took just 55 years to build, with money donated by merchants and shipbuilders. The speed – unrivalled in the Middle Ages – gave it a unity of style both inside and out. The west front has a 15th-century rose window of the Coronation of the Virgin. More stained glass, dating from the 15th to the 18th centuries, lights the wide nave and high aisles.

When the choir and furnishings were burned in the Civil War *(see p43)*, it added to the sense of space and simplicity.

Carrer Montcada ⓭

Map 5 B3. ⓴ *Jaume I.* **Museu Tèxtil i d'Indumentària** *at No. 12* 📞 *93 310 45 16.* ◐ *10am–6pm Tue–Sat, 10am–3pm Sun & public hols.* ◐ *1 & 5 Jan, Good Fri, 1 May, 24 Jun, 25 & 26 Dec.* 🖼 ⓵ 🖼 *by appointment (93 280 50 24).*

T*HE MOST AUTHENTIC* medieval street in Barcelona is a narrow lane, overshadowed by gargoyles and protruding roofs which almost touch overhead. The Gothic palaces that line it, built around magnificent courtyards, date back to Catalonia's expansion in the 13th century. A mural of the conquest of Mallorca, a rare Romanesque painting once in the Palau Berenguer d'Aguilar, is now in the Museu Nacional d'Art de Catalunya *(see p80)*.

Carrer Montcada's buildings were all modified over the years, particularly in the 17th

A wedding service in the Gothic interior of Santa Maria del Mar

Pablo Picasso, *Self-Portrait* in charcoal (1899–1900)

PABLO PICASSO IN BARCELONA

Picasso (1881–1973) was 13 when he arrived in Barcelona, where his father, José Ruiz y Blasco, had found work teaching in the city art school situated above the Llotja. The city was rich, but it also possessed a large, poor working class which was becoming organized and starting to rebel. Shortly after the family's arrival, a bomb was thrown into a Corpus Christi procession. They settled at No 3 Carrer de la Mercè, a gloomy, five-storeyed house not far from the Llotja. Picasso's precocious talent gave him admittance to the upper school, where all the other pupils were aged at least 20. Here he immediately made friends with another artist, Manuel Pallarès Grau, and the two lost their virginity to the whores of Carrer d'Avinyó, who were to inspire *Les Demoiselles d'Avignon* (1906–7), considered by many art critics to be the wellspring of modern art. Picasso travelled with Pallarès to the Catalan's home town of Horta, where he painted some early landscapes, now in the Museu Picasso. The two remained friends for the rest of their lives.

century when the Renaissance style prevailed. The only original façade is No. 25, the Casa Cervelló-Guidice. The **Museu Tèxtil i d'Indumentària** in Palau dels Marquesos de Lió at No. 12 (also called the Palau Mora) displays textiles and clothing from the 4th century AD onwards. The street also has the city's best-known champagne and *cava* bar, El Xampanyet *(see p137)*.

Museu Picasso ⑭

Carrer Montcada 15–23. **Map** 5 B2.
☎ 93 319 63 10. Ⓜ *Jaume I.*
🕐 *10am–7:30pm Tue–Sat & public hols, 10am–2:30pm Sun.* ● *1 Jan, Good Fri, 1 May, 24 Jun, 25 & 26 Dec.*
📷 ♿ Ⓦ www.museopicasso.bcn.es

O NE OF BARCELONA'S most popular attractions, the Picasso Museum is housed in five adjoining medieval palaces on Carrer Montcada: Berenguer d'Aguilar, Baró de Castellet, Meca, Mauri and Finestres.

The museum opened in 1963 showing works donated by Jaime Sabartes, a friend of Picasso. Following Sabartes' death in 1968, Picasso himself donated paintings, including early examples. These were complemented by graphic works, left in his will, and 141 ceramic pieces given by his widow, Jacqueline.

The works are divided into two sections: paintings and drawings, and ceramics. But the strength of the 3,000-piece collection are Picasso's early works. These show how, even at the ages of 15 and 16, he was painting major works

Painting in Picasso's series *Las Meninas* **(1957), Museu Picasso**

Glorious stained-glass dome, Palau de la Música Catalana

such as *The First Communion* (1896) and *Science and Charity* (1897). There are only a few pictures from his Blue and Rose periods. The most famous work is his series of 44 paintings, *Las Meninas*, inspired by Velázquez's masterpiece.

Palau de la Música Catalana ⑮

Carrer de Sant Francesc de Paula 2.
Map 5 B1. ☎ 93 295 72 00. Ⓜ *Urquinaona.* 🕐 *Sep–Jun: 10am–3:30pm daily; Jul: 10am–5pm daily; and for concerts.* ● *Aug.* 📷 ♿
🎟 *every half an hour.*
Ⓦ www.palaumusica.org

T HIS IS A real palace of music, a Modernista celebration of tilework, sculpture and glorious stained glass. It is the only concert hall in Europe lit by natural light. Designed by Lluís Domènech i Montaner, it was completed in 1908. Although a few extensions have been added, the building

still retains its original appearance. The elaborate red-brick façade is hard to appreciate fully in the confines of the narrow street. It is lined with mosaic-covered pillars topped by busts of the great composers Palestrina, Bach and Beethoven. The large stone sculpture of St George and other figures at the corner of the building portrays an allegory from Catalan folksong by Miquel Blay.

But it is the interior of the building that is truly inspiring. The auditorium is lit by a huge inverted dome of stained glass depicting angelic choristers. The sculptures of composers Wagner and Clavé on the proscenium arch were designed by Domènech but finished by Pau Gargallo.

The work of Josep Anselm Clavé (1824–74) in promoting Catalan song led to the creation of the Orfeó Català choral society in 1891, a focus of Catalan nationalism and the inspiration behind the Palau.

The pink brick façade of the late 19th-century Arc del Triomf

Arc del Triomf 16

Passeig Lluís Companys. **Map** 5 C1.
Arc de Triomf.

THE MAIN GATEWAY to the 1888 Universal Exhibition, which filled the Parc de la Ciutadella, was designed by Josep Vilaseca i Casanovas. It is built of brick in Mudéjar (Spanish Moorish) style, with sculpted allegories of crafts, industry and business. The frieze by Josep Reynés on the main façade represents the city of Barcelona welcoming foreign visitors.

Parc de la Ciutadella 17

Avda del Marquès de l'Argentera.
Map 6 D2. Barceloneta,
Ciutadella-Vila Olímpica. Nov–Feb:
10am–6pm; Mar & Oct: 10am–7pm;
Apr & Sep: 10am–8pm; May–Aug:
10am–9pm.

THIS POPULAR park has a large boating lake, orange groves and scores of parrots living in the palm trees. The 30-ha (75-acre) park was previously the site of a massive star-shaped citadel. Designed by Prosper Verboom, this was built for Felipe V between 1715 and 1720 following a 13-month siege of the city, brought about by Barcelona's opposition to the Bourbon succession *(see p41)*. The fortress was intended to house soldiers to help keep law and order, but was never used for this purpose. It was converted into a prison, which became particularly notorious during the Napoleonic occupation *(see p41)*, and during the 19th-century liberal repressions, when it was hated as a symbol of centralized power.

In 1878, under the enlightened dictator General Prim, whose statue stands in the middle of the park, the citadel was pulled down and the park given to the city, to become, in 1888, the venue of the Universal Exhibition *(see p42)*.

Three buildings, however, survived: the arsenal, which was redesigned in 1932 for use by the Catalan parliament and is today shared by the Museu d'Art Modern; the Governor's Palace, which is now a school; and the chapel.

The gardens in the Plaça de Armes were laid out by the French landscape gardener Jean Forestier. They centre on a cascade based around a triumphal arch and partly inspired by the Trevi Fountain in Rome. It was designed by architect Josep Fontseré, with the help of Antoni Gaudí, who was then still a young student.

One of the galleries inside the spacious Museu de Zoologia

Museu de Zoologia 18

Passeig de Picasso. **Map** 5 C2.
93 319 69 12. Arc de Triomf
or Jaume I. 10am–2pm Tue–Sun &
public hols (Thu till 6:30pm).
by appointment.
www.museuzoologia.bcn.es

AT THE ENTRANCE to the Parc de la Ciutadella is the fortress-like Castell dels Tres Dragons (Castle of the Three Dragons), named after a play by Frederic Soler that was popular at the time it was built.

This crenellated brick edifice was built by Lluís Domènech i Montaner for the 1888 Universal Exhibition. His inspiration was Valencia's Gothic commodities exchange. He later used it as a workshop for Modernista design, and it became a focus of the movement. It has housed the Zoological Museum since 1937.

Ornamental cascade in the Parc de la Ciutadella designed by Josep Fontseré and Antoni Gaudí

Museu de Geologia ⑲

Parc de la Ciutadella. **Map** 5 C3.
📞 93 319 68 95. 🚇 Arc de Triomf,
Jaume I. ⏱ 10am–2pm Tue–Sun &
public hols (Thu till 6pm). ⬛ 1 Jan,
Good Fri, 1 May, 25 & 26 Dec. 🎫
🎫. No children under 16.

BARCELONA'S OLDEST MUSEUM opened in 1882, the same year the Parc de la Ciutadella became a public space. It has a large collection of fossils and minerals, including specimens from Catalonia. Beside it is the Hivernacle, a glasshouse by Josep Amargós now used for concerts, and the Umbracle, a brick and wood conservatory by the park's architect, Josep Fontseré. Both date from 1884.

Glass cube of the Homenatge a Picasso, Parc de la Ciutadella

Homenatge a Picasso ⑳

Passeig de Picasso. **Map** 5 C3.
🚇 Barceloneta.

AT THE EDGE OF THE Parc de la Ciutadella, opposite Avinguda Marqués de l'Argentera, is the intriguing 1983 work *Homage to Picasso* by Catalan artist Antoni Tàpies *(see p25)*.

Built to pay homage to Picasso's Cubist works, it is an intellectual sculpture that does not immediately suggest its title. A large, plain glass cube sits in a square pond, with water streaming down the sides. The cube contains an old sofa, chairs and a sideboard skewered by metal poles and draped with a blanket. The elements have not treated it kindly, and an air conditioning system has had to be installed to prevent the glass from cracking.

Dusk on the River Loing by Alfred Sisley (1839–99), Museu d'Art Modern

Museu d'Art Modern ㉑

Parc de la Ciutadella. **Map** 6 D3.
📞 93 319 50 23. 🚇 Arc de Triomf.
⏱ 10am–7pm Tue–Sat, 10am–
2:30pm Sun & public hols. 🎫 ♿ 🎫
by appointment. 🅦 www.manac.es

THIS IS A COLLECTION of Catalan art *(see pp24–5)* of the 19th and early 20th centuries in which the main players, Miró, Picasso, Dalí and Tàpies, are under-represented as they each have separate museums. However, the collection of Modernista fine and decorative art is second to none and gives a comprehensive overview of the movement.

Among the earlier painters is Marià Fortuny i Marsal (1838–74), noted for his studies of Morocco. Two early 20th-century artists, Santiago Rusiñol (1861–1931) and Ramon Casas (1866–1932), are considered the founders of modern Catalan painting. Casas' line drawings of the great men of his day include one of Pablo Picasso newly arrived in Paris. There is also a painting Casas did of himself riding a tandem with Pere Romeu; the two men opened Els Quatre Gats café *(see p50)*, where the painting was originally hung. Picasso's contemporaries, the painters Joaquim Mir (1873–1940) and Isidre Nonell (1873–1911), are represented here. There is also a landscape by Alfred Sisley (1839–99) called *Dusk on the River Loing*.

A fine sculpture gallery exhibits works by Josep Llimona (1864–1934) and Miquel Blay (1866–1936). There are also some bold pieces of Modernista furniture acquired from houses in the Eixample.

Parc Zoològic ㉒

Parc de la Ciutadella. **Map** 6 D3.
📞 93 225 67 80. 🚇 Ciutadella-Vila Olímpica. ⏱ Oct–Feb: 10am–5pm,
Mar: 10am–6:30pm, Apr: 10am–7pm,
May–Sep: 10am–7:30pm. 🎫
🅦 www.zoobarcelona.com

BARCELONA'S ZOO was laid out in the 1940s to a relatively enlightened design in which the animals are separated by moats instead of iron bars. The zoo is strong on primates and for years its mascot has been Floquet de Neu (Snowflake), a rare albino gorilla. Dolphin and whale shows are held in one of the aquariums. Roig i Soler's 1885 sculpture by the entrance, *The Lady with the Umbrella (see p15)*, has become a symbol of Barcelona.

Floquet de Neu, Barcelona zoo's rare albino gorilla

Fashionable yachts at the Port Olímpic overlooked by Spain's two tallest skyscrapers

Port Olímpic ㉓

Map 6 F4. ⓜ Ciutadella-Vila Olímpica.

THE MOST DRAMATIC rebuilding for the 1992 Olympics was the demolition of the old industrial waterfront and the laying out of 4 km (2 miles) of promenade and pristine sandy beaches. Suddenly Barcelona seemed like a seaside resort. At the heart of the project was a 65-ha (160-acre) new estate of 2,000 apartments and parks called Nova Icària. The area is still popularly known as the Vila Olímpica because the buildings originally housed the Olympic athletes.

On the sea front there are twin 44-floor buildings, Spain's tallest skyscrapers, one occupied by offices, the other by the Arts hotel (see p117). They stand beside the Port Olímpic, which was also built for 1992. This has shops and nightclubs, but the main reasons for visiting are two levels of restaurants around the marina which have made it the latest popular place to eat out. The wonderful outdoor setting attracts business people at lunchtime and pleasure seekers in the evenings and at weekends.

Lunch can be walked off along the string of beaches that is edged by a palm-fringed promenade with cafés. Behind it, the new coastal road heads around a park that lies beside

the last three beaches, divided by rocky breakwaters. Swimming is safe on the gently sloping, sandy strands.

Barceloneta ㉔

Map 5 B5. ⓜ Barceloneta.

BARCELONA'S fishing "village", which lies on a triangular tongue of land jutting into the sea just below the city centre, is renowned for its little restaurants and cafés. The area was designed in 1753 by the architect and military engineer Juan Martín de Cermeño to rehouse people made homeless by the construction, just inland, of the Ciutadella fortress (see p62). Since then it has housed largely workers and fishermen. Laid out in a grid system with narrow two- and three-storey houses, in which each room has a window on the street, the area has a friendly, intimate air.

In the small Plaça de la Barceloneta, at the centre of the district, is the Baroque church of Sant Miguel del Port, also by Cermeño. A market is often held in the square here.

Today, Barceloneta's fishing fleet is still based in the nearby Dàrsena Industrial (Industrial Docks) by a small clock tower. On the opposite side of this harbour is the Torre de Sant Sebastià, terminus of the cable car that runs right across the port, via the World Trade Centre, to Montjuïc.

Port Vell ㉕

Map 5 A4. ⓜ Barceloneta, Drassanes.
Aquàrium 【 93 221 74 74. ◯ Oct–May: 9am–9pm Mon–Fri, 9:30am–9:30pm Sat & Sun; Jun & Sep: 9:30am–9:30pm daily; Jul–Aug: 9:30am–11pm daily. 🎫 & 🎫 by appointment.
Museu d'Història de Catalunya Plaça Pau Vila 3. 【 93 225 47 00. ◯ 10am–7pm Tue, Thu–Sat, 10am–8pm Wed, 10am–2:30pm Sun & public hols. 🎫 except 1st Sun every month. & 🎫 by appointment (93 225 42 44).

BARCELONA'S MARINA is at the foot of La Rambla, just beyond the old customs house. This was built in 1902 at the Portal de la Pau, the city's former maritime entrance. To the south, the Moll de Barcelona, with a new World Trade Centre, serves as the passenger pier for visiting liners. In front of the customs house, La Rambla is connected to the yacht clubs on the Moll d'Espanya by a swing bridge and a pedestrian jetty, known as La Rambla de Mar. The Moll d'Espanya has a new shopping and restaurant complex, the Maremàgnum, plus an IMAX cinema and the largest aquarium in Europe.

On the shore, the Moll de Fusta (Timber Wharf), with terrace cafés, has red structures inspired by the bridge at Arles painted by Van Gogh. At the end of the wharf is El Cap de Barcelona (Barcelona Head), a 20-m (66-ft) tall sculpture by Pop artist Roy Lichtenstein.

The attractive Sports Marina on the other side of the Moll d'Espanya was once lined with warehouses. The only one left,

Fishing boat moored in Barceloneta harbour

built by Elies Rogent in the 1880s, has been given a new lease of life as the Palau de Mar. Restaurants provide alfresco dining, but the building is otherwise given over to the Museu d'Història de Catalunya. Exhibits on three floors start from Lower Palaeolithic times and continue to the region's heydays as a maritime power and industrial pioneer. There is a schoolroom from the Franco era and a 1960s mock-up bar and situated outside sits a reconstructed Roman boat.

A *golondrina* tour boat departing from the Portal de la Pau

The Columbus Monument lit by fireworks during La Merce fiesta

Monument a Colom ②

Plaça del Portal de la Pau. **Map** 2 F4.
📞 93 302 52 24. 🚇 *Drassanes.* 🕐
Oct–Mar: 10am–1:30pm & 3:30–6:30pm Tue–Fri, 10am–6:30pm Sat, Sun & public hols; Apr–May: 10am–1:30pm & 3:30–7:30pm Tue–Fri, 10am–7:30pm Sat, Sun & public hols; Jun–Sep: 9am–8:30pm daily. 🖼

T HE COLUMBUS monument at the bottom of La Rambla was designed by Gaietà Buigas for the 1888 Universal Exhibition *(see p42)*. At that time Catalans considered Columbus to be Catalan rather than Italian.

The 60-m (200-ft) monument marks the spot where Columbus stepped ashore in 1493 after discovering America, bringing with him six Caribbean Indians. He was given a state welcome by the Catholic Monarchs in the Saló del Tinell *(see p54)*. The Indians' subsequent conversion to Christianity is commemorated

in the cathedral *(see pp56–7)*. A lift leads to a viewing platform at the top of the monument. The bronze statue was designed by Rafael Arché.

Golondrinas ②

Plaça del Portal de la Pau. **Map** 2 F5.
📞 93 442 31 06. 🚇 *Drassanes.*
Departures: *variable (phone for details).* 🖼

S IGHTSEEING TRIPS around Barcelona's harbour and to the Port Olímpic can be made on *golondrinas* ("swallows") – small double-decker boats that moor in front of the Columbus Monument at the foot of La Rambla.

Half-hour tours go out beneath the steep, castle-topped hill of Montjuïc towards the industrial port. They usually stop short at the breakwater, which reaches out to sea from Barceloneta, to allow passengers to disembark for a stroll.

A one-and-a-half hour trip takes in Barcelona harbour, the local beaches and finally Port Olímpic.

Museu Marítim and Drassanes ②

Avinguda de les Drassanes.
Map 2 F4. 📞 93 342 99 20.
🚇 *Drassanes.* 🕐 *10am–7pm Mon–Sun.* ● *1 & 6 Jan, 25 & 26 Dec.* 🖼 ♿ 🖼 *12:30pm Sat–Sun.*

T HE GREAT GALLEYS that were instrumental in making Barcelona a major seafaring power were built in the sheds of the Drassanes (shipyards) that now house the maritime

museum. These royal dry docks are the largest and most complete surviving medieval complex of their kind in the world. They were founded in the mid-13th century, when dynastic marriages uniting the kingdoms of Sicily and Aragón meant that better maritime communications between the two became a priority. Three of the yards' four original corner towers survive.

Among the vessels to slip from the Drassanes' vaulted halls was the *Real*, flagship of Don Juan of Austria, who led the Christian fleet to the famous victory against the Turks at Lepanto in 1571. The highlight of the museum's collection is a full-scale replica decorated in red and gold.

The *Llibre del Consolat de Mar*, a book of nautical codes and practice, is a reminder that Catalonia was once the arbiter of Mediterranean maritime law *(see p39)*. There are pre-Columbian maps, including one from 1439 that was used by Amerigo Vespucci.

Stained-glass window in the Museu Marítim

EIXAMPLE

BARCELONA CLAIMS to have the greatest collection of Art Nouveau buildings of any city in Europe. The style, known in Catalonia as Modernisme, flourished after 1854, when it was decided to tear down the medieval walls to allow the city to develop into what had previously been a construction-free military zone.

The designs of the civil engineer Ildefons Cerdà i Sunyer (1815–76) were chosen for the new expansion *(eixample)* inland. These plans called for a rigid grid system of streets, but at each intersection the corners were chamfered to allow the buildings there to overlook the junctions or squares. The few exceptions to this grid system include the Diagonal, a main avenue running from the wealthy area of Pedralbes down to the sea, and the Hospital de la Santa Creu i de Sant Pau by Modernista architect Domènech i Montaner (1850–1923). He hated the grid system and deliberately angled the hospital to look down the diagonal Avinguda de Gaudí towards Antoni Gaudí's church of the Sagrada Família, the city's most spectacular Modernista building *(see pp74–5)*. The wealth of Barcelona's commercial elite, and their passion for all things new, allowed them to give free rein to the age's most innovative architects in designing their residences as well as public buildings.

Jesus of the Column, Sagrada Família

SIGHTS AT A GLANCE

Museums and Galleries
Fundació Antoni Tàpies ②

Churches
Sagrada Família pp74–5 ⑥

Modernista Buildings
Casa Milà, "La Pedrera" ③
Casa Terrades, "Casa de les Punxes" ④
Hospital de la Santa Creu i de Sant Pau ⑤
Illa de la Discòrdia ①

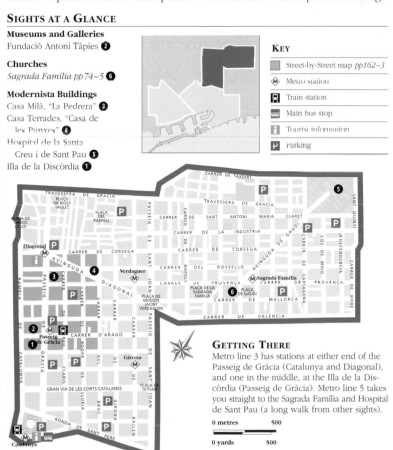

GETTING THERE
Metro line 3 has stations at either end of the Passeig de Gràcia (Catalunya and Diagonal), and one in the middle, at the Illa de la Discòrdia (Passeig de Gràcia). Metro line 5 takes you straight to the Sagrada Família and Hospital de Sant Pau (a long walk from other sights).

0 metres 500
0 yards 500

◁ **Nativity façade of the Sagrada Família – the only façade to be more or less completed in Gaudí's lifetime**

Street-by-Street: Quadrat d'Or

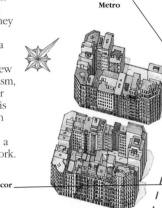

Diagonal Metro

T HE HUNDRED OR SO city blocks centring on the Passeig de Gràcia are known as the Quadrat d'Or, "Golden Square", because they contain so many of the best Modernista buildings *(see pp22–3)*. This was the area within the Eixample favoured by the wealthy bourgeoisie, who embraced the new artistic and architectural style with enthusiasm, not only for their residences, but also for commercial buildings. Most remarkable is the Illa de la Discòrdia, a single block with houses by Modernisme's most illustrious exponents. Many interiors can be visited by the public, revealing a feast of stained glass, ceramics and ornamental ironwork.

Perfume bottle, Museu del Perfum

Vinçon home decor store *(see p135)*

Passeig de Gràcia, the Eixample's main avenue, is a show-case of highly original buildings and smart shops. The graceful street lamps are by Pere Falqués (1850–1916).

RAMBLA DE CATALUNYA

PASSEIG DE GRÀCIA

Fundació Tàpies
Topped by Antoni Tàpies' wire sculpture Cloud and Chair, *this 1879 building by Domènech i Montaner houses a wide variety of Tàpies' paintings, graphics and sculptures* **2**

Casa Amatller

Museu del Perfum

Casa Ramon Mulleras

★ **Illa de la Discòrdia**
In this city block, four of Barcelona's most famous Modernista houses vie for attention. All were created between 1900 and 1910. This ornate tower graces the Casa Lleó Morera *by Domènech i Montaner* **1**

To Plaça de Catalunya

Casa Batlló

Casa Lleó Morera

Passeig de Gràcia Metro

Museu de la Música is housed in the Palau Baró de Quadras designed by Puig i Cadafalch in 1904. This carving adorns the doorway. The museum has displays of historical instruments collected from around the world.

LOCATOR MAP
See Street Finder map 3

Casa Terrades "Les Punxes"
Built in red brick with carved stone ornamentation, this 1905 house by Puig i Cadafalch echoes the Gothic buildings of northern Europe ❹

Casa Thomas

To Sagrada Família

★ Casa Milà "La Pedrera"
Gaudí put all his architectural daring into this, his most famous house. The result is a remarkable wave-like façade and a roofscape of chimneys and vents resembling abstract sculptures ❸

Palau Ramon de Montaner

0 metres   100
0 yards   100

KEY

– – – Suggested route

STAR SIGHTS

★ **Illa de la Discòrdia**

★ **Casa Milà "La Pedrera"**

Sumptuous interior of the Casa Lleó Morera, Illa de la Discòrdia

staircase beneath a stained-glass roof. The building, now used by the Institut Amatller d'Art Hispànic, has a beautiful wood-panelled library. Next door is Antoni Gaudí's Casa Batlló (1904–1906). Its façade has a fluidity typical of the movement, with tiled walls and curved iron balconies pierced with holes to look like masks or skulls. The hump-backed, scaly-looking roof is thought to represent a dragon, with St George as a chimney.

Fundació Antoni Tàpies ❷

Carrer d'Aragó 255. **Map** 3 A1. 🛈
93 487 03 15. 🚇 *Passeig de Gràcia.*
⬜ *10am–8pm Tue–Sun & public hols.*
⬛ *1 & 6 Jan, 25 & 26 Dec.* 🈂️ ♿

A NTONI TAPIES *(see p25),* born in 1923, is Barcelona's best-known living artist. Inspired by Surrealism, his abstract work is executed in a variety of materials, including concrete and metal *(see p68).* Difficult to appreciate at first, the exhibits should help viewers obtain a clearer perspective of Tàpies' work, even if there is not enough here to gain a full understanding. The collection is housed in Barcelona's first domestic building to be constructed with iron (1880), designed by Domènech i Montaner for his brother's publishing firm.

Illa de la Discòrdia ❶

Passeig de Gràcia, between Carrer d'Aragó and Carrer del Consell de Cent. **Map** 3 A4. 🚇 *Passeig de Gràcia.* **Centre del Modernisme** Casa Amatller, Passeig de Gràcia 41. 🛈 *93 488 01 39.* ⬜ *10am–7pm Mon–Sat, 10am–2pm Sun & public hols.* 🈂️

B ARCELONA'S MOST FAMOUS group of Modernista *(see pp22–3)* buildings illustrates the wide range of styles used by the movement's architects. They lie in an area known as the Illa de la Discòrdia (Island of Discord), after the startling visual argument between them.

The three finest were remodelled in the Modernista style from existing houses early in the 20th century. No. 35 Passeig de Gràcia is Casa Lleó Morera (1902–6), the first residential work of Lluís Domènech i Montaner. A shop was installed in the ground floor in 1943, but the Modernista interiors upstairs still exist. Tickets for the Modernista route *(see pp48–9),* which includes a tour of the exteriors of these houses, can

be bought in the Centre del Modernisme.

Beyond the next two houses, one of which is a beauty shop containing a perfume museum, is Casa Amatller, designed by Puig i Cadafalch in 1898. Its façade, under a stepped gable roof, features a harmonious blend of Moorish and Gothic windows. Inside the wrought-iron main doors is a fine stone

---

ANTONI GAUDÍ (1852–1926)

Born in Reus (Tarragona) into an artisan family, Antoni Gaudí i Cornet was the leading exponent of Catalan Modernisme. After a blacksmith's apprenticeship, he studied at Barcelona's School of Architecture. Inspired by a nationalistic search for a romantic medieval past, his work was supremely original. His first major achievement was the Casa Vicens (1888) at No. 24 Carrer de les Carolines *(see p48).* But his most celebrated building is the church of the Sagrada Família *(see pp74–5),* to which he devoted his life from 1914. When he had put all his money into the project, he went from house to house begging for more. He was killed by a tram in 1926 *(see p58).*

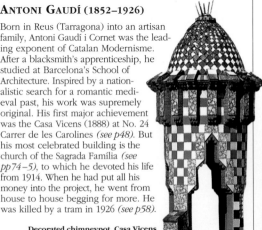

Decorated chimneypot, Casa Vicens

◁ **Extraordinary sculptured and ceramic-encrusted chimneys of Gaudí's Casa Milà**

The rippled façade of Gaudí's apartment building, Casa Milà

and gables are influenced in particular by the Gothic architecture of northern Europe. However, the deeply carved, floral stone ornamentation of the exterior, in combination with red brick used as the principal building material, are typically Modernista.

Hospital de la Santa Creu i de Sant Pau ❺

Carrer de Sant Antoni Maria Claret 167, 08025 Barcelona. **Map** 4 F1. 🎧 *93 291 91 99.* 🚇 *Hospital de Sant Pau.* **Grounds** ⏰ *daily; write in advance for permission to visit pavilions not in medical use.* 🚻 🗎 🔳 www.hspau.com

LLUIS DOMENECH I MONTANER began designing a new city hospital in 1902. His innovative scheme consisted of 26 attractive Mudéjar-style pavilions set in large gardens, as he believed that patients would recover better among fresh air and trees. All the connecting corridors and service areas were hidden underground. Also believing art and colour to be therapeutic, he decorated the pavilions profusely. The turreted roofs were tiled with ceramics, and the reception pavilion embellished with mosaic murals and sculptures by Pau Gargallo. After his death, the project was completed in 1930 by Domènech's son, Pere.

Casa Milà ❸

Passeig de Gràcia 92. **Map** 3 B3. 🎧 *93 484 59 80.* 🚇 *Diagonal.* ⏰ *10am–7:30pm daily.* 🔴 *1, 6 & 2nd week Jan, 25 & 26 Dec.* 🔳 www.casacat.es/cccc

USUALLY CALLED *La Pedrera* (the Stone Quarry), the Casa Milà is Gaudí's greatest contribution to Barcelona's civic architecture, and his last work before he devoted himself entirely to the Sagrada Família *(see pp74–5)*.

Built between 1906–10, *La Pedrera* departed from established construction principles of the time and, as a result, was ridiculed and criticized by Barcelona's intellectuals.

Gaudí designed this corner apartment block, eight floors high, around two circular courtyards. In the basement he incorporated the city's first underground car park. The intricate ironwork balconies, by Josep Maria Jujol, are like seaweed against the wave-like walls of white, undressed stone. There are no straight walls anywhere in the building.

The Milà family had an apartment on the first floor. There are tours from an office on the ground floor which take in one of the flats and the extraordinary roof. The sculptured air ducts and chimneys have such a threatening appearance they are known as *espantabruixes*, or witch-scarers.

Casa Terrades ❹

Avinguda Diagonal 416. **Map** 3 B3. 🚇 *Diagonal.* 🔴 *to public.*

THIS FREE-STANDING, six-sided apartment block by Modernista architect Josep Puig i Cadafalch gets its nickname, *Casa de les Punxes* (House of the Points), from the spires on its six corner turrets. It was built between 1903 and 1905 by converting three existing houses on the site and was Puig's largest work. It is an eclectic mixture of medieval and Renaissance styles. The towers

Spire on the main tower, Casa Terrades

Statue of the Virgin, Hospital de la Santa Creu i de Sant Pau

Sagrada Família ⑥

A carved whelk

Europe's most unconventional church, the Temple Expiatori de la Sagrada Família, is an emblem of a city that likes to think of itself as individualistic. Crammed with symbolism inspired by nature and striving for originality, it is the greatest work of Gaudí *(see pp22–3)*. In 1883, a year after work had begun on a Neo-Gothic church on the site, the task of completing it was given to Gaudí who changed everything, extemporizing as he went along. It became his life's work and he lived like a recluse on the site for 16 years. He is buried in the crypt. At his death only one tower on the Nativity façade had been completed, but work resumed after the Civil War and several more have since been finished to his original plans. Work continues today, financed by public subscription.

Bell Towers
Eight of the 12 spires, one for each apostle, have been built. Each is topped by Venetian mosaics.

THE FINISHED CHURCH

Gaudí's initial ambitions have been scaled down over the years, but the design for the completion of the building remains impressive. Still to come is the central tower, which is to be encircled by four large towers representing the Evangelists. Four towers on the Glory (south) façade will match the existing four on the Passion (west) and Nativity (east) façades. An ambulatory – like an inside-out cloister – will run round the outside of the building.

Tower with lift

The apse was the first part of the church Gaudí completed. Stairs lead down from here to the crypt below.

The altar canopy, designed by Gaudí, is still waiting for the altar.

★ Passion Façade
This bleak façade was completed in the late 1980s by artist Josep Maria Subirachs. A controversial work, its sculpted figures are angular and often sinister.

Entrance to Crypt Museum

Main entrance

Spiral Staircases
Steep stone steps – 400 in each – allow access to the towers and upper galleries. Majestic views reward those who climb or take the lift.

VISITORS' CHECKLIST

C/ Mallorca 401. **Map** 4 E3.
📞 93 207 30 31. Ⓜ️ *Sagrada Familia.* 🚌 *19, 34, 43, 50, 51, 54.*
🅿️ *Apr–Sep: 9am–9pm; Oct–Mar: 9am–6pm; daily.* ⬤ *1 & 6 Jan, 25 & 26 Dec.* ✝️ *9am, 10:30am, 11:45am, 1pm, 8:15pm daily (also 7pm Oct–Mar).*
♿ *except crypt & towers.*

Tower with lift

★ **Nativity Façade**
The most complete part of Gaudí's church, finished in 1904, has doorways which represent Faith, Hope and Charity. Scenes of the Nativity and Christ's childhood are embellished with symbolism, such as doves representing the congregation.

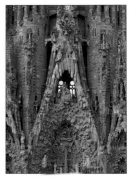

★ **Crypt**
The crypt, where Gaudí is buried, was built by the original architect, Francesc de Paula Villar i Lozano, in 1882. This is where services are held. On the lower floor a museum traces the careers of both architects and the church's history.

Nave
In the nave, which is still under construction, a forest of fluted pillars will support four galleries above the side aisles, while skylights let in natural light.

STAR FEATURES

★ **Passion Façade**

★ **Nativity Façade**

★ **Crypt**

MONTJUÏC

THE HILL OF MONTJUIC, rising to 213 m (699 ft) above the commercial port on the south side of the city, is Barcelona's biggest recreation area. Its museums, art galleries, gardens and nightclubs make it a popular place in the evenings as well as during the day.

There was probably a Celt-iberian settlement here before the Romans built a temple to Jupiter on their Mons Jovis, which may have given Montjuïc its name – though another theory suggests that a Jewish cemetery on the hill inspired the name Mount of the Jews.

The absence of a water supply meant that there were few buildings on Montjuïc until the castle was erected on the top in 1640.

Statue, gardens of the Palau Nacional

The hill finally came into its own as the site of the 1929 International Fair. With great energy and flair, buildings were erected all over the north side, with the grand Avinguda de la Reina Maria Cristina, lined with huge exhibition halls, leading into it from the Plaça d'Espanya. In the middle of the avenue is the Font Màgica (Magic Fountain), which is regularly illuminated in colour. Above it is the Palau Nacional, home of the city's historic art collections. The Poble Espanyol is a crafts centre housed in copies of buildings from all over Spain. The last great surge of building on Montjuïc was for the 1992 Olympic Games, which left Barcelona with international-class sports facilities.

SIGHTS AT A GLANCE

Historic Buildings
Castell de Montjuïc **7**

Modern Architecture
Estadi Olímpic de Montjuïc **8**
Pavelló Mies van der Rohe **4**

Museums and Galleries
Fundació Joan Miró **1**
Museu Arqueològic **2**
Museu Nacional d'Art de Catalunya **3**

Squares
Plaça d'Espanya **6**

Theme Parks
Poble Espanyol **5**

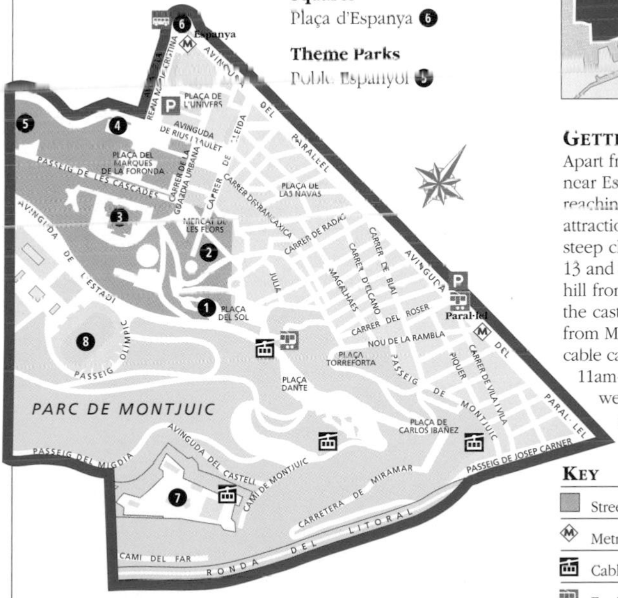

GETTING THERE

Apart from the exhibition halls near Espanya Metro station, reaching most of Montjuïc's attractions on foot involves a steep climb. However, buses 13 and 61 will take you up the hill from Plaça d'Espanya. For the castle, take the funicular from Metro Paral·lel, then the cable car. These run from 11am–7:30/8pm on winter weekends and daily in summer to 9:30/10pm.

KEY

	Street-by-Street map *pp78–9*
Ⓜ	Metro station
	Cable car station
	Funicular station
	Main bus stop
Ⓟ	Parking

0 metres   500
0 yards   500

◁ **Changing colours of the Font Màgica (Magic Fountain) on the grand avenue leading up to Montjuïc**

Street-by-Street: Montjuïc

Mᴏɴᴛᴊᴜɪᴄ ɪѕ ᴀ ѕᴘᴇᴄᴛᴀᴄᴜʟᴀʀ vantage point from which to view the city. It has a wealth of art galleries and museums, as well as theatres. Many of the buildings were designed for the 1929 International Exhibition, and the 1992 Olympics were held on its southern slopes. Montjuïc is approached from the Plaça d'Espanya between brick pillars based on the campanile of St Mark's in Venice. They give a foretaste of the eclecticism of building styles from the Palau Nacional, which houses magnificent Romanesque art, to the Poble Espanyol, which illustrates the architecture of Spain's regions.

Pavelló Mies van der Rohe
This elegant statue by Georg Kolbe stands serenely in the steel, glass, stone and onyx pavilion built in the Bauhaus style as the German contribution to the 1929 International Exhibition ❹

AVINGUDA DEL MARQUÈS DE COMILLAS

AVINGUDA DELS MONTANYANS

PASSEIG DE LES CASCA

AVINGUDA DE L'ESTADI

★ Poble Espanyol
Containing replicas of buildings from many regions of Spain, this "village" provides a fascinating glimpse of vernacular styles ❺

★ Museu Nacional d'Art de Catalunya
On show in the Palau Nacional (National Palace), the main building of the 1929 International Exhibition, is Europe's finest collection of Romanesque frescoes. These were a great source of inspiration for Joan Miró ❸

To Montjuïc castle and Olympic stadium

Sᴛᴀʀ Sɪɢʜᴛѕ

★ Poble Espanyol

★ Museu Nacional d'Art de Catalunya

★ Fundació Joan Miró

Fountains and cascades descend in terraces from the Palau Nacional. Below them is the Font Màgica (Magic Fountain). On Thursday to Sunday evenings in summer and Friday and Saturday evenings in winter, its jets are programmed to a multi-coloured music and light show. This marvel of engineering was built by Carles Buigas (1898–1979) for the 1929 International Exhibition.

LOCATOR MAP
See Street Finder map 1

Museu Arqueològic
The museum displays important finds from prehistoric cultures in Catalonia and the Balearic Islands. The Dama d'Evissa, *a 4th-century sculpture, was found in Ibiza's Carthaginian necropolis* ❷

Museu Etnològic displays artifacts from Oceania, Africa, Asia and Latin America.

To Plaça d'Espanya

Mercat de les Flors theatre (see p136)

Teatre Grec is an open-air theatre set among gardens.

★ **Fundació Joan Miró**
This tapestry by Joan Miró hangs in the centre he created for the study of modern art. In addition to Miró's works in various media, the modern building by Josep Lluís Sert is of architectural interest ❶

To Montjuïc castle and cable car

KEY
– – – Suggested route

0 metres 100
0 yards 100

Flame in Space and Naked Woman (1932) by Joan Miró

Fundació Joan Miró ❶

Parc de Montjuïc. **Map** 1 B3. ☎ *93 329 19 08.* Ⓜ *Pl. Espanya then bus 50, or Paral·lel then funicular to Montjuïc.* ⭘ *Jul–Sep: 10am–8pm Tue–Sat (till 9:30pm Thu); Oct– Jun: 10am–7pm Tue–Sat (till 9:30pm Thu), 10am–2:30pm Sun & public hols.* ● *1 Jan, 25 & 26 Dec.* 📷 ♿ ☒ www.bcn.fjmiro.es

JOAN MIRÓ (1893–1983) went to La Llotja's art school *(see p60)*, but from 1919 spent much time in Paris. Though opposed to Franco, he returned to Spain in 1940 and lived mainly in Mallorca, where he died. An admirer of Catalan art and Modernisme *(see pp22–3)*, Miró remained a Catalan painter *(see pp24–5)* but invented and developed a Surrealistic style, with vivid colours and fantastical forms. During the 1950s he concentrated on ceramics.

In 1975, after the return of democracy to Spain, his friend, the architect Josep Lluís Sert, designed this stark, white building to house a permanent collection of graphics, paintings, sculptures and tapestries lit by natural light. Miró himself donated the works and some of the best pieces on display include his *Barcelona Series* (1939–44), a set of 50 black-and-white lithographs. Exhibitions of other artists' work are also held regularly.

Museu Arqueològic ❷

Passeig Santa Madrona 39–41. **Map** 1 B3. ☎ *93 423 21 49.* Ⓜ *Espanya, Poble Sec.* ⭘ *9:30am–7pm Tue–Sat, 10am–2:30pm Sun & public hols.* ● *1 Jan, 25, 26 Dec.* 📷 *except 11 Feb, 23 Apr, 18 May, 11 & 24 Sep.* ♿ ☒ www.mac.es

HOUSED IN the 1929 Palace of Graphic Arts, the museum has artifacts from prehistory to the Visigothic period (AD 415–711). Highlights are finds from the Greco-Roman town of Empúries *(see p102)*, Hellenistic Mallorcan and Visigothic jewellery and Iberian silver treasure.

Museu Nacional d'Art de Catalunya ❸

Parc de Montjuïc, Palau Nacional. **Map** 1 A2. ☎ *93 622 03 60.* Ⓜ *Espanya.* ⭘ *10am–7pm Tue–Sat, 10am–2:30pm Sun & public hols.* 📷 ☒ ♿ ☒ *noon (book in advance on 93 622 03 75).* ☒ www.mnac.es

THE AUSTERE Palau Nacional was built for the 1929 International Exhibition, but in 1934 it was used to house an art collection that has since become the most important in the city.

The museum has probably the greatest display of Romanesque *(see pp20–21)* items in the world, centred around a series of magnificent 12th-century frescoes. Taken from Catalan Pyrenean churches, they have been pasted onto replicas of the original vaulted ceilings and apses, to save them from plunder and the ravages of time. The most remarkable are the wall paintings from Sant Climent de Taüll and Santa Maria de Taüll *(see p95)*.

There is also an impressive Gothic collection, covering the whole of Spain but particularly good on Catalonia. Notable artists include the 15th-century Spanish artists Lluís Dalmau and Jaume Huguet *(see p24)*.

Distinguished works by El Greco, Velázquez and Zurbarán are on display in the Baroque and Renaissance collection. A photographic collection, started in 1996, has room for expansion in this spacious museum.

12th-century *Christ in Majesty*, **Museu Nacional d'Art de Catalunya**

Morning by Georg Kolbe (1877–1945), Pavelló Mies van der Rohe

Pavelló Mies van der Rohe ❹

Avinguda del Marquès de Comillas. **Map** 1 B2. **[** 93 423 40 16. **⊕** *Espanya.* **🚌** 50. **□** *10am–8pm daily.* **●** *1 Jan, 25 Dec.* **📷** *except children.* **[w]** www.miesbcn.com

I F THE SIMPLE lines of this glass and polished stone pavilion look modern today, they must have shocked visitors to the 1929 International Exhibition. Designed by Ludwig Mies van der Rohe (1886–1969), director of the Bauhaus school, it included his world famous *Barcelona Chair.* The building was demolished after the exhibition, but an exact replica was built for the centenary of his birth.

Poble Espanyol ❺

Avinguda del Marquès de Comillas. **Map** 1 A2. **[** 93 508 63 00. **⊕** *Espanya.* **□** *9am–8pm Mon, 9am–2am Tue–Thu, 9am–4am Fri & Sat, 9am–midnight Sun.* **📷** **🍴** **[w]** www.poble-espanyol.com

T HE IDEA BEHIND the Poble Espanyol (Spanish Village) was to illustrate and display local Spanish architectural styles and crafts. It was laid out for the 1929 International Exhibition, but has proved to be enduringly popular.

Building styles from all over Spain are illustrated by 116 houses, arranged on streets radiating from a main square and created by many well-known architects and artists of the time. The village was refurbished at the end of the 1980s and is now a favourite place to visit for both tourists and native *barcelonins.*

Resident artisans produce crafts including hand-blown glass, ceramics, Toledo damascene and Catalan sandals *(espardenyes).* The Torres de Avila, which form the main entrance, have been converted into a nightspot, with an interior by designers Alfredo Arribas and Javier Mariscal *(see p17).* There are also shops, bars and a children's theatre.

Looking down from the Palau Nacional towards Plaça d'Espanya

Plaça d'Espanya ❻

Avinguda de la Gran Via de les Corts Catalanes. **Map** 1 B1. **⊕** *Espanya.*

T HE FOUNTAIN in the middle of this road junction, the site of public gallows until they were transferred to Ciutadella in 1715, is by Josep Maria Jujol, one of Gaudí's followers. The sculptures are by Miquel Blay. The 1899 bullring to one side is by Font i Carreras, but Catalans have never taken to bullfighting and the arena was once used as a music venue.

On the Montjuïc side of the roundabout is the Avinguda de la Reina Maria Cristina. This is flanked by two 47-m (154-ft) high brick campaniles by Ramon Raventós, modelled on the bell towers of St Mark's in Venice and built as the entrance way to the 1929 International Exhibition. The avenue, lined with exhibition buildings, leads up to Carles Buigas's illuminated *Font Màgica* (Magic Fountain) in front of the Palau Nacional.

Castell de Montjuïc ❼

Parc de Montjuïc. **Map** 1 B5. **[** 93 329 86 13. **⊕** *Paral·lel, then funicular & cable car (only Sat & public hols in winter).* **Museum □** *Nov–15 Mar: 9:30am–5pm Tue–Sun; 16 Mar–Oct: 9:30am–8pm.* **●** *1 Jan, Good Fri, 1 May, 25 & 26 Dec.* **📷**

T HE SUMMIT of Montjuïc is occupied by a huge, 18th-century castle with views over the port. The first castle was built in 1640, but destroyed by Felipe V in 1705. The present star-shaped fortress was built for the Bourbon family. During the War of Independence it was taken by French troops. After the Civil War it became a prison and the Catalan leader Lluís Companys *(see p43)* was executed here in 1940. It is now a military museum displaying ancient weaponry and model castles.

Estadi Olímpic de Montjuïc ❽

Passeig Olímpic 17–19. **Map** 1 A3. **[** 93 426 20 89. **⊕** *Espanya, Poble Sec.* **🚌** 50, 51. **□** *Jun–Sep: 10am–8pm; Oct–May: 10am–6pm; daily.* **●** *1 Jan.* **♿** **♿**

T HE ORIGINAL Neo-Classical façade has been preserved from the stadium built by Pere Domènech i Roura for the 1936 Olympics, cancelled at the onset of the Spanish Civil War. The arena's capacity was raised to 70,000 for the 1992 Olympics. Nearby are the steel-and-glass Palau Sant Jordi stadium by Japanese architect Arata Isozaki, and swimming pools by Ricard Bofill.

Entrance to the Olympic Stadium, refurbished in 1992

Altar frontal of the 13th century dedicated to the Virgin, Museu Nacional d'Art de Catalunya ▷

FURTHER AFIELD

RADICAL REDEVELOPMENTS throughout Barcelona in the late 1980s and 1990s have given it a wealth of new buildings, parks and squares. Sants, the city's main station, was rebuilt and the neighbouring Parc de l'Espanya Industrial and Parc de Joan Miró were created containing futuristic sculpture and architecture. In the east, close to the revitalized area of Poblenou, the city now has a new national theatre and concert hall. In the

Parc Güell gateway sign

west, where the streets climb steeply, are the historic royal palace and monastery of Pedralbes, and Gaudí's Torre Bellesguard and Parc Güell. Beyond, the Serra de Collserola, the city's closest rural area, is reached by two funiculars. Tibidabo, the highest point, has an amusement park, the Neo-Gothic church of the Sagrat Cor and a nearby steel-and-glass communications tower. It is a popular place among *barcelonins* for a day out.

SIGHTS AT A GLANCE

Museums and Galleries
Museu de la Ciència **8**
Museu del Futbol Club
  Barcelona **3**

Historic Buildings
Monestir de Pedralbes **5**
Palau Reial de Pedralbes **4**
Torre Bellesguard **9**

Modern Buildings
Torre de Collserola **6**

Parks and Gardens
Parc de l'Espanya Industrial **2**
Parc Güell **10**
Parc de Joan Miró **1**

Squares and Districts
Estació del Nord **11**
Plaça de les Glòries Catalanes **12**
Poblenou **13**

Theme Parks
Tibidabo **7**

KEY
▬	Street-by-Street maps
☐	Built-up area
🚉	Train station
🚋	Funicular station
═	Motorway (highway)
▬	Major road
═	Minor road

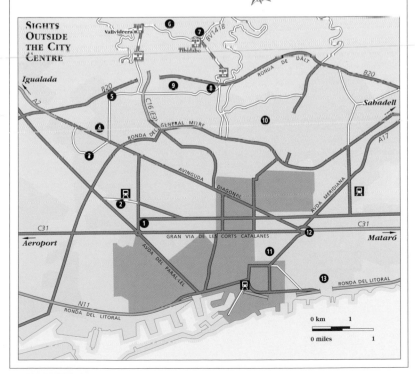

SIGHTS OUTSIDE THE CITY CENTRE

The Neo-Gothic Temple Expiatori del Sagrat Cor dominating the summit of Tibidabo

Dona i Ocell (1983) by Joan Miró in the Parc de Joan Miró

Parc de Joan Miró ❶

Carrer d'Aragó 1. ◈ *Tarragona.*

BARCELONA'S 19th-century slaughterhouse *(escorxador)* was transformed in the 1980s into this unusual park, hence its alternative name, Parc de l'Escorxador.

It is constructed on two levels, the lower of which is devoted to football pitches interspersed with landscaped sections of palms, pines, eucalyptus trees and flowers. The upper level is completely paved and is dominated by a magnificent 1983 sculpture by the Catalan artist Joan Miró *(see p25)* entitled *Dona i Ocell (Woman and Bird)*. Standing 22 m (72 ft) high in the middle of a pool, its surface is covered with colourful glazed tiles.

Parc de l'Espanya Industrial ❷

Plaça de Joan Peiró. ◈ *Sants-Estació.*

THIS MODERN PARK, designed by the Basque architect Luis Peña Ganchegui, owes its name to the textile mill that used to stand on the 5-hectare (12-acre) site.

Laid out in 1986 as part of Barcelona's policy to provide more open spaces within the city, the park has canals and a rowing lake – with a Classical statue of Neptune at its centre. Tiers of steps rise around the lake like an amphitheatre and on one side a row of ten futuristic watchtowers dominates the entire area. Their only function is to serve as public viewing platforms and lamp standards.

Six contemporary sculptors are represented in the park, among them Andrés Nagel, whose enormous metal dragon incorporates a children's slide.

Museu del Futbol Club Barcelona ❸

Avda de Arístides Maillol (7, 9). 📞 93 496 36 00. ◈ *Maria Cristina, Collblanc.* ⏱ 10am–6:30pm Mon–Sat, 10am–2pm Sun & public hols. ● 1 & 6 Jan, 24 Sep, 25 & 26 Dec. 🎫 ♿ 📷 Ⓦ www.fcbarcelona.com

CAMP NOU, Europe's largest football stadium, is home to the city's famous football club, Barcelona FC (Barça, as it is known locally). Founded in 1899, it is one of the world's richest soccer clubs, and has more than 100,000 members.

The stadium is a magnificent, sweeping structure, built in 1957

Line of watchtowers in the Parc de l'Espanya Industrial

to a design by Francesc Mitjans. An extension was added in 1982 and it can now comfortably seat 100,000 fans.

The club's museum, which displays club memorabilia and trophies on two floors, and has a souvenir shop, is one of the most popular in Barcelona. There are also paintings and sculptures of famous club footballers commissioned for the Blau-grana Biennial, an exhibition held in celebration of the club in 1985 and 1987, and others donated by Catalan artists. *Blau-grana* (blue-burgundy) are the colours of Barça's strip. The club's flags were used as an expression of local nationalist feelings when the Catalan flag was banned during the Franco dictatorship.

As well as hosting its own high-profile matches (mainly at weekends), Camp Nou also accommodates affiliated local soccer clubs and promotes other sports in its sports centre, ice rink and mini-stadium.

View across Camp Nou stadium, prestigious home of the Futbol Club Barcelona

Palau Reial de Pedralbes ❹

Avda Diagonal 686. ⓜ *Palau Reial.*
Museu de Ceràmica & Museu de Arts Decoratives 〖 93 280 50 24.
◻ 10am–6pm Tue–Sat, 10am–3pm Sun & public hols. ◼ 1 Jan, 1 May, 24 Jun, 25 & 26 Dec. 🔽 🔁 ☐ by appointment.

THE PALACE OF PEDRALBES was once the main house on the estate of Count Eusebi Güell. In 1919 he offered it to the Spanish royal family. The first visit was from Alfonso XIII in 1926, before which the interior was refurbished and a new throne, supported by golden lions, was created for him.

The building was opened to the public in 1937 and the Museu de Arts Decoratives installed. Exhibits include period furniture from other great houses in the city and fine household items from the Middle Ages to the present. A genealogical tree traces the 500-year dynasty of the count-kings of Barcelona *(see p38)*.

The palace also houses the Museu de Ceràmica, which displays old Catalan and Moorish pottery and modern ceramics, including works by Miró and Picasso *(see p80)*.

The palace gardens are well laid out with small ponds and paths. Just behind the gardens, in Avinguda de Pedralbes, is the entrance to the original Güell estate. It is guarded by a black wrought-iron gate, then forged into a great, open-jawed dragon, and two gate houses, all by Gaudí *(see pp22–3)*.

Madonna of Humility, **Monestir de Santa Maria de Pedralbes**

Monestir de Santa Maria de Pedralbes ❺

Carrer de Montevideo 14. **Thyssen-Bornemisza Collection** Baixada del Monestir 9. 〖 93 203 92 82.
🚇 *Reina Elisenda.* ◻ 10am–2pm Tue–Sun. ◼ public hols. 🔁 ☐ by appointment (93 315 11 11)

APPROACHED through an arch in its ancient walls, the lovely monastery of Pedralbes retains the air of an enclosed community. This is heightened by the good state of preservation of its furnished kitchens, cells, infirmary and refectory. But the nuns of the Order of

St Clare moved to an adjoining building back in 1983. The monastery was founded in 1326 by Elisenda de Montcada de Piños, fourth wife of Jaume II of Catalonia and Aragón. Her alabaster tomb lies in the wall between the church and the cloister. On the church side her effigy is dressed in royal robes; on the other, in a nun's habit.

The most important room in the monastery is the Capella (chapel) de Sant Miquel, with murals of the *Passion* and the *Life of the Virgin*, both painted by Ferrer Bassa in 1346, when Elisenda's niece, Francesca Saportella, was abbess.

In 1989, some 60 paintings forming part of the Thyssen-Bornemisza Collection (most of which is in Madrid) were donated to the monastery. They now hang in the former dormitory and one of Queen Elisenda's rooms. The collection is strong in Italian and Spanish works, with examples by Fra Angelico, Tiepolo, Lotto, Titian, Canaletto, Veronese, Velázquez and Zurbarán.

Torre de Collserola ❻

Carretera de Vallvidrera al Tibidabo. 〖 93 406 93 54. 🚌 *Peu del Funicular, then Funicular de Vallvidrera & bus 211.* ◻ Oct–May: 11am–2:30pm & 3:30–6pm Wed–Sun & public hols; Jul–Sep: 11am–2:30pm & 3:30–8pm Wed–Sun & public hols. ◼ 1 & 6 Jan, 25 Dec. 🔁 🔽 ⓦ www.torredecollserola.com

IN A CITY that enjoys thrills, the ultimate ride is offered by the communications tower near Tibidabo mountain *(see p88)*. A glass-sided lift takes less than two minutes to reach the top of this 288-m (944-ft) tall structure standing on the summit of a 445-m (1,460-ft) hill. The tower was designed by English architect Norman Foster for the 1992 Olympic Games. Needle-like in form, it is a tubular steel mast on a concrete pillar. There are 13 levels. The top one has an observatory with a telescope and a public viewing platform with a 360° view of the city, the sea and the mountain chain on which Tibidabo sits.

BARCELONA V REAL MADRID

FC Barcelona

Més que un club is the motto of Barcelona FC: "More than a club". It has above all, however, been a symbol of the struggle of Catalan nationalism against the central government in Madrid. To fail to win the league is one thing. To come in behind Real Madrid is a complete disaster. Each season the big question is which of the two teams will win the title. Under the Franco regime in a memorable episode in 1941, Barça won 3–0 at home. At the return match in Madrid, the crowd was so hostile that the police and referee "advised" Barça to prevent trouble. Demoralized by the intimidation, they lost 11–1. Loyalty is paramount: one Barça player who left to join Real Madrid received death threats.

Real Madrid

Merry-go-round, Tibidabo

Tibidabo ⓐ

Plaça del Tibidabo 3–4. ☎ 93 211 79
42. ⚋ Avda Tibidabo, then Tramvia
Blau & Funicular; or Peu del Funicular,
then Funicular & bus 211.
Amusement Park ◯ ring to
confirm. ● Oct–Apr: Mon–Fri. ♿
Temple Expiatori del Sagrat Cor
☎ 93 417 56 86. ◯ 10am–2pm,
3–7pm daily. ♿

THE HEIGHTS OF TIBIDABO can
be reached by Barcelona's
last surviving tram. The name,
inspired by Tibidabo's views of
the city, comes from the Latin
tibi dabo (I shall give you) – a
reference to the Temptation of
Christ when Satan took Him up
a mountain and offered Him
the world spread at His feet.

The hugely popular Parc
d'Atraccions (Amusement Park,
see p137) first opened in 1908.
The rides were renovated in
the 1980s. While the old ones
retain their charm, the newer
ones provide the latest in
vertiginous experiences. Their
hilltop location at 517 m
(1,696 ft) adds to the thrill.
Also in the park is the Museu
d'Autòmats displaying auto-
mated toys, juke boxes and
slot machines.

Tibidabo is crowned by the
Temple Expiatori del Sagrat
Cor (Church of the Sacred
Heart), built with religious zeal
but little taste by Enric Sagnier
between 1902 and 1911. A lift
takes you up to the feet of an
enormous figure of Christ.

Just a short bus ride away is
another viewpoint worth
visiting – the Torre de
Collserola *(see p87)*.

Museu de la Ciència ⓑ

Carrer Teodor Roviralta 55. ☎ 93 212
60 50. ⚋ Avinguda del Tibidabo, then
Tramvia Blau. ◯ 10am–8pm Tue–
Sun. ● 1, 5 & 6 Jan, 25 & 26 Dec. ⚋
except 1st Sun every month. ♿

THE CITY'S science museum
provides hands-on experi-
ences, particularly popular with
children. You can test your
senses and physical abilities,
and learn about world ecology.
Two floors look at sound and
optics. There is a weather station, and a planetarium staging
35-minute shows. Outside is a
submarine you can explore.

**Wrought-iron entrance door at
Antoni Gaudí's Torre Bellesguard**

Torre Bellesguard ⓒ

Carrer de Bellesguard 16. ⚋ Avinguda
del Tibidabo. ● closed to public.

BELLESGUARD means
"beautiful spot" and
here, half way up the
Collserola hills, is the
place chosen by the
medieval Catalan kings
as their summer home.
Their castle, built in
1408, was in particular a
favourite residence of
Barcelona's Martí the
Humanist *(see p55)*.

The surrounding district
of Sant Gervasi was
developed in the 19th
century after the coming
of the railway. In 1900
Gaudí built the present
house on the site of the
castle, which had fallen
badly into ruin. Its castel-
lated look and the elon-
gated, Gothic-inspired
windows refer clearly to

the original castle. Gaudí kept
the vestiges of its walls in his
structure. The roof, with a
walkway behind the parapet, is
topped by a distinctive Gaudí
tower. Ceramic fish mosaics
by the main door symbolize
Catalonia's past sea power.

Parc Güell ⓓ

Carrer d'Olot. ☎ 93 424 38 09. Ⓜ
Lesseps. ◯ Nov–Feb: 10am–6pm;
Mar & Oct: 10am–7pm; Apr & Sep:
10am–8pm; May–Aug: 10am–9pm;
daily. ♿ ⚋ **Casa-Museu Gaudí** ☎
93 219 38 11. ◯ Oct–Mar: 10am–
6pm; Apr–Sep: 10am–8pm; daily.
● 1 & 6 Jan, 25 & 26 Dec. ⚋

PARC GÜELL is Antoni Gaudí's
(see pp22–3) most colourful creation. He was com-
missioned in the 1890s by
Count Eusebi Güell to design
a garden city on 20 hectares
(50 acres). In the event, little
of the grand design for public
buildings and 60 houses in
landscaped gardens became
reality. What we see today
was completed between 1910
and 1914 and the park
opened in 1922.

Most atmospheric is the
Room of a Hundred Columns,
a cavernous market hall of 84
crooked pillars, brightened by
glass and ceramic mosaics. Up
a flight of steps flanked by
ceramic animals is the Gran
Plaça Circular, an open space

**Mosaic-encrusted chimney by Gaudí at
the entrance of the Parc Güell**

Catalonia's new National Theatre near the Plaça de les Glòries Catalanes

with a snaking balcony of coloured mosaics, whose contours are bordered by a bench that measures 152 m (499 ft), said to be the longest in the world. It was made by Josep Jujol. The view from here is panoramic.

The two mosaic-decorated pavilions at the entrance are by Gaudí, but the gingerbread-style house where he lived from 1906 to 1926, now the Casa-Museu Gaudí, is by Francesc Berenguer. It contains Gaudí furniture and drawings.

Estació del Nord ⓫

Avinguda de Vilanova. **Map** 6 D1.
Ⓜ Arc de Triomf.

ONLY THE 1861 façade overlooking a park and the grand 1915 entrance remain of this former railway station. The rest has been remodelled as a sports centre, a police headquarters, and the city's bus station. Two elegant, blue-tiled sculptures, *Espiral arbrada (Branched Spiral)* and *Cel obert (Open Sky)* by Beverley Pepper (1992) sweep through the pleasant park. In front of

the station, at Avinguda de Vilanova 12, is a carefully restored building occupied by Catalonia's power generating company. It was built as a power station in 1897 by the architect Pere Falqués. Though the great machinery inside is not visible, the exterior of this iron and brick structure is unmistakably Modernista.

Plaça de les Glòries Catalanes ⓬

Gran Via de les Corts Catalanes.
Map 4 F5. Ⓜ Glòries.

THIS WHOLE AREA, where the Diagonal crosses the Gran Via de les Corts Catalanes, has recently been redeveloped as the city expands northeastwards and the Diagonal is extended down to the sea, completing the vision of the Eixample's planner Ildefons Cerdà *(see p67)*. On the north side, a new shopping centre contrasts with the Encants Vells flea market *(see p135)*, which sprawls beside the highway heading north out of town. It is open 8am–8pm four days a week, and much

of the merchandise of furniture, clothes, and bric-à-brac is simply laid out on the ground. It is busiest early in the day and bartering is all part of the fun.

To the south of the *plaça* is the new Teatre Nacional de Catalunya, a vast temple to culture by the Barcelona architect Ricard Bofill. Beside it is the Auditori de Barcelona, with two concert halls by Rafael Moneo which were inaugurated in 1999. The Museu de la Música *(see p69)* will move here after the millennium.

La Rambla del Poblenou, a good place for a stroll and a cup of coffee

Poblenou ⓭

Rambla del Poblenou. Ⓜ Poblenou.

POBLENOU IS the trendy part of town where artists and photographers have built their studios in the defunct warehouses of the city's former industrial heartland. The area is centred on the Rambla del Poblenou, a quiet avenue of plane trees which now extends from Avinguda Diagonal down to the sea. Here palm trees back a stretch of sandy beach.

Halfway down the Rambla, at the crossroads with Carrer de Ramon Turró is the Casino de l'Aliança, an historic social and cultural centre next to a good restaurant and, opposite, El Tio Che, a well-known ice cream parlour. A walk around the quiet streets leading from the Rambla will reveal a few protected pieces of industrial architecture, legacies from the time Barcelona was known as "the Manchester of Spain".

At the bottom of the Rambla along the parallel Carrer del Ferrocarril is the pretty, tree-shaded Plaça de Prim with low, whitewashed houses reminiscent of a small country town.

Blue-tiled sculpture by Beverley Pepper, Parc de l'Estació del Nord

CATALONIA

···

LLEIDA · ANDORRA · GIRONA
BARCELONA PROVINCE · TARRAGONA

THERE IS A *wealth of natural beauty in Catalonia's four provinces, plus the small Catalan-speaking country of Andorra. They offer rocky coasts and mountains, fertile plains and sandy shores. Many who visit don't stray far from the coast, but the rewards for venturing further afield are immense.*

Beyond the constant bustle of Barcelona, Catalonia is essentially a rural region, with no large cities and few industrial blights. Of the four provinces, all named after their principal city, Lleida is the largest and least populated. Among its jewels are the Romanesque churches of the Boí valley and the Aigüestortes National Park.

Santa Maria, Ripoll

The province of Girona is blessed with mountains and sea. This eastern end of the Pyrenees has the magical Cerdanya valley and the ancient monasteries of Ripoll and Sant Joan de les Abadesses, as well as medieval villages and a handsome and too-often overlooked capital city. Its coast, the Costa Brava, is rocky and full of delights.

Barcelona province has its own coasts; the Maresme to the north is rather spoiled by the railway running beside the sea, but the Garraf to the south is more exciting – Sitges is a highly fashionable spot. Inland are the Holy Mountain of Montserrat (Catalonia's spiritual heart), the Penedès winelands, and the country town of Vic.

Tarragona, the most southerly of the provinces, has one of the peninsula's former Roman capitals. Here the land rolls more gently, supporting fruit and nut orchards and the monastic communities of Poblet and Santes Creus, before falling away towards the rice lands of the Ebre. The coastline is more gentle, too, with long, sandy beaches.

Aigüestortes y E. Sant Maurici National Park in the central Pyrenees, in the province of Llerida

◁ A fisherman inspects his nets in Cadaqués on the Costa Brava

Exploring Catalonia

CATALONIA INCLUDES a long stretch of the Spanish Pyrenees, whose green, flower-filled valleys hide picturesque villages with Romanesque churches. The Parc Nacional d'Aigüestortes and Vall d'Aran are paradises for naturalists, while Baqueira-Beret offers skiers reliable snow. Sun-lovers can choose between the rugged Costa Brava or the long sandy stretches of the Costa Daurada. Tarragona is rich in Roman monuments. Inland are the monasteries of Poblet and Santes Creus and the well-known vineyards of Penedès.

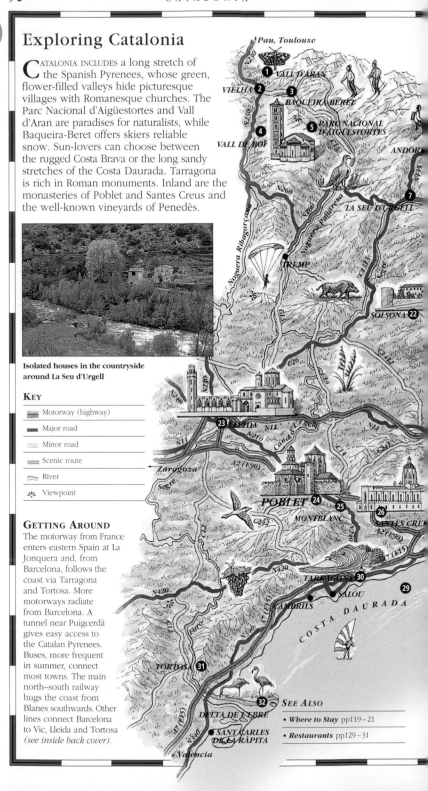

Isolated houses in the countryside around La Seu d'Urgell

KEY

▨▨▨	Motorway (highway)
▬▬	Major road
⋯⋯	Minor road
▨▨▨	Scenic route
⤳	River
☀	Viewpoint

GETTING AROUND

The motorway from France enters eastern Spain at La Jonquera and, from Barcelona, follows the coast via Tarragona and Tortosa. More motorways radiate from Barcelona. A tunnel near Puigcerdà gives easy access to the Catalan Pyrenees. Buses, more frequent in summer, connect most towns. The main north–south railway hugs the coast from Blanes southwards. Other lines connect Barcelona to Vic, Lleida and Tortosa *(see inside back cover).*

Map labels:
Pau, Toulouse
VALL D'ARAN
VIELHA
BAQUEIRA-BERET
PARC NACIONAL D'AIGÜESTORTES
VALL DE BOÍ
ANDOR
LA SEU D'URGELL
TREMP
SOLSONA
LLEIDA
Zaragoza
Sogre
POBLET
MONTBLANC
SANTES CRE
TARRAGONA
SALOU
CAMBRILS
COSTA DAURADA
TORTOSA
DELTA DE L'EBRE
SANT CARLES DE LA RÀPITA
Valencia

SEE ALSO

• Where to Stay pp119–21

• Restaurants pp129–31

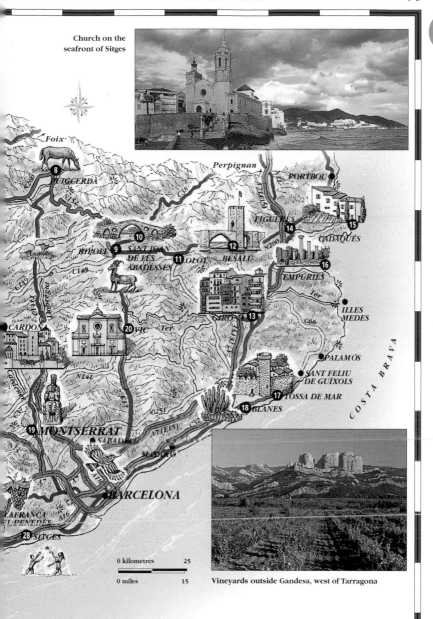

Church on the seafront of Sitges

Vineyards outside Gandesa, west of Tarragona

SIGHTS AT A GLANCE

Andorra 6
Baqueira-Beret 3
Besalú 12
Blanes 18
Cadaqués 15
Cardona 21
Costa Daurada 29
Delta de l'Ebre 32
Empúries 16

Figueres 14
Girona 13
Lleida 23
Montblanc 25
Montserrat pp104–5 19
Olot 11
Parc Nacional
    d'Aigüestortes 5
Poblet pp108–9 24

Puigcerdà 8
Ripoll 9
Santes Creus 26
Sant Joan de les
    Abadesses 10
La Seu d'Urgell 7
Sitges 28
Solsona 22
Tarragona 30

Tortosa 31
Tossa de Mar 17
Vall d'Aran 1
Vall de Boí 4
Vic 20
Vielha 2
Vilafranca del
    Penedès 27

The Vall d'Aran, surrounded by the snow-capped mountains of the Pyrenees

BUTTERFLIES OF THE VALL D'ARAN

A huge variety of butter-flies and moths is found high in the valleys and mountains of the Pyrenees. The isolated Vall d'Aran is the home of several unique and rare subspecies. The best time of the year in which to see the butterflies is between May and July.

Chequered Skipper
(Carterocephalus palemon)

Clouded Apollo
(Parnassins mnemosyne)

Grizzled Skipper (underside)
(Pyrgus malvae)

Vall d'Aran ❶

Lleida N230. 🚌 *Vielha.*
🛈 *Vielha (973 64 01 10).*

THIS VALLEY OF VALLEYS – *aran* means valley – is a lovely 600-sq km (230-sq mile) haven of forests and meadows filled with flowers, surrounded by towering mountain peaks.

The Vall d'Aran was formed by the Riu Garona, which rises in the area and flows out to France as the Garonne. With no proper link to the outside world until 1924, when a road was built over the Bonaigua Pass, the valley was cut off from the rest of Spain for most of the winter. Snow blocks the narrow pass from November to April, but today access is easy through the Túnel de Vielha from El Pont de Suert.

The fact that the Vall d'Aran faces north means that it has a climate similar to that on the Atlantic coast. Many rare wild flowers and butterflies flourish in the perfect conditions that are created by the shady slopes and damp breezes. It is also a famous habitat for many species of narcissus.

Tiny villages have grown up beside the Riu Garona, often around Romanesque churches, notably at **Bossòst**, **Salardú**, **Escunhau** and **Arties**. The valley is also ideal for outdoor sports such as skiing and is popular with walkers.

Vielha ❷

Lleida. 🏃 *2,700.* 🚌 🛈 *Carrer Sarriulera 10 (973 64 01 10).* 🛒 *Thu.* 🎉 *Festa de Vielha (8 Sep), Feria de Vielha (8 Oct).*

NOW A modern ski resort, the capital of the Vall d'Aran holds on to its medieval past. The Romanesque church of **Sant Miquel** has an octag-onal bell tower and a superb 12th-century crucifix, the *Mig Aran Christ.* It formed part of a larger carving representing the Descent from the Cross. The **Museu de la Vall d'Aran** is devoted to Aranese culture.

🏛 **Museu de la Vall d'Aran**
Carrer Major 26. 📞 *973 64 18 15.* 🕐 *10am–1pm, 5–8pm Tue– Sat, 10am–1pm Sun.* ● *1 & 6 Jan, 8 Sep, 8 Oct, 25 & 26 Dec.* 🖥 *www.aran.org*

Mig Aran Christ (12th-century),
Sant Miquel church, Vielha

Baqueira-Beret ❸

Lleida. 🏔 *100.* 🚉 🛈 *Baqueira-Beret (973 63 90 00).* 🎭 *Romeria de Nostra Senyora de Montgarri (2 Jul).*

THIS EXTENSIVE ski resort, one of the best in Spain, is popular with both the public and the Spanish royal family. There is reliable winter snow cover and a choice of over 40 pistes at altitudes from 1,520 m to 2,470 m (4,987 ft to 8,104 ft).

Baqueira and Beret were separate mountain villages before skiing became popular, but they have now merged to form a single resort. The Romans took full advantage of the thermal springs located here, which are nowadays appreciated by tired skiers.

Vall de Boí ❹

Lleida N230. 🚉 *La Pobla de Segur.* 🚉 *El Pont de Suert.* 🛈 *Barruera (973 69 40 00).*

THIS SMALL VALLEY on the edge of the Parc Nacional d'Aigüestortes is dotted with tiny villages, many of which are built around magnificent Catalan Romanesque churches.

Dating from the 11th and 12th centuries, these churches are distinguished by their tall belfries, such as the six storey bell tower of the **Església de Santa Eulàlia** at Erill-la-Vall.

The two churches at Taüll, **Sant Climent** *(see p20)* and **Santa Maria**, have superb frescoes. Between 1919 and 1923 the originals were taken for safekeeping to the Museu Nacional d'Art de Catalunya in Barcelona *(see p80)*. Replicas now stand in their place. You can climb the towers of Sant Climent for superb views of the surrounding countryside.

Other churches in the area worth visiting include those at **Coll**, for its fine ironwork, **Barruera**, and **Durro**, which has another massive bell tower.

At the head of the valley is the hamlet of **Caldes de Boí**, popular for its thermal springs and ski facilities. It is also a good base for exploring the Parc Nacional d'Aigüestortes, the entrance to which is only 5 km (3 miles) from here.

The tall belfry of Sant Climent church at Taüll in the Vall de Boí

Parc Nacional d'Aigüestortes ❺

Lleida. 🚉 *La Pobla de Segur.* 🚉 *El Pont de Suert, La Pobla de Segur.* 🛈 *Barruera (973 69 40 00).*

THE PRISTINE mountain scenery of Catalonia's only national park is among the most spectacular to be seen anywhere in the Pyrenees.

Established in 1955, the park covers an area of 102 sq km (40 sq miles). Its full title is Parc Nacional d'Aigüestortes i Estany de Sant Maurici, named after the lake *(estany)* of Sant Maurici in the east and the Aigüestortes (literally, twisted waters) area in the west. The main village is the mountain

settlement of Espot, on the park's eastern edge. Dotted around the park are waterfalls and the sparkling, clear waters of around 150 lakes and tarns which, in an earlier era, were scoured by glaciers to depths of up to 50 m (164 ft).

The finest scenery is around Sant Maurici lake, which lies beneath the twin shards of the Serra dels Encantats, (Mountains of the Enchanted). From here, there is a variety of walks, particularly along the string of lakes that leads north to the towering peaks of Agulles d'Amitges. To the south is the dramatic vista of Estany Negre, the highest and deepest tarn in the park.

Early summer in the lower valleys is marked by a mass of pink and red rhododendrons, while later in the year wild lilies bloom in the forests of fir, beech and silver birch.

The park is also home to a variety of wildlife. Chamois (also known as izards) live on the mountain screes and in the meadows, while beavers and otters can be spotted by the lakes. Golden eagles nest on mountain ledges, and grouse and capercaillie are found in the woods.

During the summer the park is popular with walkers, while in winter, the snow-covered mountains are ideal for cross-country skiing.

A crystal-clear stream, Parc Nacional d'Aigüestortes

LES QUATRE BARRES

The four red bars on the *senyera*, the Catalan flag, are said to represent the four provinces: Barcelona, Girona, Lleida and Tarragona. The design derives from a legend of Guifré el Pelós, first Count of Barcelona *(see p38)*. It relates how he received a call for help from Charles the Bald, who was King of the West Franks and grandson of Charlemagne. Guifré went to his aid and turned the tide of battle, but was mortally wounded. As he lay dying, Charles dipped his fingers in Guifré's blood and dragged them across his plain gold shield, giving him a grant of arms.

Catalonia's national emblem

Andorra ❻

Principality of Andorra. 🏛 *65,000.* 🚌 *Andorra la Vella.* ℹ *Calle Dr Vilanova, Andorra la Vella (376 82 02 14).* ⓦ *www.andorra.ad*

ANDORRA OCCUPIES 464 sq km (179 sq miles) of the Pyrenees between France and Spain. In 1993, it became fully independent and held its first ever democratic elections. Since 1278, it had been an autonomous feudal state under the jurisdiction of the Spanish bishop of La Seu d'Urgell and the French Count of Foix (a title adopted by the President of France). These are still the ceremonial joint heads of state.

Andorra's official language is Catalan, though French and Castilian are also spoken by most residents.

For many years Andorra has been a tax-free paradise for shoppers, a fact reflected in the crowded shops and supermarkets of the capital **Andorra la Vella**. Les Escaldes (near the capital), as well as Sant Julià de Lòria and El Pas de la Casa (the towns nearest the Spanish and French borders), have also become shopping centres.

Most visitors never see Andorra's rural charms, which match those of other parts of the Pyrenees. The region is excellent for walkers. One of the main routes leads to the **Cercle de Pessons**, a bowl of lakes in the east, and past Romanesque chapels such as **Sant Martí** at La Cortinada. In the north is the picturesque Sorteny valley where traditional farmhouses have been converted into snug restaurants.

La Seu d'Urgell ❼

Lleida. 🏛 *13,000.* 🚌 ℹ *Avenida Valles de Andorra 33 (973 35 15 11).* 🗓 *Tue & Sat.* 🎉 *Festa major (last week of Aug).*

THIS PYRENEAN TOWN was made a bishopric in the 6th century. Feuds between the bishops of Urgell and the Counts of Foix over land, gave rise to Andorra in the 13th century. The **cathedral** has a Romanesque statue of Santa Maria d'Urgell. The **Museu Diocesà** contains a 10th-century copy of St Beatus of Liébana's *Commentary on the Apocalypse*.

🏛 Museu Diocesà

Plaça del Deganat. ☎ *973 35 32 42.* ⏰ *Oct–May: noon–1pm Mon–Fri, 11–1pm Sat & Sun; Jun–Sep: 10am–1pm & 4–7pm Mon–Sat, 10am–1pm Sun.* ● *1 Jan, 25 Dec & public hols.* 🏛 ♿

Carving, La Seu d'Urgell cathedral

Puigcerdà ❽

Girona. 🏛 *7,000.* 🚌 🚉 ℹ *Carrer Querol 1 (972 88 05 42).* 🗓 *Sun.* 🎉 *Festa del Llac (third Sun of Aug); Festa del Roser (third week of Jul).* ⓦ *www.puigcerda.com*

PUIG IS CATALAN for hill. Despite sitting on a relatively small hill compared with the encircling mountains, which

rise to 2,900 m (9,500 ft), Puigcerdà nevertheless has a fine view down the beautiful Cerdanya valley.

Puigcerdà was founded in 1177 by Alfons II as the capital of Cerdanya, an important agricultural region, which shares a past and its culture with the French Cerdagne. The Spanish enclave of **Llívia**, an attractive little town with a medieval pharmacy, lies 6 km (3.75 miles) inside France.

Cerdanya is the largest valley in the Pyrenees. At its edge is the **Cadí-Moixeró** nature reserve *(see p138)*, a place for ambitious walks.

Portal of Monestir de Santa Maria

Ripoll ❾

Girona. 🏛 *11,000.* 🚌 🚉 ℹ *Plaça del Abat Oliva (972 70 23 51).* 🗓 *Sat.* 🎉 *Festa major (11–12 May), La Llana y Casament a Pagès (Sun after Festa major).* ⓦ *www.elripolles.com*

ONCE A TINY mountain base from which raids against the Moors were made, Ripoll is now best known for the **Monestir de Santa Maria** *(see p20)*, founded in 879. The town is called the "cradle of Catalonia" as the monastery was the power base of Guifré el Pelós (Wilfred the Hairy), founder of the House of Barcelona *(see p38)*. He is also buried here. In the later 12th century, the west portal was decorated with what are regarded as the finest Romanesque carvings in Spain. This and the cloister are the only parts of the medieval monastery to have survived.

ENVIRONS: In the mountains to the west is **Sant Jaume de Frontanyà** *(see p20)*, another superb Romanesque church.

The medieval town of Besalú on the banks of the Riu Fluvià

Sant Joan de les Abadesses ❿

Girona. 🚗 3,800. 🚌 🚶 Plaça de Abadia 9 (972 72 05 99). 🚐 Sun. 🎆 Festa major (second week of Sep). 🌐 www.santjoandelesabadesses.com

A FINE, 12th-century Gothic bridge arches over the Riu Ter to this unassuming market town, whose main attraction is its **monastery**.

Founded in 885, it was a gift from Guifré, first count of Barcelona, to his daughter, the first abbess. The church has little decoration except for a wooden calvary, *The Descent from the Cross*. Though made in 1150, it looks modern. The figure of a thief on the left was burnt in the Civil War and replaced so skilfully that it is hard to tell it is new. The museum has Baroque and Renaissance altarpieces.

12th-century calvary, Sant Joan de les Abadesses monastery

ENVIRONS: To the north are **Camprodon** and **Beget**, both with Romanesque churches *(see p21)*. Camprodon also has some grand houses, and its region is noted for sausages.

Olot ⓫

Girona. 🚗 28,000. 🚌 🚶 Carrer del Bisbe Lorenzana 15 (972 26 01 41). 🚐 Mon. 🎆 Feria de mayo (1 May), Corpus Christi (Jun), Festa del Tura (8 Sep). 🌐 www.agtat.es

T HIS SMALL MARKET TOWN is at the centre of a landscape pockmarked with extinct volcanoes. But it was an earthquake in 1474 that destroyed its medieval past.

During the 18th century the town's textile industry spawned the "Olot School" of art *(see p24)*. Cotton fabrics were printed with drawings, and in 1783 the Public School of Drawing was founded. Much of the school's work, which includes paintings such as Joaquim Vayreda's *Les Falgueres*, is in the **Museu Comarcal de la Garrotxa**. There are also pieces by *Modernista* sculptor Miquel Blay, whose damsels support the balcony at No. 38 Passeig Miquel Blay.

🏛 **Museu Comarcal de la Garrotxa**
Calle Hospici 8. 📞 972 27 91 30. 🕐 11am–2pm, 4–7pm Mon, Wed–Sat, 11am–2pm Sun & public hols. 🔴 1 Jan, 25 Dec. 🎫 ♿

Besalú ⓬

Girona. 🚗 2,000. 🚌 🚶 Plaça de la Llibertat 1 (972 59 12 40). 🚐 Tue. 🎆 Sant Vicenç (22 Jan), Festa major (last weekend of Sep).

A MAGNIFICENT medieval town, with a striking approach across a fortified bridge over the Riu Fluvià, Besalú has two fine Romanesque churches: **Sant Vicenç** and **Sant Pere** *(see p21)*. The latter is the sole remnant of a Benedictine monastery founded in 977, but pulled down in 1835 leaving a big, empty square.

In 1964 a **mikvah**, a Jewish ritual bath, was discovered by chance. It was built in 1264 and is one of only three of that period to survive in Europe. The tourist office has the keys to all the town's attractions.

To the south, the sky-blue lake of **Banyoles**, where the 1992 Olympic rowing contests were held, is ideal for picnics.

Shop selling *llonganisses* in the mountain town of Camprodon

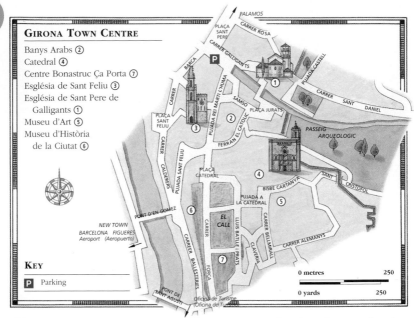

GIRONA TOWN CENTRE

Banys Arabs ②
Catedral ④
Centre Bonastruc Ça Porta ⑦
Església de Sant Feliu ③
Església de Sant Pere de
    Galligants ①
Museu d'Art ⑤
Museu d'Història
    de la Ciutat ⑥

KEY

P Parking

0 metres   250

0 yards   250

Girona ⑬

Girona. 🏘 *75,000.* ✈ 🚃 🚌
ℹ *Rambla de la Llibertat 1 (972 22
65 75).* 🛒 *Tue, Sat.* 🎉 *El Pedal
(bike race, last fortnight of Sep),
Sant Narcís (29 Oct for a week).*
Ⓦ *www.ajuntament.gi*

THIS HANDSOME TOWN puts
on its best face beside the
Riu Onyar, where tall, pastel-
coloured buildings rise above
the water. Behind them, in the
old town, the Rambla de la
Llibertat is lined with busy
shops and street cafés.

The houses were built in the
19th century to replace sections of the city wall damaged
during a seven-month siege
by French troops in 1809. Most

of the rest of the ramparts, first
raised by the Romans, are still
intact and have been turned
into the Passeig Arqueològic
(Archaeological Walk), which
runs right round the city.

The walk's starting point is
on the north side of the town,
near the **Església de Sant
Pere de Galligants** (St Peter
of the Cock Crows) *(see p21).*
The church now houses the
city's archaeological collection.

From here, a narrow street
goes through the north gate,
where huge Roman foundation
stones are still visible. They
mark the route of the Via
Augusta, the road which once
ran from Tarragona to Rome.
The most popular place of
devotion in the town is the

Església de Sant Feliu. The
church, begun in the 14th
century, was built over the
tombs of St Felix and St
Narcissus, both patrons of the
city. Next to the high altar are
eight Roman sarcophagi.

Despite their name, the
nearby **Banys Àrabs** (Arab
Baths), lit by a fine octagonal
lantern, were built in the late
12th century, about 300 years
after the Moors had left.

🏛 Centre Bonastruc Ça Porta

Carrer de la Força 8. 📞 *972 21
67 61.* ⊙ *daily.* ● *1 & 6 Jan, 25 &
26 Dec.* 🏷 ♿
This centre charts the history of
Jews in Girona. The buildings it
occupies in the maze of alley-
ways and steps in the old town
were once part of El Call, the
Jewish ghetto, which was in-
habited by the city's Jews from
the late 9th century until their
expulsion from Spain in 1492.

⛪ Catedral
Girona Cathedral's west face is
pure Catalan Baroque, but the
rest of the building is Gothic.
The single nave, built in 1416
by Guillem Bofill, possesses
the widest Gothic span in the
Christian world. Behind the
altar is a marble throne known
as "Charlemagne's Chair". It is
named after the Frankish king

Painted houses packed tightly along the bank of the Riu Onyar in Girona

whose troops took Girona in 785. In the chancel is a 14th-century jewel-encrusted silver and enamel altarpiece, the best example in Catalonia. Among the fine Romanesque paintings and statues in the cathedral's museum are a 10th-century illuminated copy of St Beatus of Liébana's *Commentary on the Apocalypse*, and a 14th-century statue of the Catalan king, Pere the Ceremonious.

The collection's most famous item is a tapestry, called *The Creation*, decorated with lively figures. The rich colours of this large 11th- to 12th-century work are well preserved.

Tapestry of *The Creation*

Museu d'Art
Pujada de la Catedral 12. (972 20 95 36. (Tue–Sun. (1 & 6 Jan, 25 & 26 Dec.
This is one of Catalonia's best art galleries, with works from the Romanesque period to the 20th century. The many items from churches ruined by war or neglect tell of the richness of church interiors long ago.

Museu del Cinema
Carrer Sèquia 1. (972 41 27 77 (Tue–Sun. (1 & 6 Jan, 25 & 26 Dec.
Next to Església de Mercadel, this collection includes film and artifacts from the mid-19th century to the present day.

Museu d'Història de la Ciutat
Carrer de la Força 27. (972 22 22 29. (Tue–Sun. (1 & 6 Jan, 25 & 26 Dec.
The city's history museum is in an 18th-century former convent. Recesses where the decomposing bodies of members of the Capuchin Order were placed can still be seen. Exhibits include old *sardana* (*see p111*) instruments.

Figueres ⑭

Girona. 35,000. Plaça del Sol (972 50 31 55). Thu. Santa Creu (3 May), Sant Pere (29 Jun).

FIGUERES IS THE market town of the Empordà plain. Beside the plane-tree-shaded Rambla is the former Hotel de Paris, now home to the **Museu de Joguets** (Toy Museum). At the bottom of the Rambla is a statue of Narcís Monturiol i Estarriol (1819–95) who, it is said, invented the submarine.

Figueres was the birthplace of Salvador Dalí, who in 1974 turned the town theatre into the **Teatre-Museu Dalí**. Under its glass dome are works by Dalí and other painters. The whole place, from *Rainy Taxi* to the Mae West room, is a monument to Catalonia's most eccentric artist.

ENVIRONS: The **Casa-Museu Castell Gala Dalí**, 55 km (35 miles) south of Figueres, is the medieval castle Dalí bought in the 1970s. It contains some of his paintings. East of Figueres is the Romanesque monastery, **Sant Pere de Rodes** (*see p21*).

***Rainy Taxi*, a monument in the garden of the Teatre-Museu Dalí**

Museu de Joguets
C/ Sant Pere 1. (972 50 45 85. (Jun–Sep: daily; Oct–May: Tue–Sun.
Teatre-Museu Dalí
Pl Gala-Salvador Dalí. (972 67 75 05. (Jul–Sep: daily; Oct–Jun: Tue–Sun. (1 Jan, 25 Dec. by appointment.
Casa-Museu Castell Gala Dalí
C/ Gala Dalí, Púbol (La Pera). (972 48 86 55. (mid-Mar–Nov: Tue–Sun; Dec–mid-Mar: only for groups by appointment.

THE ART OF DALÍ

Salvador Dalí i Domènech was born in Figueres in 1904 and mounted his first exhibition at the age of 15. After studying at the Escuela de Bellas Artes in Madrid, and dabbling with Cubism, Futurism and Metaphysical painting, the young artist embraced Surrealism in 1929, becoming the movement's best-known painter. Never far from controversy, the self-publicist Dalí became famous for his hallucinatory images – such as *Woman-Animal Symbiosis* – which he described as "hand-painted dream photographs". Dalí's career also included writing and film-making, and established him as one of the 20th century's greatest artists. He died in his home town in 1989.

Ceiling fresco in the Wind Palace Room, Teatre-Museu Dalí

Cadaqués ⓯

Girona. 🏘 *2,000.* 🚌 ℹ️ *Carrer Cotxe 2 (972 25 83 15).* 🚍 *Mon.* 🎉 *Fiesta major de Verano (Sep), Santa Esperança (18 Dec).*

THIS PRETTY, whitewashed resort, overlooked by the Baroque **Església de Santa Maria**, is the most easterly in the Iberian peninsula. In the 1960s it was dubbed the "St Tropez of Spain", largely because of the young crowd that sought out Salvador Dalí in nearby Port Lligat. The house where he lived from 1930 until his death in 1989 is open to the public as the **Casa-Museu Salvador Dalí**. In summer, a "bus-train" takes visitors there from (but not back to) Cadaqués. The 15-minute walk is also pleasant.

The **Centre d'Art Perrot-Moore** contains examples of Dalí's works, some excellent Picassos, and a room dedicated to contemporary artists.

🏛 **Casa-Museu Salvador Dalí**
Port Lligat. 📞 *972 25 10 15.* 📠 *972 25 10 83.* ◻ *by appointment.* 📷
🏛 **Centre d'Art Perrot-Moore**
Carrer Vigilant 1. 📞 *972 25 82 31.* ◻ *Easter–Oct: Tue–Sun.* 📷 ♿

Empúries ⓰

Girona. 🚌 *L'Escala.* 📞 *972 77 02 08.* ◻ *Easter, Jun–Sep: 10am–8pm daily; Oct–May: 10am–6pm daily.* 📷 *ruins.* 🎭 *only for groups by appointment.*

THE EXTENSIVE ruins of this Greco-Roman town *(see p37)* occupy an imposing site beside the sea. Three separate

An excavated Roman pillar in the ruins of Empúries

Looking south along the Costa Brava from Tossa de Mar

settlements were built between the 7th and 3rd centuries BC: the old town (known to archaeologists as Palaiapolis); the new town (Neapolis); and the Roman town, which Julius Caesar founded in 49 BC.

The **old town** was founded by the Greeks in 600 BC as a trading port. It was built on what was then a small offshore island, and is now the site of the tiny walled hamlet of Sant Martí de Empúries. In 550 BC this was replaced by a larger new town on the shore which the Greeks named Emporion, meaning "trading place". In 218 BC, the Romans landed at Empúries and built a city next to the new town. From here they began their subjugation of the Iberian peninsula.

A nearby museum exhibits some of the site's finds, but the best are in the Museu Arqueològic of Barcelona *(see p80).*

Tossa de Mar ⓱

Girona. 🏘 *4,000.* 🚌 ℹ️ *Avinguda Pelegrí 25 (972 34 01 08).* 🚍 *Thu.* 🎉 *Festa de hivern (22 Jan), Festa de estiu (29 Jun).* 🌐 *www.tossademar.com*

AT THE END of a tortuous corniche, the Roman town of Turissa is one of the prettiest along the Costa Brava. Above the modern town is the **Vila Vella** (old town), a protected national monument. The medieval walls enclose fishermen's cottages, a 14th-century church and countless bars.

The **Museu Municipal** in the old town exhibits local

archaeological finds and modern art including *The Flying Violinist* by Marc Chagall.

🏛 **Museu Municipal**
Plaça Roig y Soler 1. 📞 *972 34 07 09.* ◻ *Tue–Sun.* 📷

Blanes ⓲

Girona. 🏘 *30,000.* 🚌 🚍 ℹ️ *Plaça de Catalunya 21 (972 33 03 48).* 🚍 *Mon.* 🎉 *Santa Ana (26 Jul).* 🌐 *www.blanes.net*

THE WORKING PORT of Blanes has one of the longest beaches on the Costa Brava. However, the highlight of the town is the **Jardí Botànic Mar i Murtra**. These gardens, designed by the German Karl Faust in 1928, are spectacularly sited above cliffs. There are around 7,000 species of Mediterranean and tropical plants, including African cacti.

🌿 **Jardí Botànic Mar i Murtra**
Pg Karl Faust 10. 📞 *972 33 08 26.* ◻ *daily.* ● *1 & 6 Jan, 24 & 25 Dec.*

A few of the many species of cacti, Jardí Botànic Mar i Murtra

◁ **Surrealist decoration on one of the buildings of the Teatre-Museu Dalí in Figueres**

The Costa Brava

THE COSTA BRAVA ("wild coast") runs for some 200 km (125 miles) from Blanes northwards to the region of Empordà, which borders France. It is a mix of rugged cliffs, pine-backed sandy coves, golden beaches and crowded, modern resorts. The busiest resorts – Lloret de Mar, Tossa de Mar and Platja d'Aro – are to the south. Sant Feliu de Guíxols and Palamós are still working towns behind the summer rush. Just inland there are medieval villages to explore, such as Peralada, Peratallada and Pals. Wine, olives and fishing were the mainstays of the area before the tourists came in the 1960s.

Cadaqués *retains an air of seclusion as it is accessible only by a steep road. It has an arty atmosphere and its small, stony beaches are relatively unspoiled and uncrowded.*

L'Estartit *is a good base for the Illes Medes, a former pirates' lair, which now form a marine reserve with clear waters perfect for skin diving.*

Palamós is a working port with modern hotels to the south, and secluded beaches and coves lapped by clear water to the north.

Platja d'Aro's long and sandy beach is lined with modern hotels. It is one of the most popular resorts on the coast.

Tossa de Mar has a golden beach in a small cove beneath the fortified old town.

Roses lies at the head of a sweeping bay. Its sandy beach, the longest on the Costa Brava, has become a mecca for lovers of water sports.

L'Escala is a small resort, popular mainly with local tourists. It has fine beaches and a small port where fishing nets dry in the sun.

Begur is a hilltop town just inland. It has good views of the coast, and small coves are tucked at its feet.

Llafranc, a whitewashed resort, with a promenade leading to neighbouring Calella, is one of the coast's most pleasant resorts.

Lloret de Mar *has more hotels than anywhere else on the coast. But there are unspoiled beaches nearby, such as Santa Cristina.*

Cadaqués
Roses
L'Escala
L'Estartit
Illes Medes
Begur
Llafranc
Calella de Palafrugell
Palamós
Platja d'Aro
S'Agaró
Sant Feliu de Guíxols
Tossa de Mar
Lloret de Mar
Blanes

0 kilometres 10
0 miles 5

Monestir de Montserrat ⑲

THE "SERRATED MOUNTAIN" (mont serrat), its highest peak rising to 1,236 m (4,055 ft), is a superb setting for Catalonia's holiest place, the Monastery of Montserrat, which is surrounded by chapels and hermits' caves. The monastery was first mentioned in the 9th century, enlarged in the 11th century, and in 1409 became independent of Rome. In 1811, when the French attacked Catalonia in the War of Independence (see p41), the monastery was destroyed. Rebuilt and repopulated in 1844, it was a beacon of Catalan culture during the Franco years. Today Benedictine monks live here. Visitors can hear the Escolania singing the *Salve Regina y Virolai* (the Montserrat hymn) at 1pm and 7:10pm every day (Sundays noon only), except in July and during the Christmas period, in the basilica.

A Benedictine monk

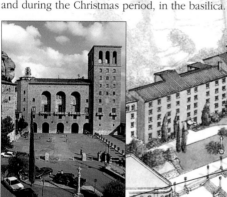

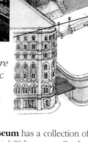

Plaça de Santa Maria
The focal points of the square are two wings of the Gothic cloister built in 1477. The modern monastery façade is by Francesc Folguera.

Plaça de la Creu   Gothic cloister

The Museum has a collection of 19th- and 20th-century Catalan paintings and many Italian and French works. It also displays liturgical items from the Holy Land.

The Way of the Cross
This path passes 14 statues representing the Stations of the Cross. It begins near the Plaça de l'Abat Oliba.

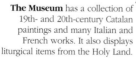

STAR FEATURES
★ **Basilica Façade**
★ **Black Virgin**

View of Montserrat
The complex includes shops, cafés and a hotel. Funicular railways take visitors from the Plaça de la Creu to the Cova Santa and the hermitage of Sant Joan.

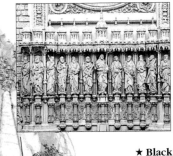

★ Basilica Façade
Agapit and Venanci Vallmitjana sculpted Christ and the Apostles on the basilica's Neo-Renaissance façade. It was built in 1900 to replace the Plateresque façade of the original church, consecrated in 1592.

VISITORS' CHECKLIST

Montserrat (Barcelona province).
93 877 77 77. Aeri de Montserrat, then cable car. from Barcelona. **Basilica** Oct–Jun: 7:30am–7:30pm; Jul–Sep: 7:30am–8:15pm; daily. from 9am Mon–Fri, from 7:30am Sat, from 8am Sun & religious hols. **Museum** 10am–6pm Mon–Fri, 9:30am–6:30pm Sat–Sun & public hols (phone ahead to confirm times).

★ Black Virgin
La Moreneta looks down from behind the altar, protected behind glass; her wooden orb protrudes for pilgrims to touch.

Basilica Interior
The sanctuary in the domed basilica is adorned by a richly enamelled altar and paintings by Catalan artists.

The Escolania is the famous choir of 50 boy choristers, who sing twice a day in the basilica.

Terminus for cable car from Aeri de Montserrat railway station

Inner Courtyard
On one side of the courtyard is the baptistry (1902), with sculptures by Carles Collet. Pilgrims may approach the Virgin through a door to the right.

THE VIRGIN OF MONTSERRAT
The small wooden statue of La Moreneta (the dark maiden) is the soul of Montserrat. It is said to have been made by St Luke and brought here by St Peter in AD 50. Centuries later, the statue is believed to have been hidden from the Moors in the nearby Santa Cova (Holy Cave). Carbon dating suggests, however, that the statue was carved around the 12th century. In 1881 Montserrat's Black Virgin became patroness of Catalonia.

The blackened Virgin of Montserrat

Vic ⑳

Barcelona. ▲ *31,000.* ▣ ▣ **i** *C/
Ciutat 4 (93 886 20 91).* ▣ *Tue & Sat.*
▣ *Mercat del Ram (Sat before Easter),
Sant Miquel (5–15 Jul), Música Viva (3
days mid-Sep), Mercat medieval (6–8
Dec).* W *www.ajvic.es*

MARKET DAYS are the best
time to go to this small
country town. This is when
the excellent local sausages
(embotits), for which the area
is renowned, are piled high in
the large Gothic Plaça Major,
along with other produce
from the surrounding plains.

In the 3rd century BC Vic
was the capital of an ancient
Iberian tribe, the Ausetans. The
town was then colonized by
the Romans – the remains of
a Roman temple survive today.
Since the 6th century the town
has been a bishop's see. In the
11th century, Abbot Oliva commissioned El Cloquer tower,
around which the cathedral
was built in the 18th century.
The interior is covered with
vast murals by Josep-Maria
Sert (1876–1945, *see p25*).
Painted in reds and golds,
they represent Biblical scenes.

Adjacent to the cathedral is
the **Museu Episcopal de Vic**
(see p21), which has one of
the best Romanesque collections in Catalonia. The large
display of mainly religious art
and relics includes bright,
simple murals and wooden
carvings from rural churches.
Also on display are 11th- and
12th-century frescoes and
some superb altar frontals.

Cardona dominating the surrounding area from its hilltop site

🏛 **Museu Episcopal**
Plaça Bisbe Oliba, 3. **C** *93 889 44
17.* ⭘ *Tue–Sun.* ▣ ▣ ▣

Cardona ㉑

Barcelona. ▲ *6,000.* ▣ **i** *Avinguda
Rastrillo (93 869 27 98).* ▣ *Sun.* ▣
*Carnival (Feb), Festa major (second
Sun of Sep).*

THIS 13TH-CENTURY, ruddy-
stoned castle of the Dukes
of Cardona, constables to the
crown of Aragón, is set on the
top of a hill. The castle was
rebuilt in the 18th century and
is now a luxurious parador
(see p114). Beside the castle
is an elegant, early 11th-
century church, the **Església
de Sant Vicenç**.

The castle gives views of
the town and of the Muntanya
de Sal (Salt Mountain), a huge
salt deposit beside the Riu
Cardener that has been mined
since Roman times.

Twelfth-century altar frontal, Museu Episcopal de Vic

Solsona ㉒

Lleida. ▲ *7,000.* ▣ **i** *Carretera de
Bassella 1 (973 48 23 10).* ▣ *Tue &
Fri.* ▣ *Carnival (Feb); Corpus Christi
(May/Jun), Festa major (8–11 Sep).*
W *www.elsolsonesinvita.com*

NINE TOWERS and three gate-
ways remain of Solsona's
moated fortifications. Inside the
walls is an ancient town of
noble mansions. The cathedral
houses a beautiful black stone
Virgin. The **Museu Diocesà i
Comarcal** contains Romanesque paintings and archaeological finds. **Museu Ganivets**
has a fine collection of knives.

🏛 **Museu Diocesà i Comarcal**
Plaça del Palau 1. **C** *973 48 21 01.*
⭘ *Tue–Sun.* ▣
🏛 **Museu Ganivets**
Travesia Sant Josep de Calasanç 9. **C**
973 48 15 69. ⭘ *Tue–Sun.* ● *25, 26
Dec, 6 Jan.* ▣ ▣

Lleida ㉓

Lleida. ▲ *112,000.* ▣ ▣ **i** *Avda
de Madrid 36 (973 27 09 97).* ▣ *Thu
& Sat.* ▣ *Sant Anastasi (11 May),
Sant Miquel (29 Sep).*
W *www.lleidatur.es*

DOMINATING LLEIDA, the
capital of Catalonia's only
inland province, is **La Suda**, a
fort, now in ruins, taken from
the Moors in 1149. The cathedral, founded in 1203, lies
within the fort's walls, above
the town. It was transformed
into barracks by Felipe V in
1707. Today it is desolate, but
remains imposing, with magnificent Gothic windows.

A lift descends from La Seu

Vella to the Plaça de Sant Joan in the busy, pedestrianized shopping street that sweeps round the foot of the hill. The new cathedral is here, as is the reconstructed 13th-century town hall, the **Paeria**.

Poblet ㉔

See pp108–9.

Montblanc ㉕

Tarragona. 🏠 6,000. 🚌 🚊 🛈
Antigua Iglesia de Sant Francesca (977 86 17 33). 🚐 *Tue & Fri.* 🎊 *Festa major (8–11 Sep).*

T HE MEDIEVAL grandeur of Montblanc lives on within its walls – possibly Catalonia's finest piece of military architecture. At the **Sant Jordi** gate St George allegedly slew the dragon. The **Museu Comarcal de la Conca de Barberà** has displays on local crafts.

🏛 **Museu Comarcal de la Conca de Barberà**
Carrer de Josa 6. 🏠 977 86 03 49.
🔲 *Tue–Sun & public hols* 🎨

Santes Creus ㉖

Tarragona 🏠 150. 🚊 🛈 *Plaça de Sant Bernard 1 (977 63 83 01).* 🚐
Sat & Sun. 🎊 *Santa Llúcia (13 Dec).*

T HE TINY VILLAGE of Santes Creus is home to the prettiest of the "Cistercian triangle"

monasteries. The other two, Vallbona de les Monges and Poblet, are nearby. The **Monestir de Santes Creus** was founded in 1150 by Ramon Berenguer IV *(see p38)* during his reconquest of Catalonia. The Gothic cloisters are decorated with figurative sculptures, a style first permitted by Jaume II, who ruled from 1291 to 1327. His carved tomb is in the 12th-century church whose interior is decorated with a rose window.

🛈 **Monestir de Santes Creus**
🏠 977 63 83 29. 🔲 *Tue- Sun & public hols.* ⬤ *1 Jan, 25 Dec.* 🎨 ♿

Vilafranca del Penedès ㉗

Barcelona. 🏠 30,000. 🚌 🚊
🛈 *Carrer Cort 14 (93 892 03 58).*
🚐 *Sat.* 🎊 *Fira de Mayo (2nd week of May), Festa major (end Aug).*
🌐 www.ajvilafranca.es

T HIS MARKET TOWN is set in the heart of Penedès, the main wine-producing region of Catalonia. The **Museu del Vi** (Wine Museum) documents the history of the area's wine trade. Local *bodegues* can be visited for wine tasting.
Sant Sadurní d'Anoia, the capital of Spain's sparkling wine, *cava (see pp28–9)*, is 8 km (5 miles) to the north.

🏛 **Museu del Vi**
Plaça de Jaume I. 🏠 93 890 05 82.
🔲 *Tue -Sun & public hols.* 🎨

Anxaneta climbing to the top of a tower of casCtellers

HUMAN TOWERS

The province of Tarragona is famous for its *casteller* festivals, in which teams of men stand on each other's shoulders in an effort to build the highest human tower *(castell)*. Configurations depend on the number of men who form the base. Teams wear similar colours, and often have names denoting their home town. The small boy who has to undertake the perilous climb to the top, where he makes the sign of the cross, is called the *anxaneta* (weathercock). *Castellers* assemble in competition for Tarragona province's major festivals throughout the year. In the wine town of Vilafranca del Penedès they turn out for Sant Fèlix (30 August), and in Tarragona city for Santa Tecla, its *festa major* on 23 September. Rival teams in Valls appear on St John's Day (24 June), but strive for their best achievement at the end of the tower-building season on St Ursula's Day (21 October), when teams from all over Catalonia converge on the town square.

Monestir de Santes Creus, surrounded by poplar and hazel trees

Monestir de Poblet ㉔

THE MONASTERY OF SANTA MARIA DE POBLET is a haven of tranquillity and a resting place of kings. It was the first and most important of three sister monasteries, known as the "Cistercian triangle" *(see p107)*, that helped to consolidate power in Catalonia after it had been recaptured from the Moors by Ramon Berenguer IV. In 1835, during the Carlist upheavals, it was plundered and seriously damaged by fire. Restoration of the impressive ruins, largely complete, began in 1930 and monks returned in 1940.

The dormitory is reached by stairs from the church. The vast 87-m (285-ft) gallery dates from the 18th century. Half of it is still in use by the monks.

The 13th-century refectory is a vaulted hall with an octagonal fountain and a pulpit.

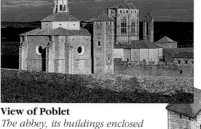

View of Poblet
The abbey, its buildings enclosed by fortified walls that have hardly changed since the Middle Ages, is in an isolated valley near the Riu Francolí's source.

Museum

Wine cellar

Library
The Gothic scriptorium was converted into a library in the 17th century, when the Duke of Cardona donated his book collection.

Former kitchen

Royal doorway

Royal palace

TIMELINE

1157 Founding of sister monastery at Vallbona de les Monges			*Royal tombs*			**1812** Poblet desecrated by French troops		**1940** Monks return
	1168 Santes Creus founded – third abbey in Cistercian triangle	**14th century** Main cloister finished		**1479** Juan II, last king of Aragón, buried here				
1100	**1300**		**1500**		**1700**		**1900**	
	1196 Alfonso II is the first king to be buried here	**1336–87** Reign of Pere the Ceremonious, who designates Poblet a royal pantheon					**1953** Tombs reconstructed. Royal remains returned	
				1788–1808 Reign of Carlos IV, who has main reredos installed				
	1151 Poblet monastery founded by Ramon Berenguer IV					**1835** Disentailment *(p41)* of monasteries. Poblet ravaged		

Chapterhouse

This perfectly square room, with slender columns, has tiers of benches for the monks. It is paved with the tombstones of 11 abbots who died between 1393 and 1693.

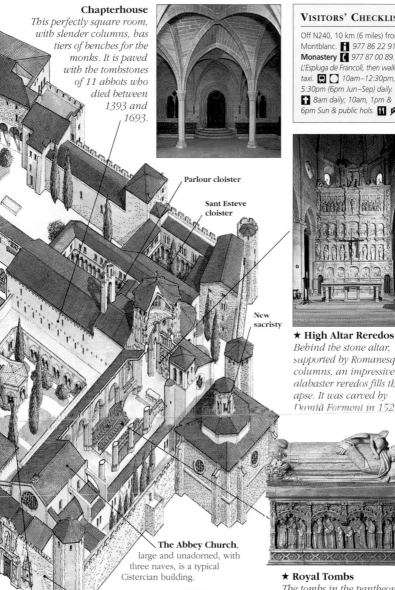

Parlour cloister

Sant Esteve cloister

New sacristy

★ High Altar Reredos

Behind the stone altar, supported by Romanesque columns, an impressive alabaster reredos fills the apse. It was carved by Damià Forment in 1527.

The Abbey Church, large and unadorned, with three naves, is a typical Cistercian building.

Baroque church façade

★ Cloisters

The evocative, vaulted cloisters were built in the 12th and 13th centuries and were the centre of monastic life. The capitals are beautifully decorated with carved scrollwork.

★ Royal Tombs

The tombs in the pantheon of kings were begun in 1359. In 1950 they were reconstructed by the sculptor Frederic Marès.

STAR FEATURES

★ High Altar Reredos

★ Royal Tombs

★ Cloisters

Palm trees lining the waterfront at Sitges

Sitges ㉘

Barcelona. 🏃 20,000. 🚊 🚌
ℹ C/ Sínia Morera 1 (93 894 50 04).
🚢 Thu (in summer). 🎭 Festa major
(23–24 Aug). ⓦ www.sitges.org

LIVELY BARS line the seafront at Sitges, where Modernista artist Santiago Rusiñol *(see p25)* spent much time. He bequeathed his collection of ceramics, sculptures and paintings to the **Museu Cau Ferrat**, which also has works by El Greco.

Sitges is also now a popular gay resort.

🏛 **Museu Cau Ferrat**
Carrer Fonollar. 📞 93 894 03 64.
🕐 Tue–Sun. ● public hols. 🎫

Costa Daurada ㉙

Tarragona. 🚊 🚌 Calafell, Sant Vicenç
de Calders, Salou. ℹ Tarragona
(977 23 34 15).

THE COAST OF Tarragona province, with its long, sandy beaches, is known as the Costa Daurada (the Golden Coast). **Vilanova i la Geltrú** and **El Vendrell** are two of the active ports along its coastline. The **Museu Pau Casals** in Sant Salvador (El Vendrell) is dedicated to the famous cellist.

Port Aventura, south of Tarragona, is one of Europe's largest theme parks. Its attractions are exotically-inspired and named Mediterrània, Wild West, México, Polynesia and China. **Cambrils** and **Salou** to the south are the liveliest resorts – the others are mostly low-key, family holiday spots.

🏛 **Museu Pau Casals**
Avinguda Palfuriana 59–61.
📞 977 68 42 76. 🕐 Tue–Sun.
📽 **Port Aventura**
Autovia Salou–Vila-seca. 📞 977 77
90 00. 🕐 mid-Mar–6 Jan. 🎫 ♿

Tarragona ㉚

Tarragona. 🏃 110,000. ✈ 🚊 🚌
ℹ Carrer Fortuny 4 (977 23 34 15).
🚢 Tue & Thu. 🎭 Sant Magí (19
Aug), Santa Tecla (23 Sep).

TARRAGONA IS NOW a major industrial port, but it has preserved many remnants of its Roman past. As the capital of Tarraconensis, the Romans used it as a base for the conquest of the peninsula in the 3rd century BC *(see p37)*.

The avenue of Rambla Nova ends abruptly on the clifftop Balcó de Europa, in sight of the ruins of the **Amfiteatre Romà** and the ruined 12th-century church of **Santa Maria del Miracle**.

Nearby is the Praetorium, a Roman tower that was converted into a palace in medieval times. It is sometimes known as the Castell de Pilato (named after Pontius Pilate), and it now houses the **Museu de la Romanitat**. This displays Roman and medieval finds, and gives access to the cavernous passageways of the excavated Roman circus, built in the 1st century AD. Adjoining the Praetorium is the

The remains of the Roman amphitheatre, Tarragona

Museu Nacional Arqueo-lògic, containing the most important collection of Roman artifacts in Catalonia. It has an extensive collection of bronze tools and beautiful mosaics, including a *Head of Medusa*.

Among the most impressive remains are the huge pre-Roman stones on which the Roman wall is built. An archaeological walk stretches 1-km (1,100-yd) along the wall to its towers.

Behind the wall lies the 12th-century **cathedral**, built on the site of a Roman temple to Jupiter and a subsequent Arab mosque. This evolved over many centuries, as seen from the blend of styles of the exterior. Inside is an alabaster altarpiece of St Tecla, carved by Pere Joan in 1434. The 13th-century cloister, which is filled with orange trees, has early Gothic vaulting, but the doorway is Romanesque *(see pp20–21)* in its decoration.

In the west of town is a 3rd- to 6th-century Christian cemetery (ask about opening times in the archaeological museum). Some of the sarcophagi were originally used as pagan tombs.

Environs: The **Aqüeducte de les Ferreres** lies just outside the city, next to the A7 motorway (there is a lay-by for viewing). This 2nd-century aqueduct was built to bring water to the city from the Riu Gaià, 30 km (19 miles) to the north. The **Arc de Berà**, a 1st-century triumphal arch on the Via Augusta, is 20 km (12 miles) northeast on the N340.

🏛 **Museu Nacional Arqueològic de Tarragona**
Plaça del Rei 5. 📞 977 23 62 09. ◯ *10am–2pm Sun & public hols; Jun–Sep: 10am–8pm Tue–Sat; Oct–May: 10am–1:30pm & 4–7pm Tue–Sat.* 🏷 *(free Tue).* ♿ 🌐 *www.mnat.es*
🏛 **Museu de la Romanitat**
Plaça del Rei. 📞 977 24 19 52. ◯ *Jun–Sep: 9am–9pm Tue–Sat, 9am–3pm Sun & public hols; Oct–May: 9am–7pm Tue–Sat, 10am–3pm Sun & public hols.* 🏷

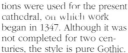

Ruins of the Palaeo-Christian Necropolis

Tortosa ❸❶

Tarragona. 👥 *30,000.* 🛈 *Avda Generalitat (977 51 08 22).* 🚌 *Mon.* 🎉 *Nostra Senyora de la Cinta (1st week Sep).* 🌐 *www.tortosa.altanet.org*

A RUINED CASTLE and medieval walls are clues to Tortosa's historical importance. Sited at the lowest crossing point on the Riu Ebre, it has been strategically significant since Iberian times. The Moors held the city from the 8th century until 1148. The old Moorish castle, known as La Suda, is all that remains of their defences. It has now been renovated as a parador *(see p121)*. The Moors also built a mosque in Tortosa in 914. Its foundations were used for the present cathedral, on which work began in 1347. Although it was not completed for two centuries, the style is pure Gothic.

Tortosa was badly damaged in 1938–39 during one of the fiercest battles of the Civil War *(see p43)*, when the Ebre formed the front line between the opposing forces,

Delta de L'Ebre ❸❷

Tarragona. 🚉 *Aldea.* 🚌 *Deltebre, Aldea.* 🛈 *Deltebre (977 48 96 79).* 🌐 *www.ebre.com/delta*

T HE DELTA of the Riu Ebre is a prosperous rice-growing region and wildlife haven. Some 70 sq km (27 sq miles) have been turned into a nature reserve, the **Parc Natural del Delta de L'Ebre**. In Deltebre there is an information centre and an interesting **Eco-Museu**, with an aquarium containing species found in the delta.

The main towns in the area are **Amposta** and **Sant Carles de la Ràpita**, both of which serve as good bases for exploring the reserve.

The best places to see the variety of wildlife are along the shore, from the Punta del Fangar in the north to the Punta de la Banya in the south. Everywhere is accessible by car except the Illa de Buda. Flamingoes breed on this island and, together with other water birds such as herons and avocets, can be seen from tourist boats that leave from Riumar and Deltebre.

🏛 **Eco-Museu**
Carrer Martí Buera 22. 📞 977 4896 79. ◯ *by appointment.* 🏷 ♿

The Sardana

Catalonia's national dance is more complicated than it appears. Its success depends on the dancers forming a circle and accurately counting the complicated short- and long-step skips and jumps, which accounts for their serious faces. Music is provided by a *cobla*, an 11-person band consisting of a leader playing a three-holed flute *(flabiol)* and a little drum *(tamborí)*, five woodwind players and five brass players. The *sardana* is performed during most *festes* and at special day-long gatherings called *aplecs*. In Barcelona it is danced every Sunday evening at 6:30 in the Plaça de Sant Jaume.

A group of *sardana* dancers captured in stone

TRAVELLERS' NEEDS

WHERE TO STAY 114-121
RESTAURANTS, CAFÉS AND BARS 122-133
SHOPPING IN BARCELONA 134-135
ENTERTAINMENT IN BARCELONA 136-137
SPORTS AND OUTDOOR ACTIVITIES 138-139

WHERE TO STAY

CATALONIA HAS AN unrivalled variety of accommodation to offer visitors. The Barcelona and Catalonia tourist authorities have complete listings of hotels, country houses and camp sites as well as information on a range of other options. In Barcelona you can stay in the modern luxury of Spain's highest skyscraper,

Sign for a luxury five-star hotel

while on the coast you can try a self-catering holiday village (efficiencies) with all sorts of sports and entertainments provided. Family-run *cases de pagès,* which are stone-built farm or village houses or country manors, are Catalonia's most distinctive alternative. Some of the best hotels in every price range are listed on pages 116–21.

Façade of the Hotel Lloret in Barcelona's Rambla de Canaletes

HOTEL GRADING AND FACILITIES

THE DIFFERENT TYPES of hotel in Catalonia are denoted by the blue plaques near their doors. These show a star-rating which reflects the number and range of facilities available rather than quality of service. *Hotels* (H) and *hotel-residències* (HR) are graded from one to five stars; *motels* (M), *hostals* (H) and *hostal-residències* HR) from one to three stars; and *pensions* (P), with the simplest accommodation, have one or two stars. Hotels, *hostals, pensions* and motels have restaurants that are open to non-residents. *Hotel-residències* and *hostal-residències* do not have full dining rooms, but some serve breakfast.

PRICES AND PAYING

SPANISH LAW requires all hotels to display their prices at reception and in every room. As a rule, the higher the star-rating, the greater the price. Rates are almost invariably quoted per room (but meal prices per person). A double room in a one-star *hostal* can be as little as 18 euros a night; one in a five-star hotel will cost more than 120 euros a night. Prices vary according to region, season or special feature such as a view or balcony. The prices given on pages 116–21 are based on mid-season or high (tourist)-season rates. Prices for rooms and meals are usually quoted without including VAT *(IVA),* currently seven per cent.

BOOKING AND CHECK-IN

HOTELS IN BARCELONA can be very busy during the many trade fairs held all year round, so booking in advance is advisable. Off-season in rural Catalonia there is rarely any need to book ahead, but if you want a room in a busy season or in a particular hotel it is a good idea to do so. Resort hotels on the Costa Brava often close from autumn to spring. On the warmer Costa Daurada, hotels may have a shorter winter closing period. You will not normally be asked for a deposit when you book a room. However, a deposit of 20–25 per cent may be levied for bookings during peak periods or for a stay of more than a few nights. You may lose all or some of it if you cancel at less than a week's notice. Most hotels will honour a booking only until 8pm. If you are delayed, telephone to tell them when to expect you.

When checking in you will be asked for your passport or identity card to comply with police regulations. It will normally be returned as soon as your details have been copied.

PARADORS

THERE ARE seven paradors in Catalonia – at Aiguablava, Artíes, Cardona, Seu de Urgell, Vic, Vielha and Tortosa. They form part of Spain's chain of high-quality, government-run hotels in historic buildings, or in purpose-built, new buildings in spectacular settings. Reservations for paradors can be made through the **Central de Reservas** (Madrid), **Keytel International** (London) and **Marketing Ahead** (New York).

The spacious and comfortable interior of the parador at Vic

◁ **Christmas market in front of the cathedral, Barcelona**

Solid, stone-built architecture typical of traditional Catalan farmhouses

RURAL ACCOMMODATION

CASES DE PAGÈS are Catalan farmhouses (*masies*) or country houses that accept visitors. Some do B&B, some an evening meal or full board. Tourist offices have the *Guia residències-casa de pagès*, published by the Generalitat de Catalunya. You can book directly or through **Turisverd**.

The **Associació Fondes de Catalunya** is a group of *cases fonda* (simple country hotels, offering wholesome regional cuisine). The facility closes for two weeks during August, so if you plan to visit Catalonia in that month, you should make a reservation before setting off.

The **Xarxa d'Albergs de Catalunya** runs youth hostels, which also cater for adults and families, and the **Federació d'Entitats Excursionistes de Catalunya** runs mountain refuges for hikers.

SELF-CATERING

VILLAS AND apartments let by the week are plentiful on the Costa Daurada and Costa Brava. *Aparthotels* (or *hotels-apartament*) and *residències-apartament* are a new breed of self-catering accommodation (efficiencies). Ranked from one to four stars, each apartment has a kitchen, but each complex also has a restaurant and often a swimming pool and other facilities. Generalitat de Catalunya tourist offices (*see p142*) and most travel agents have details of all types of villas and apartments.

Holiday (vacation) villages (*ciutats de vacances*), such as Cala Montjoi and Club-Hotel Giverola on the Costa Brava, are similar, but accommodation is in bungalows and includes sports and entertainments.

Gites de Catalunya are superior country houses rented out on a week-by-week basis by Turisverd or **The Individual Travellers' Spain**. Many *cases de pagès* are also self-catering (run as efficiencies).

CAMP SITES

CATALONIA HAS over 300 camp sites, classified as deluxe (L), 1-star, 2-star, 3-star, or farm (M, *càmpings-masia*). All have basic amenities, guards and a safe. *Catalunya Càmpings*, published by the Generalitat (*see p142*), is available from tourist offices. Many sites in Barcelona are grouped under the **Associació de Càmpings de Barcelona** (which closes for three weeks in August, so ring in advance). A camping carnet from your home camping association can be used instead of a passport at sites and also covers you for third-party insurance. Camping is permitted only at official sites.

Sign for a camp site

DISABLED TRAVELLERS

FEW HOTELS are well equipped for disabled guests, although some youth hostels are. The **Federació ECOM** and Viajes 2000 (*see p143*) will advise on hotels throughout Catalonia for visitors with special needs.

Choosing a Hotel

THE HOTELS in this guide have been selected across a wide price range for the excellence of their facilities, location or character. Many have a highly recommended restaurant. The chart below first lists hotels in Barcelona by area, followed by a selection in the rest of Catalonia. For more details on restaurants see pages 126–131.

	Credit Cards	Number of Rooms	Private Parking	Swimming Pool	Garden or Terrace

OLD TOWN

HOSTAL D'AVINYO. Map 5 B2. W www.hostalavinyo.com €
Avinyo 42, 08002. **(** 93 318 79 45. FAX 93 318 68 93.
This simple, recently renovated hotel has a very central position, near Port Vell, La Ramblas and the Picasso Museum. 🛏
Credit Cards: MC V — Number of Rooms: 28

REMBRANDT. Map 5 A2. €€
Carrer de Portaferrissa 23, 08002. **(** 93 318 10 11. FAX 93 318 10 11.
A clean, simple hotel in the Barri Gòtic, popular with students. A tiled courtyard is a sitting area. Some bedrooms share bathrooms. 🛏
Number of Rooms: 24 — Garden or Terrace: ■

LLORET. Map 5 A1. €€
Rambla de Canaletes 125, 08002. **(** 93 317 33 66. FAX 93 301 92 83.
There are views of the city from the foyer of this popular hotel near the Plaça de Catalunya – but streetside bedrooms can be noisy. 🛏 ▤ 📺
Credit Cards: MC V — Number of Rooms: 56

PENINSULAR. Map 2 F3. €€
Carrer de Sant Pau 34, 08001. **(** 93 302 31 38. FAX 93 412 36 99.
Rooms are truly basic in this former Carmelite convent, but good value. Just off La Rambla behind the Liceu opera house, this hotel's charms lie in its luminous inner courtyard and Modernista dining room. 🛏 ▤ 🍴
Credit Cards: MC V — Number of Rooms: 80

ESPAÑA. Map 2 F3. W www.hotelespanya.com €€€
Carrer de Sant Pau 9–11, 08001. **(** 93 318 17 58. FAX 93 317 11 34.
Lluís Domènech i Montaner, the outstanding Modernista architect, designed this hotel. The bedrooms are all modern. 🛏 ▤ ♿
Credit Cards: AE DC MC V — Number of Rooms: 84

JARDÍ. Map 5 A2. @ hoteljardi@retemail.es €€€
Plaça Sant Josep Oriol 1 (beside Plaça del Pi), 08002. **(** 93 301 59 00. FAX 93 342 57 33.
A popular hotel overlooking a leafy square. Some bedrooms have been renovated and have good views; the others are cheaper. 🛏 ▤
Credit Cards: AE DC MC V — Number of Rooms: 40

GAUDÍ. Map 2 F3. W www.hotelgaudi.es €€€€
Carrer Nou de la Rambla 12, 08001. **(** 93 317 90 32. FAX 93 412 26 36.
A pleasant hotel near Gaudí's Palau Güell in a street close to La Rambla with comfortable, well-equipped rooms. 🛏 ▤ 📺 ♿ 🍴
Credit Cards: AE DC MC V — Number of Rooms: 73 — Private Parking: ■

MESÓN CASTILLA. Map 2 F1. €€€€
Carrer de Valdonzella 5, 08001. **(** 93 318 21 82. FAX 93 412 40 20.
A comfortable hotel, if a little old-fashioned, in a building with a Modernista façade near the Casa de la Caritat arts centre. 🛏 ▤ 📺 ♿
Credit Cards: AE DC MC V — Number of Rooms: 57 — Private Parking: ■ — Garden or Terrace: ■

ORIENTE. Map 2 F3. @ horiente@husa.es €€€€
La Rambla 45-47, 08002. **(** 93 302 25 58. FAX 93 412 38 19.
A former Franciscan friary makes a romantic setting for the recently restored Oriente. The cloister has been converted into a ballroom. 🛏 📺 🍴
Credit Cards: AE DC MC V — Number of Rooms: 142

SAN AGUSTÍN. Map 2 F3. @ hotelsa@hotelsa.com €€€€
Plaça de Sant Agustí 3, 08001. **(** 93 318 16 58. FAX 93 317 29 28.
An attractive hotel with a pleasant lounge and bar looking across a square. Some bedrooms are decorated with traditional Catalan furniture. 🛏 ▤ 📺 ♿
Credit Cards: AE DC MC V — Number of Rooms: 75

ARTS. Map 6 E4. W www.harts.es €€€€€
Carrer de la Marina 19–21, 08005. **(** 93 221 10 00. FAX 93 221 10 70.
A modern, super-luxurious beachside hotel at the Port Olímpic in one of Spain's tallest buildings. 🛏 ▤ 📺 ♿ 🍴
Credit Cards: AE DC MC V — Number of Rooms: 482 — Private Parking: ■ — Swimming Pool: ● — Garden or Terrace: ■

ATLANTIS. Map 2 F1. @ hotelatlantis@retemail.es €€€€€
Carrer de Pelai 20, 08001. **(** 93 318 90 12. FAX 93 412 09 14.
This modern, inexpensive hotel is centrally located near the Plaça de Catalunya. The bedrooms have a range of facilities. 🛏 ▤ 📺 ♿
Credit Cards: AE DC MC V — Number of Rooms: 42 — Private Parking: ■

<table>
<tr><td colspan="2">

Price categories for a standard double room per night, with tax, breakfast and service included:

€ under 50 euros
€€ 50–75 euros
€€€ 75–100 euros
€€€€ 100–125 euros
€€€€€ over 125 euros

</td><td>

CREDIT CARDS
Indicates which credit cards are accepted: *AE* American Express; *DC* Diners Club; *MC* MasterCard/Access; *V* VISA
PARKING
Parking provided by the hotel in a private car park or a private garage on the hotel site or very close by. Some hotels charge for use of private parking facilities.
SWIMMING POOL
Hotel pool outdoors unless otherwise stated.
GARDEN
Hotel with garden, courtyard or terrace, often providing tables for eating outdoors.

</td></tr>
</table>

	CREDIT CARDS	NUMBER OF ROOMS	PRIVATE PARKING	SWIMMING POOL	GARDEN OR TERRACE
COLÓN. Map 5 B2. [w] www.hotelcolon.es €€€€€ Avinguda de la Catedral 7, 08002. 93 301 14 04. FAX 93 317 29 15. From the Colón's front windows guests can watch the *sardana*, the traditional Catalan folk dance, performed in the Plaça de la Catedral, opposite, on Sunday mornings. Ask for a room with a terrace.	AE DC MC V	147			■
LE MERIDIEN. Map 5 A1. @ meridien@meridienbarcelona.com €€€€€ La Rambla 111, 08002. 93 318 62 00. FAX 93 301 77 76. An elegant hotel on La Rambla, popular with rock and film stars. It has an enormous presidential suite and a business centre.	AE DC MC V	208	■		
NOUVEL. Map 5 A1. €€€€€ Carrer de Santa Anna 18–20, 08002. 93 301 82 74. FAX 93 301 83 70. In a street off La Rambla, near the Plaça de Catalunya, this well managed, old-style hotel is tastefully decorated and furnished.	MC V	71			
PARK HOTEL. Map 5 C3. @ parkhotel@parkhotelbarcelona.com €€€€€ Avda Marquès de l'Argentera 11, 08003. 93 319 60 00. FAX 93 319 45 19. A rare gem of 1950s architecture, designed by Antonio Moragas in 1951 and well preserved during his son's award-winning renovations in 1990.	AE DC MC V	91			
RIVOLI RAMBLAS. Map 5 A1. @ reservas@rivolihotels.com €€€€€ Rambla dels Estudis 128, 08002. 93 302 66 43. FAX 93 317 50 53 or 93 318 8760. An elegant hotel on La Rambla decorated in contemporary style, with spacious bedrooms and city views from a roof terrace.	AE DC MC V	129	■		■
ROYAL. Map 5 A1. @ hotelroyal@hroyal.com €€€€€ La Rambla 117, 08002. 93 301 94 00. FAX 93 317 31 79. This hotel, near the top of La Rambla, has friendly staff and simple but elegant rooms with spacious marble bathrooms.	AE DC MC V	108	■		

EIXAMPLE

	CREDIT CARDS	NUMBER OF ROOMS	PRIVATE PARKING	SWIMMING POOL	GARDEN OR TERRACE
FELIPE II. Map 3 C4. [w] www.lasquias.com/felipe2 € Carrer de Mallorca 329, 08037. 93 458 77 58. FAX 93 207 21 04. A basic, clean hotel in an old apartment block in the Eixample, with a particularly fine antique elevator. Breakfast is not available.		11			
HOSTAL CIUDAD CONDAL. Map 3 A4. €€€ Carrer de Mallorca 255, 00008. 93 215 10 40. FAX 93 487 04 59. A modest *hostal* on one of Eixample's most elegant streets. Rear rooms on the second floor are quieter than those closer to street level. No breakfasts.	DC MC V	11	■		
GRAN VIA. Map 3 A5. @ hgranvia@nuhotels.es €€€€ Gran Via de les Corts Catalanes 642, 08007. 93 318 19 00. FAX 93 318 99 97. A hotel in a late 19th-century building with an ageing grandeur, north of the Plaça de Catalunya adjoining the Passeig de Gràcia.	AE DC MC V	53			■
ALEXANDRA. Map 3 A4. @ informacion@hotel-alexandra.com €€€€€ Carrer de Mallorca 251, 08008. 93 467 71 66. FAX 93 488 02 58. A stylish, modern interior behind a 19th-century façade sets the tone in this hotel, which is well equipped for business meetings.	AE DC MC V	99	■		
CATALUNYA PLAZA. Map 5 A1. @ catalunya@city-hotels.es €€€€€ Plaça de Catalunya 7, 08002. 93 317 71 71. FAX 93 317 78 55. A city-centre hotel popular with business people. The 19th-century building has large sitting rooms decorated with some intricate frescoes.	AE DC MC V	46			
CLARIS. Map 3 B4. @ claris@derbyhotels.es €€€€€ Carrer Pau Claris 150, 08009. 93 487 62 62. FAX 93 215 79 70 Antique kilims and elegant English and French furniture ornament this hotel off the Passeig de Gràcia. It occupies the converted Vedruna Palace and has a private museum of pre-Columbian art.	AE DC MC V	120	■	●	■

For key to symbols see back flap

Price categories for a standard double room per night, with tax, breakfast and service included:

€ under 50 euros
€€ 50–75 euros
€€€ 75–100 euros
€€€€ 100–125 euros
€€€€€ over 125 euros

CREDIT CARDS
Indicates which credit cards are accepted: *AE* American Express; *DC* Diners Club; *MC* MasterCard/Access; *V* VISA
PARKING
Parking provided by the hotel in a private car park or a private garage on the hotel site or very close by. Some hotels charge for use of private parking facilities.
SWIMMING POOL
Hotel pool outdoors unless otherwise stated.
GARDEN
Hotel with garden, courtyard or terrace, often providing tables for eating outdoors.

	CREDIT CARDS	NUMBER OF ROOMS	PRIVATE PARKING	SWIMMING POOL	GARDEN OR TERRACE
CONDES DE BARCELONA. Map 3 A4. [W] www.condesdebarcelona.com €€€€€ — Passeig de Gràcia 73–75, 08008. (93 467 47 80. FAX 93 467 47 85 or 93 467 47 81. This Modernista hotel has an impressive pentagonal lobby with a marble floor, illuminated by a skylight. Book well in advance so as not to miss the aesthetic thrill.	AE DC MC V	183	■	●	■
DUCS DE BERGARA. Map 5 A1. [W] www.hoteles-catalonia.es €€€€€ — Carrer de Bergara 11, 08002. (93 301 51 51. FAX 93 317 34 42. A luxury hotel in an Modernista building, with original halls and stairways, just off the Plaça de Catalunya. It has spacious, well-furnished bedrooms and modern public rooms.	AE DC MC V	149		●	
GALLERY. Map 3 A3. [W] www.galleryhotel.com €€€€€ — Carrer Rosselló 249, 08008. (93 415 99 11. FAX 93 415 91 84. A modern, efficient, comfortable hotel which is well situated and retains the personal atmosphere of a family-run business. An attractive terrace-garden restaurant leads into a public garden. Rooms are soundproofed.	AE DC MC V	113	■		■
GRAN HOTEL CALDERÓN. Map 3 A5. [W] www.hh.hoteles.com €€€€€ — Rambla de Catalunya 26, 08007. (93 301 00 00. FAX 93 412 41 93. A modern hotel near the Plaça de Catalunya with spacious, comfortable rooms, indoor and rooftop pools, and a good restaurant.	AE DC MC V	253	■	●	
GRAN HOTEL HAVANA. Map 3 B5. [@] hotelhavana@hoteles-silken.com €€€€€ — Gran Via de les Corts Catalanes 647, 08010. (93 412 11 15. FAX 93 412 26 11. Stunning light from a central glass atrium floods the avant-garde interior of this efficient and friendly hotel. Its most popular suite is behind the large clock face on the façade. Some rooms have a terrace.	AE DC MC V	145	■		
MAJESTIC. Map 3 A4. [W] www.hotelmajestic.es €€€€€ — Passeig de Gràcia 68, 08007. (93 488 17 17. FAX 93 488 18 80. A hotel in Neo-Classical style in a chic street (adjoining the Carrer de València). The bedrooms are well equipped and soundproofed.	AE DC MC V	303	■	●	
REGENTE. Map 3 A4. [W] www.hccwap.com €€€€€ — Rambla de Catalunya 76, 08008. (93 487 59 89. FAX 93 487 32 27. A hotel in a Modernista building, with magnificent stained-glass decoration and a small, rooftop pool overlooking Montjuïc.	AE DC MC V	79		●	
RITZ. Map 3 B5. [W] www.ritzbcn.com €€€€€ — Gran Via de les Corts Catalanes 668, 08010. (93 318 52 00. FAX 93 318 01 48. The most elegant of Barcelona's grand hotels, recently refurbished. The large, luxurious bedrooms are decorated in classic style.	AE DC MC V	122	■		■

FURTHER AFIELD

	CREDIT CARDS	NUMBER OF ROOMS	PRIVATE PARKING	SWIMMING POOL	GARDEN OR TERRACE
LES CORTS: *Gran Derby.* [W] www.derbyhotels.es €€€€€ — Carrer de Loreto 28, 08029. (93 322 20 62. FAX 93 419 68 20. Attractive suites are the only accommodation offered here. There is no restaurant; guests may dine in the Hotel Derby over the road.	AE DC MC V	40	■	●	■
PEDRALBES: *Princesa Sofía Intercontinental.* €€€€€ — Plaça de Pius XII 4, 08028. (93 508 10 00. FAX 93 508 10 01. A vast, luxury hotel decorated in marble, wood and bronze, with a restaurant, and bar. Also with facilities for conferences.	AE DC MC V	500	■	●	■
SARRIA-SANT GERVASI: *Rekor'd.* €€€€ — Carrer de Muntaner 352, 08021. (93 200 19 53. FAX 93 414 50 84. A small, modern hotel oriented towards business travellers in the uptown shopping area. Large rooms with office space. Some with mini-gym.	AE DC MC V	15	■		

CATALONIA

ANDORRA LA VELLA: *Andorra Park Hotel.* €€€€€
Les Canals 24 (Andorra). 376 82 09 79. FAX 376 82 09 83.
One of Andorra's most luxurious hotels, it is modern and built into a steep, wooded hillside. It has a library, a swimming pool hewn out of rock, and is beside a department store.

AE DC MC V — 40

ARTIES: *Parador Don Gaspar de Portolà.* €€€€
Ctra a Baqueira-Beret, 25599 (Lleida). 973 64 08 01. FAX 973 64 10 01.
A modern, warm, comfortable parador, near the Vall d'Aran ski resorts, ideal for après-ski rest. Beside it is a medieval chapel.

AE DC MC V — 57

AVINYONET DE PUIGVENTÓS: *Mas Pau.* www.maspau.com €€€
Despoblado, 17742 (Girona). 972 54 61 54. FAX 972 54 63 26.
A beautiful hotel in a 17th-century house, surrounded by wooded farmland. The bedrooms and suites open onto a garden. 7 Jan–15 Mar.

AE DC MC V — 20

BAQUEIRA-BERET: *Royal Tanau.* www.solmelia.com €€€€€
Carretera de Beret, 25598 (Lleida). 973 64 44 46. FAX 973 64 43 44.
A luxurious hotel in the Tanau skiing area, with a ski lift to the pistes. It has full après-ski facilities and apartments as well as rooms.
Apr–Jun & Sep–Nov.

AE DC MC V — 30

BEGUR: *Aigua Blava.* €€€€
Platja de Fornells, 17255 (Girona). 972 62 20 58. FAX 972 62 21 12.
A charming hotel on a small beach in an attractive spot on the Costa Brava. It has marvellous sea views. 7 Nov–19 Feb.

AE MC V — 85

BEUDA: *Can Felicià.* www.canfelicia.com €€€
Segueró, 17851 (Girona). 972 59 05 23. FAX 972 59 05 23.
Beautiful views make this charming, rural hotel in a former school a good place to stay. Simple, pleasing decor. Price includes home-cooked dinners.

6

BOLVIR DE CERDANYA: *Torre del Remei.* www.torredelremei.com €€€€€
Camí Reial, 17539 (Girona). 972 14 01 82. FAX 972 14 04 49.
An Art Nouveau mansion with a large garden has become a refined hotel full of comforts, such as video players (VCRs) in bedrooms.

AE DC MC V — 11

CADAQUÉS: *Misty.* €€
Carretera Nova Port Lligat, 17488 (Girona). 972 25 89 62. FAX 972 15 90 90.
Three houses and a swimming pool surrounded by gardens make up this appealing hotel, one of the most unusual on the Costa Brava. Jan.

DC MC V — 11

CARDONA: *Prador de Cardona.* www.paradores.es €€€€€
Castell s/n (Cardona, Barcelona). 93 869 12 75. FAX 93 869 16 36.
This luxurious converted medieval castle dominates Cardona and has lovely views from its hillside setting. It has a fine Catalan restaurant.

AE DC V — 54

CASTELLDEFELS: *Gran Hotel Rey Don Jaime.* €€€€€
Avinguda del Hotel 22, 08860 (Barcelona). 93 665 13 00. www.grup-saleras.com
This Mediterranean-style hotel has arches and white-washed walls. It is on a hilltop giving views over the coast.

AE DC MC V — 234

CASTELLÓ D'EMPÚRIES: *Allioli.* €€
Urbanització Castell Nou, 17486 (Girona). 972 25 03 00. FAX 972 25 03 00.
A 17th-century Catalan farmhouse, just off the main Roses–Figueres road. The restaurant is popular for Sunday lunch among the local people.

AE DC MC V — 42

L'ESPLUGA DE FRANCOLÍ: *Hostal del Senglar.* www.hostaldelsenglar.com €€
Pl de Montserrat Canals 1, 43440 (Tarragona). 977 87 01 21. FAX 977 87 01 27.
A three-storey, whitewashed hotel with a garden. A menu of delicious dishes traditional to the area is served in the restaurant.

AE DC MC V — 40

L'ESPLUGA DE FRANCOLÍ: *Masia del Cadet.* @ masiadelcadet@yahoo.es €€
Les Masies de Poblet, 43449 (Tarragona). 977 87 08 69. FAX 977 87 08 69.
An inexpensive hotel near the monastery of Poblet in a tastefully renovated, 15th-century house. The bedrooms are austere and quiet. Traditional Catalan food is served in the restaurant. Nov.

AE DC MC V — 12

LA GARRIGA: *Blancafort.* www.balnearioblancafort.com €€€€
Carrer Banys 59, 08530 (Barcelona). 93 871 46 00. FAX 93 871 57 50.
A 19th-century hotel in a relaxing spa town near Barcelona. There are simple bedrooms and games facilities in the lounges.

MC V — 56

Price categories for a standard double room per night, with tax, breakfast and service included: € under 50 euros €€ 50–75 euros €€€ 75–100 euros €€€€ 100–125 euros €€€€€ over 125 euros	**CREDIT CARDS** Indicates which credit cards are accepted: *AE* American Express; *DC* Diners Club; *MC* MasterCard/Access; *V* VISA **PARKING** Parking provided by the hotel in a private car park or a private garage on the hotel site or very close by. Some hotels charge for use of private parking facilities. **SWIMMING POOL** Hotel pool outdoors unless otherwise stated. **GARDEN** Hotel with garden, courtyard or terrace, often providing tables for eating outdoors.			

	CREDIT CARDS	NUMBER OF ROOMS	PRIVATE PARKING	SWIMMING POOL	GARDEN OR TERRACE
LA GARRIGA: *La Garriga*. 🖥 www.termes.com　€€€€€ Carrer Banys 23, 08530 (Barcelona). 📞 93 871 70 86. 📠 93 871 78 87. Affluent people from Barcelona have been taking the waters here since 1876. Children under 12 years old are not admitted to the hotel. 🛏 🍴 📺 ♿ 🍴	AE MC V	22	■	●	■
GRANOLLERS: *Fonda Europa*.　€€€ Carrer Anselm Clavé 1, 08400 (Barcelona). 📞 93 870 03 12. 📠 93 870 79 01. This small hotel has been an inn for travellers since 1714. The bedrooms are on the second floor and are decorated in Art Deco style. 🛏 🍴 📺 🍴	AE DC MC V	7			
LLORET DE MAR: *Santa Marta*. 🖥 www.hstamarta.com　€€€€€ Platja Santa Cristina, 17310 (Girona). 📞 972 36 49 04. 📠 972 36 92 80. Recently refurbished, this hotel has tennis courts and other sporting facilities. It is set in a pine wood that extends down to a cove. 🛏 🍴 📺 ♿ ● *mid-Dec–mid-Feb.*	AE DC MC V	78	■	●	■
MONTSENY: *Sant Bernat*. 🖥 www.husa.es　€€€€ Finca El Cot, Carretera de Santa María de Palautordera a Seva, Km 20.7, 08460 (Barcelona). 📞 93 847 30 11. 📠 93 847 32 20. A big country house in the Serra de Montseny, with a façade cloaked in greenery. There are beautiful grounds with lawns and a pond. 🛏 📺 🍴	AE DC MC V	20	■		■
PERAMOLA: *Can Boix de Peraluola*. 🖥 www.lugaresdivinos.com　€€€€ Afueras, 25790 (Lleida). 📞 973 47 02 66. 📠 973 47 02 81. This good-value, family-run hotel has rooms and apartments convenient for walking in the Pyrenean foothills. 🛏 🍴 📺 ♿ 🍴 ● *mid-Jan–mid-Feb, 1–15 Nov.*	AE DC MC V	41	■	●	■
S'AGARÓ: *Hostal de la Gavina*. 🖥 www.lagavina.com　€€€€€€ Plaça de la Rosaleda, 17248 (Girona). 📞 972 32 11 00. 📠 972 32 15 73. This elegant Mediterranean-style beach mansion is set in its own exclusive estate, with beautiful gardens and a sea water pool. 🛏 🍴 📺 🍴 ● *15 Oct–Holy Week.*	AE DC MC V	74	■	●	■
SA TUNA (BEGUR): *Hotel Sa Tuna*. 🖥 www.postalsatuna.com　€€€ Passeig de Ancora 6, 17255 (Girona). 📞 & 📠 972 62 21 98. A simple, white-washed, small hotel on one of the Costa Brava's prettiest coves. Recent improvements by the grandson of the original owner have added to its charms. Rooms with own terrace overlooking the bay. 🛏 🍴 ● *Oct–Feb.*	MC V	5			■
SANTA CRISTINA D'ARO: *Mas Torrellas*.　€€ Carretera Sta Cristina-Platja d'Aro, 17246 (Girona). 📞 972 83 75 26. 📠 972 83 75 27. An 18th-century country house hotel. Its most comfortable bedroom is in a distinctive yellow tower, built at a later date. 🛏 🍴 📺 ● *1 Nov–1 Mar.*	AE DC MC V	17	■		■
SANTA PAU: *Cal Sastre*. 🖥 www.calsastre.com　€€€ Cases Noves 1, 17811 (Girona). 📞 972 68 01 32. 📠 972 68 04 81. This 18th-century rural house has been converted into a comfortable hotel. Dinner in the village square is included. 🛏 🍴 ● *end Jun, 20 Dec–7 Jan.*	AE DC MC V	10			■
SANT PERE DE RIBES: *Els Sumidors*. 🖥 www.sumidors.com　€€€ Carretera de Vilafranca Km 2.4, 08810 (Barcelona). 📞 & 📠 93 896 20 61. On the slope of a hill, with views across the Penedès wine region, this rustic 18th-century house has atmosphere and charm, but few luxuries. 🛏 🍴	MC V	9	■	●	■
LA SEU D'URGELL: *Parador de La Seu d'Urgell*. 🖥 www.parador.es　€€€€ Carrer Sant Domènec 6, 25700 (Lleida). 📞 973 35 20 00. 📠 973 35 23 09. Only the cloister, now used as the lounge, remains of a convent that occupied this site close to the 12th-century cathedral of La Seu. The dining room and indoor swimming pool have glass ceilings. 🛏 🍴 ♿ 🍴 📺	AE DC MC V	80	■	●	■
LA SEU D'URGELL: *El Castell*. 🖥 www.hotelelcastell.com　€€€€€ Carretera N260, Km 229, 25700 (Lleida). 📞 973 35 07 04. 📠 973 35 15 74. This sumptuous hotel is a low, modern building beneath the medieval castle of Seu d'Urgell. There are impressive views across the mountains of El Cadí and the ski slopes of Andorra are nearby. 🛏 🍴 📺 🍴	AE DC MC V	38	■	●	■

SITGES: *La Santa María.* €€
Passeig Ribera 52, 08870 (Barcelona). 93 894 09 99. FAX 93 894 78 71.
A cheery, modern hotel hidden behind an older moulded- plaster frontage.
The restaurant has tables on the seafront. 🛏 ☰ TV ⬛ ▮ ⬤ 15 Dec–15 Feb.
AE DC MC V — 53

SITGES: *Capri Veracruz.* €€€
Avinguda de Sofia 13–15, 08870 (Barcelona). 93 811 02 67. FAX 93 894 51 88.
Built in the 1950s near the beach, in one of the quieter parts of Sitges, this hotel
has simple bedrooms, a family atmosphere and a games room. 🛏 ☰ TV ⬛
AE MC V — 69

SITGES: *Romàntic.* w www.hotelromantic.com €€€
Sant Isidre 33, 08870 (Barcelona). 93 894 83 75. FAX 93 894 81 67.
Well-known in Sitges, this memorable hotel lives up to its name. Bedrooms are
simple, but attractively decorated with antiques and paintings. A gloriously
shady garden is perfect for breakfast, and evening cocktails. 🛏 ⬤ 1 Nov–1 Apr.
AE MC V — 70

SITGES: *San Sebastián Playa.* w www.solmelia.com €€€€€
Carrer Port Alegre 53, 08870 (Barcelona). 93 894 86 76. FAX 93 894 04 30.
This new hotel on the beach near the old part of town has attentive staff and
comfortable bedrooms, as well as a restaurant and meeting rooms. 🛏 ☰ TV ⬛
AE DC MC V — 51

TARRAGONA: *Lauria.* w www.hlauria.es €€
Rambla Nova 20, 43004. 977 23 67 12. FAX 977 23 67 00.
A modern, functional hotel in the town centre and close to the sea, with an
elegant entrance under balustraded stone stairs. 🛏 ☰ TV
AE DC MC V — 72

TAVÉRNOLES: *El Banús.* w www.elbanus.com €€€€€
El Banús, 08519 (Barcelona). 93 812 20 91. FAX 93 888 70 12.
A small farmhouse, furnished with Banús family heirlooms, offering
apartments with kitchen facilities. Minimum stay is two days. ⬤ Nov–Mar.
AE MC V — 3

TAVERTET: *El Jufré.* €€
Tavertet, 08511 (Barcelona). & FAX 93 856 51 67.
This converted farmhouse with stunning mountain views has been in the same
family for over 800 years. Warm, comfortable rooms have replaced the animal
quarters. A perfect base for walking and exploring Osona. 🛏 ⬤ 22 Dec–9 Jan.
— 8

TORRENT: *Mas de Torrent.* €€€€€
Afueras, 1/123 (Girona). 972 30 32 92. FAX 9/2 30 32 93.
A superbly converted, 18th-century country house in large, terraced gardens.
It has magnificent views 🛏 ☰ TV ⬛ ▮
AE DC MC V — 39

TORTOSA: *Parador Castillo de la Zuda.* w www.parador.es €€€€
Castillo de la Zuda, 43500 (Tarragona). 977 44 44 50. FAX 977 44 44 58.
A medieval Moorish castle makes a superb hilltop parador with views of the
town and valley of the Riu Ebre. Swimming pool in summer only. 🛏 ☰ TV ▮
AE DC MC V — 72

TREDÒS: *Hotel de Tredòs.* w www.hoteldetredos.com €€€
Carretera a Baqueira-Beret, 25598 (Lleida). 973 64 40 14. FAX 973 64 43 00.
Skiers and mountain walkers find this hotel in the Vall d'Aran good value. It
is built of stone and slate in the local style. 🛏 TV ⬛ ⬤ Oct, Nov & May, Jun.
M V — 43

VIC: *Parador de Turismo de Vic.* w www.parador.es €€€
Paratge Bac de Sau, 08500 (Barcelona). 93 812 23 23. FAX 93 812 23 68.
This recently refurbished and comfortable parador, 14 km (9 miles) from Vic,
has magnificent views over the Sau reservoir. A peaceful retreat amid pine
forests and dramatic rock formations. Swimming pool in summer. 🛏 ☰ TV ⬛
AE DC MC V — 39

VIELHA (VIELLA): *Parador Valle de Arán.* @ viella@parador.es €€€
Carretera Pont de Suert, 25530 (Lleida). 973 64 01 00. FAX 973 64 11 00.
This modern parador has a semicircular lounge dominated by a large
window from which there are magnificent mountain views. 🛏 ☰ TV ⬛ ▮
AE DC MC V — 118

VILADRAU: *Hostal de la Glòria.* @ hostalgloria@infomail.lacaixa.es €€
Carrer Torreventosa 12, 17406 (Girona). 93 884 90 34. FAX 93 884 94 65.
A hotel with a family atmosphere in a traditional Catalan house above the
Serra de Montseny. It is full of copper pots.
🛏 TV ⬤ three weeks at Christmas.
DC MC V — 23

VILANOVA I LA GELTRÚ: *César.* @ hotelcesar@terra.es €€
Carrer Isaac Peral 8, 08800 (Barcelona). 93 815 11 25. FAX 93 815 67 19.
This hotel, near the Ribes Roges beach, is owned by two sisters who pay
great attention to detail, from the furniture and the fabrics in the bedrooms to
the well-known restaurant. 🛏 ☰ TV ⬛
AE DC MC V — 36

Restaurants, Cafés and Bars

Wall tile advertising a Barcelona restaurant

ATING OUT remains both a common practice and one of the convivial joys of life in Catalonia. Catalans are proud of their regional cuisine and expect to eat well in restaurants, not only at celebratory dinners, but also at work-day meal breaks or at family Sunday lunches out. Country restaurants in particular are packed on Sundays. Barcelona has an unusually large number of restaurants. From the sophisticated feast to the simple tapa, fresh ingredients are usually in evidence as Catalans tend to despise convenience food. The restaurants and cafés listed on pages 126–33 have been selected for their food and atmosphere. Pages 26–7 and 124–5 illustrate some of Catalonia's best dishes.

Bodegues are bars that specialize in wines and do not serve food

RESTAURANTS AND BARS

BARCELONA AND Catalonia possess some of Spain's best restaurants, testifying to the quality of Catalan cooking, but the cheapest and quickest places to eat are the bars and cafés that serve *tapes* (tapas). Some bars, however, especially *pubs* (late-opening bars for socializing) do not serve food. Family-run *bars i restaurants*, *hostals* and *fondes* – old Catalan words for the various types of inn – serve inexpensive, sit-down meals. *Xiringuitos* are beachside bars that are open only during the busy summer season.

Most restaurants close one day a week, some for lunch or dinner only, and most for an annual holiday. They also close on some public holidays. The main closing times of the restaurants on pages 126–31 are listed at the end of each entry. Always check the opening times, however, when phoning to book a table.

EATING HOURS

CATALANS, in common with other Spaniards, often eat a light breakfast *(el esmorzar)* of biscuits or toast with butter and jam and *cafè amb llet* (milky coffee), then follow with a second breakfast or snack between 10 and 11am, perhaps in a café. This may consist of a croissant, or an *entrepà* (sandwich) with sausage, ham or cheese, or a slice of the ubiquitous *truita de patates* (potato omelette). Fruit juice, coffee or beer are the usual accompaniments.

From about 1pm onwards, people will stop in the bars for a beer or an *aperitivo* with tapas. By 2pm those who can will have arrived home from work for *dinar* (lunch), which is the main meal of the day. Others will choose to have lunch in a restaurant.

The cafés, *salons de te* (tea rooms) and *pastisseries* (pastry shops) fill up by about 5:30 or

Decoration, Barcelona bar

6pm for *el berenar* (tea) of sandwiches, pastries or cakes, with coffee, tea or fruit juice. Snacks such as *xurros* (fried, sugar-coated batter sticks) can also be bought from stalls.

By 7pm, bars are crowded with people having tapas with sherry, wine or beer. In Catalonia *el sopar* (dinner or supper), begins at about 9pm. However, restaurants sometimes begin serving earlier for tourists. In summer, however, families and groups of friends often do not sit down to dinner until as late as 11pm. At weekend lunch times, especially in the summer, you will often find that restaurants are filled by large and noisy family gatherings.

HOW TO DRESS

A JACKET AND TIE are rarely required, but Catalans dress smartly, especially for city restaurants. Day dress is casual in beach resorts, but shorts are frowned on in the evenings.

Eating out at Barcelona's Port Olímpic, a busy venue all year round

Outdoor tables at a *cafeteria* in Cadaqués on the Costa Brava

READING THE MENU

ASIDE FROM TAPAS, perhaps the cheapest eating options in Catalan restaurants are the fixed-price *plats combinats* and the *menú del dia*. A *plat combinat* (meat or fish with vegetables and, usually, fried potatoes) is offered only by cheaper establishments. Most restaurants – but not all – offer an inexpensive, fixed-price *menú del dia*, normally of three courses, but with little choice. Some gourmet restaurants offer a *menú de degustació* consisting of a choice of six or seven of the head chef's special dishes.

The Catalan word for menu is *la carta*. It starts with *sopes* (soups), *amanides* (salads), *entremesos* (hors d'oeuvres), *ous i truites* (eggs and omelettes) and *verdures i llegums* (vegetable dishes).

Main courses are *peix i marisc* (fish and shellfish) and *carns i aus* (meat and poultry). Daily specials are chalked on a board or clipped to menus. *Paella* and other rice dishes may be served as the first course. A useful rule is to follow rice with meat, or start with *fuet* or *secallona* (two popular types of sausage) or salad and follow with *paella*.

Desserts are called *postres*. All restaurants offer fresh fruit, but otherwise the range of *postres* is often limited – perhaps the famous *crema catalana* (*crème brûlée*) or *flam* (crème caramel) and *natillas* (custard). Gourmet restaurants have more creative choices.

Vegetarians are rather poorly catered for. Some vegetable, salad and egg dishes will be vegetarian, but may contain pieces of ham or fish, so ask before you order.

All eating places welcome children and will serve small portions if requested.

Las Torres de Ávila *(see p137)*, a distinctive Barcelona bar

WINE CHOICES

DRY FINO WINES are perfect with shellfish, sausage, olives, soups and most first courses. Main dishes are often accompanied by wines from Penedès or Terra Alta *(see p28)* in Catalonia, or from Spain's other wine areas such as Rioja, Ribera del Duero and Navarra. Oloroso wines are often drunk as a *digestif*. *Cava (see pp28–9)* is popular for Sunday lunch.

SMOKING

IN FINE RESTAURANTS customers are offered cigars with their coffee and brandy. Many people in Spain smoke and very few restaurants have no-smoking areas or tables.

PRICES AND PAYING

IF YOU ORDER from *la carta* in a restaurant, your bill can soar way above the price of the *menú del dia*, especially if you order pricey items, such as fresh seafood, fish or *ibérico* ham. If there is an expensive fish such as sole or swordfish on the menu at a bargain price, it may be frozen. Sea bass and other popular fish and shellfish, such as large prawns, lobster and crab, are generally priced by weight.

El compte (the bill) includes service charges and perhaps a small cover charge. Prices on menus do not include seven per cent VAT *(IVA)*, which is usually added when the bill is calculated. Clients hardly ever tip restaurant waiters more than five per cent, often just rounding up the bill.

Cheques are rarely used in restaurants. Traveller's cheques are usually accepted, but you might not be given change. The major credit cards and international direct debit cards are now accepted in most restaurants. However, do not expect to pay by credit card in smaller eating or drinking places like tapas bars, cafés, village *hostals*, roadside *pubs* or *bodegues*.

WHEELCHAIR ACCESS

SINCE RESTAURANTS are rarely designed for wheelchairs, phone in advance (or ask the hotel staff to call) to check on access to tables and toilets.

Interior of Set Portes restaurant *(see p127)*, Port Vell, Barcelona

A Glossary of Typical Dishes

Olives

CATALAN CUISINE AT ITS BEST, using fresh food, is known as *cuina de mercat* (market cuisine) and there is nowhere better to see produce laid out than at Barcelona's Boqueria market *(see p135)*. Peppers glisten, fish sparkle and no meat is wasted – even cock's combs are sold for the pot. Olives come in all sorts of varieties. Spring brings *calçot* onions and broad (fava) beans, while strawberries, from Easter onwards, are eaten with *cava*. In autumn 30 varieties of mushroom spill across the stalls.

TAPES (TAPAS – SNACKS)

Bar-hopping around Barcelona is a delightful way to spend an evening, and a good way to try the many local dishes laid out on the counters.
Anxoves: anchovies.
Berberechos: cockles.
Bunyols de bacallà: salt cod fritters.
Calamars a la romana: fried squid rings.
Pa amb tomàquet: bread rubbed with tomato, garlic and olive oil – a good filler.
Panadons d'espinacs: small spinach pasties or pies.
Patatas bravas: potato chunks in spicy tomato sauce.
Pernil: ham – leg of pork seasoned and hung to dry.
Pescaditos: small fried fish.
Popets: baby octopus.
Truita: omelette.
Truita de patates: traditional potato and onion omelette.

Pa amb tomàquet (bread with tomato), often served with ham

ENTRANTS (STARTERS)

These are often unusual dishes and two may be enough for a meal. Some may appear as main courses.
Amanida catalana: Catalan mixed salad *(see p26)*.
Arròs negre: black rice *(see p26)*. Can be a main course.

Produce at La Boqueria, Barcelona's huge covered market on La Rambla

Cargols a la llauna: snails in a spicy sauce.
Empedrat: salad of salt cod and white beans.
Escalivada: char-grilled or roasted aubergines (eggplant) and peppers, all drizzled with olive oil.
Espinacs a la catalana: spinach with pine nuts, raisins and anchovies; sometimes made with chard *(bledes)*.
Esqueixada: raw salt cod salad *(see p27)*.
Faves a la catalana: a broad (fava) bean stew of black pudding, bacon, onion and garlic.
Fideus: noodles, usually served with fish and meat.
Garotes: raw sea urchins, from the Costa Brava, eaten with bread, garlic or spring onions.
Musclos: mussels.
Ous remenats amb camasecs: scrambled eggs with wild mushrooms.
Pa de fetge: liver pâté.
Sardines escabetxades: pickled sardines.
Xató: salt cod and tuna salad with *romesco* sauce *(see p26)*.

SOPES (SOUPS)

Caldereta de llagosta: spiny lobster soup.
Escudella i carn d'olla: the liquid from Catalonia's traditional hotpot; the meat and vegetables *(carn i olla)* are served as a main course.
Gaspatxo: a clear, cold soup with added raw vegetables.
Sopa de farigola: thyme soup.
Sopa de bolets: mushroom soup.

MAIN DISHES

Methods of cooking are: *a la brasa* (over open flames); *bullit* (boiled); *cremat* (crisp fried or caramelized); *estofat* (stewed); *farcit* (stuffed); *al forn* (in the oven); *a la graella/ planxa* (cooked on a griddle, pan-fried or barbecued); *a la pedra* (on a hot stone).

PEIX I MARISCOS (FISH AND SHELLFISH)

Allipebre d'anguiles: spicy eel stew.
Anfós al forn: baked stuffed grouper.
Calamars farcits: squid stuffed with pork, tomatoes and onions.
Cassola de peix: fish casserole.
Congre amb pèsols: conger eel with peas.
Escamarlans bullits: boiled Dublin Bay prawns.
Gambes a la planxa: prawns cooked on a griddle.
Graellada de peix: mixed seafood grill.
Llagosta a la brasa: lobster cooked over open flames.
Llagostins amb maionesa: king prawns and mayonnaise.
Llobarro al forn a rodanxes: baked, sliced sea bass.
Lluç a la planxa: hake cooked on a griddle.
Molls a la brasa: red mullet cooked over open flames.
Orada a la sal: gilthead bream baked in salt, which is removed on serving.
Paella valenciana: paella with chicken and seafood.
Rap a l'all cremat: angler fish with crisped garlic.
Romesco de peix: seafood with the famous *romesco* sauce *(see p26)*. Tarragona's master *romesco* makers compete each summer.
Sarsuela: fish, shellfish and spices, everything goes into

the pot that gives its name to a light Spanish opera.

Sèpia amb pèsols: cuttlefish with peas.

Suquet de peix: Catalonia's principal fish stew, made with various fish, tomatoes, peppers, potatoes and almonds.

Verats a la brasa: mackerel cooked over open flames.

CARN (MEAT)

Ànec amb naps: duck with turnips, ideally the "black" turnips of the Empordà region; also sometimes served with pears (*ànec amb peres*).

Boles de picolat: meatballs in tomato sauce. Meatballs with cuttlefish (*sèpia*) is classic *mar i muntanya* food (*see p26*).

Botifarra amb mongetes: sausage and beans (*see p27*).

Bou a l'adoba: beef casserole.

Costelles a la brasa amb allioli: flame-roast lamb cutlets with garlic mayonnaise.

Costelles de cabrit rostides: roast goat kid cutlets.

Cuixa de xai al forn: roast leg of lamb.

Estofat de bou: beef stew with sausages, potatoes, herbs and sometimes a little chocolate.

Aubergines (eggplant) and peppers, used in abundance

Estofat de quaresma: a filling Lenten vegetable stew.

Freginat: calf's liver with onions.

Fricandó: braised veal with wild mushrooms.

Llom de porc: pork chops.

Oca amb peres: goose with pears – traditional village festival fare.

Niu: a huge fish and meat stew from Palafrugell, Costa Brava, with pigeon, cuttlefish, cod tripe, pig's trotters, egg and garlic mayonnaise.

Peus de porc a la llauna: pig's trotters in a spicy sauce.

Pollastre amb samfaina: chicken with *samfaina* (*see p26*).

Pota i tripa: lamb's trotters and tripe.

Tripa a la catalana: tripe in *sofregit* (*see p26*) and wine with pine nuts and almonds.

Xai amb pèsols: lamb with peas.

Barcelona's cheese and honey market (*see p135*) in the Plaça del Pi

CAÇA (GAME)

Although the hunting season is from October to February, some game is available all year round, especially rabbit.

Becada amb coc: woodcock in a bread roll.

Civet de llebre: jugged hare.

Conill a la brasa amb allioli: rabbit with garlic mayonnaise.

Conill amb cargols: rabbit with snails.

Conill amb xocolata: rabbit with garlic, liver, almonds, fried bread, chocolate and old wine.

Estofat de porc senglar amb bolets: wild boar casserole with wild mushrooms.

Guatlles amb salsa de magrana: quail in pomegranate sauce.

Perdiu: partridge.

Perdius amb farcellets de col: partridge with cabbage dumplings.

VERDURES (VEGETABLES)

Albergínies: aubergines (eggplant).

Bledes: chard.

Bolets: mushrooms.

Calçots: leek-sized green onions, roasted on an open fire and dipped in a spicy tomato sauce. A spring-time speciality of the Tarragona region.

Carbassó arrebossat: battered courgettes (zucchini).

Carxofes: artichokes.

Julivert: parsley.

Mongetes tendres i patates: French beans and potatoes.

Pastanagues: carrots.

Pebrots: red peppers.

POSTRES (DESSERTS)

Although *pastisseria* (pastries) and *dolços* (sweets) are very popular in Catalonia, desserts in restaurants are generally uneventful. The choice may be simply ice cream or fruit: apple (*poma*), peach (*préssec*), banana (*plàtan*), orange (*taronja*), grapes (*raïm*).

Crema catalana: rich egg custard (*see p27*).

Figues amb aniset: figs in anise.

Flam: crème caramel.

Formatge: cheese. There is little local cheese.

Gelat: ice cream.

Mató: fresh goat's cheese, eaten with honey, sugar or jam.

Menjar blanc: an almond blancmange.

Peres amb vi negre: pears in red wine.

Postre de músic: a bowl of mixed nuts and dried fruit, once given as a reward to itinerant musicians.

Recuit: curdled sheep's (or cow's) milk in a small pot.

Mel i mató – a traditional dessert of soft cheese served with honey

Choosing a Restaurant

THE RESTAURANTS in this guide have been selected across a wide range of price categories for their good value, exceptional food and interesting location. The chart below lists restaurants in Barcelona by area; those in the *Further Afield* section are listed under their respective districts; and restaurants in the rest of Catalonia are arranged by town.

	Credit Cards	Tapas Bar	Fixed-Price Menu	Good Wine List	Outdoor Tables
OLD TOWN					
AGUT. Map 5 A3. € — Carrer d'En Gignàs 16. 93 315 17 09. Painters used to exchange their artwork for a hearty Catalan meal here. Specialities include aubergine (eggplant) terrine and steaks. ● *Sun D, Mon; Aug.*	MC V		■	●	
CAFÉ SCHILLING. Map 2 F3. € — Calle Ferrán 23. 93 317 67 87. Although the speciality of this café is its coffee, they also serve excellent sandwiches. Art and photography are displayed on the walls. ● *D.*					
CAN CULLERETES. Map 5 A2. € — Carrer d'En Quintana 5. 93 317 30 22. The city's oldest restaurant, established in 1786, serves traditional Catalan dishes such as *peix variat* (a seafood medley). ● *Sun D, Mon & 3 weeks Jul.*	MC V		■	●	
EGIPTE. Map 5 A2. € — La Rambla 79. 93 317 74 80. This popular, lively place with a good-value menu serves Mediterranean specialities and salt cod prepared in ten different ways.	AE DC MC V		■	●	
FONDA SENYOR PARELLADA. Map 5 B3. € — Carrer de l'Argenteria 37. 93 310 50 94. With wooden benches and old chandeliers, this atmospheric restaurant is a great choice for authentic Catalan cuisine.	AE DC MC V			●	
PLA DE LA GARSA. Map 5 B2. € — Carrer dels Assaonadors 13. 93 315 24 13. This pretty restaurant, once the stables of a medieval palace, offers an exceptional-value lunch menu. Wide choice of quality pâtés and cheeses at night, and an interesting range of red wines. ● *24 Dec L.*	AE MC V		■	●	
LES QUINZE NITS. Map 5 A3. € — Plaça Reial 6. 93 317 30 75. Conveniently located, this attractive restaurant draws a young crowd and offers good Catalan dishes at reasonable prices. ● *24 Dec D & 25 Dec.*	AE DC MC V		■	●	■
ROMESCO. Map 2 F3. € — Carrer de Sant Pau 28. 93 318 93 81. A popular spot just off La Rambla with home-style cooking, a lively atmosphere and unbeatable prices. The house speciality is *frijoles* (a Cuban dish of rice, black beans, fried banana and eggs). ● *Sun; Aug.*		●	■		
LA VERONICA. Map 5 A3. € — Carrer d'Avinyó 30. 93 412 11 22. Functional but fun, this trendy spot has delicious *pizzes* (pizzas) which change according to season. Hot soups in winter, chilled soups in summer. Lively terrace day and night. ● *Mon L, Tue L.*	MC V			●	■
AGUA. Map 6 D4. €€ — Passeig Marítim de la Barceloneta 30. 93 225 12 72. A fashionable place to eat, this designer restaurant on the beach offers a wide range of rice dishes, Mediterranean food and an appealing terrace.	AE MC V	●		●	■
AMAYA. Map 5 A1. €€ — La Rambla 20-24. 93 302 10 37. This classic, popular Basque-Catalan restaurant offers a good selection of tapas at the bar and half-portions of many dishes that appear on the encyclopedic menu. Fantastic wine list.	AE DC MC V	●	■	●	■

Price categories for a three-course evening meal for one, including a half-bottle of house wine, tax and service: € under 20 euros €€ 20–30 euros €€€ 30–40 euros €€€€ over 40 euros	**TAPAS BAR** In addition to the main dining room, there is a bar serving tapas and *racions* (larger portions). **FIXED-PRICE MENU** A good-value, fixed-price menu is offered at lunch or dinner, or both, usually with three courses. **GOOD WINE LIST** Denotes a wide range of good wines, or a more specialized selection of local wines. **OUTDOOR TABLES** Facilities for eating outdoors – on a terrace or in a garden or courtyard – often with a good view.	**CREDIT CARDS**	**TAPAS BAR**	**FIXED-PRICE MENU**	**GOOD WINE LIST**	**OUTDOOR TABLES**

CAFÈ DE L'ACADÈMIA. Map 5 B3. €€
Carrer de Lledó 1. **[** *93 315 00 26.*
This attractive restaurant gives a new interpretation to traditional Catalan cooking. Modern paintings combine with ancient stone walls. ● *Sat, Sun & public hols.* ▤ &
Credit Cards: AE DC MC V · Fixed-Price Menu ■ · Outdoor Tables ■

CAL PEP. Map 5 B3. €€
Plaça de les Olles 8. **[** *93 310 79 61.*
According to some seafood fanatics, Pep's *peixet fregit* (fried fish) is the best in the world. Other recommended seafood dishes include clams with ham, fried baby squid, and crayfish with onion. ● *Sun, Mon L, public hols, Easter, Aug, 24–26 Dec.* ▤
Credit Cards: AE DC MC V · Tapas Bar ●

EL SALÓN. Map 5 B3. €€
Carrer de l'Hostal d'En Sol 6–8. **[** *93 315 21 59.*
A refreshingly different restaurant-cum-bar with a great atmosphere and situated in a little street just off Plaça de Traginers. Its eclectic, ever-changing menu is mostly Mediterranean with a dash of Oriental charm. ● *Sun & public hols.* ▤
Credit Cards: AE MC V · Good Wine List ● · Outdoor Tables ■

ESTEVET. Map 2 F1. €€
Carrer de Valldonzella 46. **[** *93 302 41 86.*
A traditional, welcoming restaurant decorated with the original tiles and customers' paintings. The ebullient owner will guide you with the starters. Try the roast shoulder of young goat. ● *Sun, 2 weeks in Aug & public hols.* ▤ &
Credit Cards: AE DC MC V · Fixed-Price Menu ■ · Good Wine List ●

CAN MAJÓ. Map 5 B5. €€€
Carrer de l'Almirall Aixada 23. **[** *93 221 54 55.*
This renowned seafood restaurant in Barceloneta serves great rice dishes such as shellfish paella and *suquet* (a delicious fish and potato stew). ● *Sun D, Mon.* ▤ &
Credit Cards: AE DC MC V · Fixed-Price Menu ■ · Good Wine List ● · Outdoor Tables ■

LOS CARACOLES. Map 5 A3. €€€
Carrer dels Escudellers 14. **[** *93 302 31 85.*
Los Caracoles is Spanish for snails, and the snail-shaped bread is a tasty reminder. Serves excellent, simple dishes such as paella and spit-roasted chicken. ▤ &
Credit Cards: AE DC MC V · Tapas Bar ● · Good Wine List ●

REIAL CLUB MARÍTIM DE BARCELONA. Map 5 A4. €€€
Moll d'Espanya. **[** *93 221 62 56.*
A classic nautical club restaurant with spectacular views of the port. The elaborate cuisine includes dishes such as aubergine (eggplant) terrine with goat's cheese, and gilthead with apples and a cider sauce. ● *Sun D, 24–25 Dec.* ▤
Credit Cards: AE DC MC V · Good Wine List ● · Outdoor Tables ■

SET PORTES. Map 5 B3. €€€
Passeig de Isabel II 14. **[** *93 319 29 50.*
This lavishly decorated restaurant is reminiscent of an elegant Parisian café. It serves 11 types of paella, and delicious home-made cannelloni. ▤
Credit Cards: AE DC MC V · Good Wine List ●

CARBALLEIRA. Map 5 B3. €€€€
Carrer Reina Cristina 3. **[** *93 310 10 06.*
The first Galician seafood restaurant in Barcelona, and one of the best. For a superior lunchtime tapa at the bar, try the *arròs a la banda* – rice cooked in fish stock and served with *allioli* (garlic mayonnaise). ● *Sun D, Mon, public hols D.* ▤ &
Credit Cards: AE DC MC V · Good Wine List ●

TALAIA. Map 6 E5. €€€€
Anexo Torre Mapfre, Carrer de la Marina 16. **[** *93 221 90 90.*
This stunning, sleek restaurant overlooking the Port Olímpic marina offers wonderful food. You can order half portions *(pica-pica)* of most dishes. ▤ &
Credit Cards: AE DC MC V · Tapas Bar ● · Good Wine List ●

EIXAMPLE

BILBAO. Map 3 B2. €€
Carrer del Perill 33. **[** *93 458 96 24.*
A classic, bustling restaurant where little has changed since it opened in the early 1950s. Traditional seasonal Catalan home cooking. The wine list includes more than 30 types of *cava (see pp28–9).* ● *Sun, & public hols; Aug.* ▤ &
Fixed-Price Menu ■ · Good Wine List ●

Price categories for a three-course evening meal for one, including a half-bottle of house wine, tax and service:

€ under 20 euros
€€ 20–30 euros
€€€ 30–40 euros
€€€€ over 40 euros

TAPAS BAR
In addition to the main dining room, there is a bar serving tapas and *racions* (larger portions).

FIXED-PRICE MENU
A good-value, fixed-price menu is offered at lunch or dinner, or both, usually with three courses.

GOOD WINE LIST
Denotes a wide range of good wines, or a more specialized selection of local wines.

OUTDOOR TABLES
Facilities for eating outdoors – on a terrace or in a garden or courtyard – often with a good view.

	Credit Cards	Tapas Bar	Fixed-Price Menu	Good Wine List	Outdoor Tables
EL TRAGALUZ. Map 3 A3. €€€ Passatge de la Concepció 5. *93 487 06 21.* Two different dining concepts are on offer here: one building houses a sushi bar, while the restaurant behind has Mediterranean cuisine. The restaurant logo is by graphic designer Javier Mariscal *(see p17)*. 🍽 ♿	AE DC MC V	●	■	●	
ROIG ROBÍ. Map 3 A2. €€€€ Carrer de Sèneca 20. *93 218 92 22, 93 217 97 38.* Small, intimate restaurant offering authentic Catalan cuisine, with a lovely interior courtyard for summer. The terrines, fresh salads and any of the rice or seafood dishes are excellent. ● *Sat L, Sun & public hols.* 🍽	AE DC MC V		■	●	■

FURTHER AFIELD

	Credit Cards	Tapas Bar	Fixed-Price Menu	Good Wine List	Outdoor Tables
EIXAMPLE ESQUERRA: *Chicoa.* €€ Carrer d'Aribau 73. *93 453 11 23.* A haven for lovers of salt cod, with more than ten different preparations of the celebrated *bacallà* on offer. As well as other seafood and meat dishes, there is a good Penedès rosé house wine. ● *Mon D, Sun; Aug & public hols.* 🍽 ♿	AE MC V			●	
EIXAMPLE ESQUERRA: *Jaume de Provença.* €€€€ Carrer de Provença 88. *93 430 00 29.* The chef's original and creative Catalan cuisine has established his restaurant as among the city's finest. Despite the business-like decor the food is excellent and the service attentive. ● *Sun D, Mon; Aug.* 🍽 ♿	AE DC MC V		■	●	
GRÀCIA: *Envalira.* **Map 3 B1.** €€ Plaça del Sol 13. *93 218 58 13.* Some would claim this family-run restaurant is the only place to sample Catalonia's famous rice dishes. The most unusual is *arròs a la milanesa.* They also serve individual paellas – a rarity. ● *Sun D, Mon, Easter, Christmas; Aug.* 🍽 ♿	AE MC V			●	
GRÀCIA: *Giardinetto Notte.* **Map 3 A2.** €€€ Carrer Granada del Penedès 22. *93 218 75 36.* Mediterranean and Italian dishes are served in this romantic setting. Try the home-made pasta with a bottle of Catalan wine. ● *Sat L, Sun & public hols; Aug.* 🍽	AE DC MC V		■	●	
GRÀCIA: *Botafumeiro.* **Map 3 A2.** €€€€ Carrer Gran de Gràcia 81. *93 218 42 30.* Fine seafood and Galician specialities are served in this stylish restaurant. Mouthwatering desserts and an extensive wine list. ● *3 weeks in Aug.* 🍽 ♿	AE DC MC V	●		●	
GRÀCIA: *Ot.* **Map 3 C2.** €€€€ Carrer Torres 25. *93 284 77 52.* Very small (eight tables). The customer has no choice here but is guaranteed a gourmet experience, thanks to the cooking of its New Generation Catalan chefs. Booking essential. ● *Sat L, Sun & public hols; 3 weeks in Aug, 1 week in Dec.* 🍽	AE DC MC V		■	●	
PEDRALBES: *Neichel.* €€€€ Beltrán i Rózpide 1–5. *93 203 84 08.* European haute cuisine with Catalan touches is served in one of the city's most prestigious establishments. It has an excellent selection of cheeses and over 300 wine labels. ● *Sun, Mon; Aug & public hols.* 🍽	AE DC MC V		■	●	
POBLENOU: *Els Pescadors.* €€€ Plaça de Prim 1. *93 225 20 18.* Once a fisherman's tavern, this restaurant serves fish fresh from the quayside, excellent *a la llauna* (baked), especially *llobarro* (sea bass) or *dorada* (bream). Seasonal game and over 150 wines. ● *Holy Week, 24–26 Dec, 31 Dec–1 Jan.* 🍽 ♿	AE DC MC V			●	■
SANT GERVASI: *La Balsa.* €€€ Carrer de la Infanta Isabel 4. *93 211 50 48.* As well as exquisite Catalan and international cuisine, including an excellent goose liver starter, there are great views from the terrace of this restaurant. ● *Sun & Mon L; Holy Week, 25 & 26 Dec; Aug L.*	AE DC MC		■	●	■

SANTS: *Peixerot.*   €€€
Torre Catalunya, Carrer de Tarragona 177. [93 424 69 69.
First-class seafood predominates in this modern restaurant. Great rice dishes
and shellfish – serves *pica-pica* (half portions). ● Sat D, Sun; Aug. ▤

| | AE DC MC V | | ● | |

TIBIDABO: *El Asador de Aranda.*   €€€
Avinguda del Tibidabo 31. [93 417 01 15.
At the foot of Tibidabo, in a striking Modernista house, this very Castilian
restaurant is a carnivore's dream: lamb roasted in a wood-burning oven is the
speciality. Excellent wine list. ● Sun D, public hols D, Holy Week. ▤ ▧

| | AE DC MC V | | ● | ■ |

TIBIDABO: *La Venta.*   €€€
Plaça Doctor Andreu. [93 212 64 55.
An attractive restaurant at the foot of Tibidabo. Its glass-covered terraces, with
views of the city, are open in summer and provide a bright, greenhouse setting
in winter. Seasonal and Catalan-French cuisine. ● Sun; 1 Jan, 25 Dec. ▤

| | AE DC MC V | | ● | ■ |

CATALONIA

ALTAFULLA: *Faristol.*   €€
Carrer de Sant Martí 5 (Tarragona). [977 65 00 77.
Wine was once made in this delightful, 18th-century house, now decorated with
antiques. Try the superb chocolate mousse. ● Oct–May: Mon–Thu, Jun–15 Sep: L.

| | DC MC V | | ● | ■ |

ANDORRA LA VELLA: *Borda Estevet.*   €€€€
Carretera de la Comella 2 (Andorra). [(00–376) 86 40 26.
This old country house, decorated in rustic style, is still used for the traditional
practice of drying the tobacco that is grown nearby. Ask for the meat *a la
llosa* (brought to you on a hot slate). ▤ ▧ ● 1 Jan.

| | AE MC V | | ● | ■ |

ARENYS DE MAR: *Hispania.*   €€€€
Carrer Real 54, Carretera NII (Barcelona). [93 791 04 57.
Authentic Catalan cuisine which has won accolades from near and far. The
classic clam *suquet*, similar to a fricassee, and the *crema catalana* (a rich
caramel custard) are both delicious. ● Sun D, Tue, Easter & Oct. ▤ ▧

| | AE DC MC V | | ● | |

ARTIES: *Casa Irene.*   €€€€
Hotel Valarties, Carrer Major 3 (Lleida). [973 64 43 64.
Located in a picturesque village, this restaurant offers wonderful, French-
influenced food and three *menús de desgustació*. ● Mon, Tue L & Nov. ▤ ▧

| | AE DC MC V | ■ | ● | ■ |

BEGUR: *La Pizzeta.*   €
Ventura i Sabater 2 (Girona). [972 62 38 84.
It is essential to book in this popular alternative pizzeria in an elegant village
house. It also serves unusual salads, pasta and grilled meat. Ideal for families.
Interesting wines. ● Tue, 9 Dec–Feb. ▧

| | AE MC V | | ● | ■ |

BERGA: *Sala.*   €€€
Passeig de la Pau 27 (Barcelona). [93 821 11 85.
Classic Catalan dishes are offered here, many of which feature mushrooms.
Game is available in season. ● Sun D, Mon. ▤

| | AE DC MC V | | ● | |

BOLVIR DE CERDANYA: *Torre del Remei.*   €€€€
Camí Reial (Girona). [972 14 01 82.
This stunning palace surrounded by gardens has been impeccably restored and
now houses an elegant restaurant and hotel. Superb gourmet dishes and great
wine selection. ▤ ▧

| | AE DC MC V | ■ | ● | ■ |

CALAFELL PLATJA: *Giorgio.*   €€
Carrer Ángel Guimerá 4 (Tarragona). [977 69 11 59.
Delicious Italian food, served on a terrace overlooking the sea. The lasagne or
bouillons or broths are legendary. ☐ Fri–Sun & public hols; daily in summer.

| | | | ■ | ● | ■ |

CAMBRILS: *Joan Gatell-Casa Gatell.*   €€€€
Passeig Miramar 26, Cambrils Port (Tarragona). [977 36 00 57.
This restaurant is known for its seafood. The rice dishes, shellfish and lobster
casserole are all first class. ● Sun D, Mon & mid-Dec–mid-Jan, 1–15 May. ▤

| | AE DC MC V | ■ | ● | ■ |

CASTELL-PLATJA D'ARO: *Cal Rei.*   €€
Barri de Crota 3 (Girona). [972 81 79 25.
A lovely, 14th-century *masia* (farmhouse) serving the innovative cuisine of the
Empordà region. ● Mon D, Tue, Nov. ▤ ▧

| | AE DC MC V | ■ | ● | ■ |

For key to symbols see back flap

Price categories for a three-course evening meal for one, including a half-bottle of house wine, tax and service:

€ under 20 euros
€€ 20–30 euros
€€€ 30–40 euros
€€€€ over 40 euros

TAPAS BAR
In addition to the main dining room, there is a bar serving tapas and *racions* (larger portions).

FIXED-PRICE MENU
A good-value, fixed-price menu is offered at lunch or dinner, or both, usually with three courses.

GOOD WINE LIST
Denotes a wide range of good wines, or a more specialized selection of local wines.

OUTDOOR TABLES
Facilities for eating outdoors – on a terrace or in a garden or courtyard – often with a good view.

	Credit Cards	Tapas Bar	Fixed-Price Menu	Good Wine List	Outdoor Tables
FALSET: *El Cairat.* €€ Carrer Nou 3 (Tarragona). 977 83 04 81. One of the best restaurants in the Priorat wine-growing region. Creatively adapted local dishes include salt cod with aubergines (eggplant) and meatballs with wild mushrooms. Excellent local wines. ● Sun D, Mon & Nov. ▤	AE MC V			●	
FIGUERES: *Emporda.* €€€€ Hotel Empordà, Carretera NII (Girona). 972 50 05 62. Gourmets congregate here to enjoy the legacy of chef Jaime Subirós' cuisine. The fresh broad beans (fava beans) with mint and the salt cod with a garlic mousseline are both exquisite. Delightful terrace for dining in summer. ▤ ♿	AE DC MC V		■	●	
LA FLORESTA: *Casa Blava.* € Avinguda de Montserrat 1 (Barcelona). 93 674 93 51. Paellas are cooked here on open log fires. Also grilled meats and *calçots* in season (large spring onions grilled and served with a delicious sauce). Garden for children. Very close to Barcelona. ● Sun–Thu D, Wed.	AE DC MC V	●	■		■
GIRONA: *Cal Ros.* €€ Cort Reial 9. 972 21 73 79. Typical Catalan food and other regional specialities are available at very reasonable prices in this old, charming, establishment. ● Sun D, Mon. ▤ ♿	AE DC MC V		■	●	
GIRONA: *El Celler de Can Roca.* €€€€ Carretera Taialá 40. 972 22 21 57. The capital's best restaurant, where Juan Roca creates dishes such as lamb stuffed with sweetbreads and cinnamon. ● Sun & Mon, 1–15 Jul, 25 Dec. ▤ ♿	AE DC MC V		■	●	
LLEIDA: *Forn del Nastasi.* €€€ Carrer Salmeron 10. 973 23 45 10. Excellent regional cuisine including chargrilled vegetables *(escalivada)* and snails *a la llauna* (oven-baked). ● Sun D, Mon & 1st two weeks in Aug. ▤ ♿	AE DC MC V		■	●	
LLORET DE MAR: *El Trull.* €€€ Ronda Europa, Cala Canyellas (Girona). 972 36 49 28. Rustic dining room serving grilled lobster which you can choose from the aquarium. The *arrosat* (noodles with seafood) are also good. ▤ ♿	AE DC MC V		■	●	■
MARTINET: *Boix.* €€€ Carretera N260 km264 (Lleida). 973 51 50 50. A famous Catalan restaurant, located on the banks of the Riu Segre, serving roast leg of lamb so tender you can eat it with a spoon. ▤ ♿	AE DC MC V		■	●	■
MONT-RAS: *La Cuina de Can Pipes.* €€€€ Barri Canyellas (Girona). 972 30 66 77. This elegant, 18th-century farmhouse serves exquisitely delicate regional dishes. Try the *tournedo de foie.* ● Jan & Feb; Jul & Aug: Mon–Fri L. ▤ ♿	AE MC V		■	●	■
PERALADA: *Castell de Peralada.* €€€ Casino Castell de Peralada (Girona), C/ San Joan. 972 53 81 25. Dine in the incomparable medieval setting of this castle and try any of the dishes of the Empordà region and the castle's own house wine. ▤	AE DC MC V		■	●	■
PERATALLADA: *Bonay.* €€ Plaça de les Voltes 13 (Girona). 972 63 40 34. A timeless restaurant in an attractive village. The succulent dishes include *oca amb naps* (goose with turnips). ● Mon, 15 Oct–30 Nov. ▤ ♿	MC V			●	●
PORRERA: *Lo Teatret.* € Carrer del Onze de Setembre 4 (Tarragona). 977 82 81 61. This restaurant in the former village theatre serves traditional dishes with a modern touch: enjoy salt cod, herring, lamb or wild-mushroom cannelloni. Priorat wines – difficult to find in other parts of Catalonia. ● Mon. ▤	DC MC V		■	●	

REUS: *El Pa Torrat.*   €€
Avinguda Reus 24, Castellvell del Camp (Tarragona). 977 85 52 12.
Home cooked dishes such as roast rabbit with *allioli* (garlic mayonnaise) and
stuffed squid. ● Sun D, Mon D, Tue; last two weeks Aug & 22 Dec–6 Jan.

| | AE DC MC V | | | ● | |

ROSES: *El Bulli.*   €€€€
Cala Montjoi (Girona). 972 15 04 57.
Considered by many to be one of Spain's best restaurants and perhaps one of
Europe's most beautiful. Expensive, but worth it. ● Oct–Mar.

| | AE DC MC V | | ■ | ● | ■ |

SANT CARLES DE LA RÀPITA: *Miami Can Pons.*   €€€
Avinguda Constitució nr. 37 (Tarragona). 977 74 05 51.
Good-quality Catalan cooking is served here by the Pons family. Seafood, the
suquet and the *crema catalana* are specialities. Playground. ● 3 weeks in Jan.

| | AE DC MC V | | ■ | ● | |

SANT CELONI: *El Racó de Can Fabes.*   €€€€
Carrer de Sant Joan 6 (Barcelona). 93 867 28 51.
Santi Santamaría is considered one of Spain's best chefs and this delightful
country restaurant is a gastronomic paradise. The seasonal menu combines
many types of fresh regional produce. ● Sun D & Mon, 2 weeks in Feb.

| | AE DC MC V | | ■ | ● | |

SANT FELIU DE GUÍXOLS: *Can Toni.*   €€
Carrer Garrofers 54 (Girona). 972 32 10 26.
Enjoy the traditional cooking of the Empordà region here. Many dishes
include mushrooms when in season (September–March). ● Mon.

| | MC V | ● | ■ | ● | |

SANT SADURNÍ D'ANOIA: *El Mirador de les Caves.*   €€€
Carretera Sant Sadurní-Ordal Km 4, Subirats (Barcelona). 93 899 31 78
The duck with a foie gras and truffle sauce is one of the superb dishes served
here. ● Sun D & Mon D, Aug 8-23, 23 Dec–7 Jan.

| | AE DC MC V | | ■ | ● | |

LA SEU D'URGELL: *El Castell*   €€€€
Carretera N260 Km 229 (Lleida). 973 35 07 04.
At the foot of La Seu d'Urgell castle, surrounded by beautiful countryside, lies
this idyllic hotel-restaurant serving modern Catalan cuisine. The wine list will
delight the most sophisticated wine lovers.

| | AE DC MC V | | | ● | ■ |

SITGES: *Al Fresco.*   €€
Pau Barrabeitg 4 (Barcelona). 93 894 06 00.
Mediterranean and Oriental cuisines are expertly combined here. Superb
desserts. ● Mon & Tue in winter, 19 Dec–26 Jan.

| | AE DC MC V | | | ● | ■ |

SITGES: *El Velero.*   €€€
Passeig de la Ribera 38 (Barcelona). 93 894 20 51.
A seaside restaurant whose imaginative creations include sole fillets on a bed
of mushrooms topped with crab sauce, and lobster with a chickpea sauce.
● Sun & Mon D (in winter), Mon & Tue L (in summer); 23 Dec–1 Jan.

| | AE DC MC V | | ■ | ● | |

TARRAGONA: *El Merlot.*   €€€
Carrer Caballers 6. 977 22 06 52.
Situated in the old part of town, this restaurant serves Mediterranean cuisine,
with specialities including dishes of game in season and home-made desserts.
● Sun, Mon L.

| | AE DC MC V | | ■ | | |

TAVERTET: *Can Baumes.*   €
Calle de Abajo 2. 93 856 52 07.
Family-run restaurant serving traditional Catalan dishes such as *canelones de
boletes* (mushroom canneloni) and rabbit. ● Mon, 22 Dec–22 Jan.

| | V | ● | ■ | ● | ■ |

VALLS: *Masia Bou.*   €€
Carretera Lleida Km 215 (Tarragona). 977 60 04 27.
Many interesting dishes are on offer, but the speciality is *calçotadas* (onions
charred over embers, with *romesco* sauce – see p26). ● Tue in summer.

| | MC AE V | | ■ | ● | ■ |

VIC: *Ca L'U.*   €€
Plaça Santa Teresa 4 (Barcelona). 93 886 35 04.
Archetypal market-town restaurant serving wholesome stews and game. Famed
for its sole with prawns. Saturday market-day breakfasts, such as pigs' trotters
and bean stews, are not for the faint-hearted. ● Sun D & Mon; 24–25 Dec.

| | DC MC V | | ■ | ● | |

VIC: *Floriac.*   €€
Carretera Manresa-Vic N141 Km 39, 5, Collsuspina (Barcelona). 93 743 02 25.
16th-century *masia* (farmhouse) serving quality regional cuisine and excellent
game dishes when available. Check winter opening. ● 2 weeks Feb, 2 weeks Jul.

| | AE DC MC V | | ■ | ● | ■ |

For key to symbols see back flap

Cafés and Bars

THE RESTAURANTS in this guide have been selected across a wide range of price categories for their good value, exceptional food and interesting location. This chart lists restaurants in Barcelona by area – those in the *Further Afield* section are listed under their respective districts. Restaurants in the rest of Catalonia are arranged by town.

	Café	Bar	Tapas Served	Regional or Themed	Nightclub	Outdoor Tables	Live Music
OLD TOWN							
Bar Ra: Map 2 F2 — Plaça de la Garduña 1. ☎ 93 301 41 63. A small bar/restaurant behind La Boqueria market serving delicious food and natural juices. Good value set lunch. ◖ 10am–12:30am.		●				●	
Boadas: Map 5 A1 — Carrer dels Tallers 1. ☎ 93 318 88 26. Barcelona's oldest and most atmospheric cocktail bar is run by Maria Dolors Boadas, daughter of the Cuban-Catalan founder. Slick waiters mix heady potions – try a *mojito* (white rum with lemon juice, mint leaves and lots of ice). ◖ noon–2am Mon–Wed, noon–3am Thu–Sat.		●					
Bodega La Palma: Map 5 B3 — Carrer de la Palma de Sant Just 7. ☎ 93 315 06 56. A well restored *bodega* (wine cellar), where wine from barrels is served in ceramic pitchers. Excellent *truites* and *pa amb tomàquet (see p124)*. Bustling at breakfast time. ◖ 8am–3:30pm & 7–10pm Mon–Sat. ◗ Sun; Aug.		●	■				
Café El Bosc de les Fades: Map 2 F4 — Pasaje de Banca 7. ☎ 93 317 26 49. An imaginatively decorated café/bar, resembling a nymph's woodland grotto. It is located near Las Ramblas. ◖ Mon–Wed 10:30am–1am, Fri–Sat 11am–3am, Sun 11am–1am.	■						
Café Zurich: Map 5 A1 — Plaça de Catalunya 1. ☎ 93 317 91 53. Reopened in 1998 as a replica of the legendary café demolished to build El Triangle commercial centre, it is rapidly reclaiming its status as a landmark and meeting place. ◖ May–Oct: 8am–1am; Nov–Apr: 8am–11pm.	■					●	
Castells: Map 5 A1 — Plaça Bonsuccés 1. ☎ 93 302 10 54. A friendly, bustling, local bar that has been in the same family since the 19th century. Fresh, home-made tapas. Busy on nights when Barça has won a match. ◖ 8am–1am Mon–Thu (2:30am Fri & Sat). ◗ Sun; Jul.		●	■			●	
Granja M Viader: Map 5 A1 — Carrer d'En Xuclà 4–6. ☎ 93 318 34 86. The oldest *granja* (milk bar) in Barcelona, where Cacaolat (chocolate drink) was invented. *Suizos* (hot chocolate topped with cream), *mel i mató* (see p125) and *crema catalana* (see p27) are among its fattening delights. ◖ 9am–1:45pm & 5–8:45pm. ◗ Mon am, Sun & public hols.	■						
Irati: Map 5 A2 — Carrer del Cardenal Casañas, nr 15–17. ☎ 93 302 30 84. One of the first in a new wave of bars in Barcelona, serving genuine Basque *pinchos* (tapas). Join the crush at the bar, take your pick, sip Basque Txakoli wine and count up the sticks to pay. Great fun. ◖ noon–midnight daily.		●	■	●			
Jamboree: Map 5 A3 — Plaça Reial 17. ☎ 93 319 17 89. Once a convent, this establishment is now one of the best jazz clubs in town, with a busy programme of national and international musicians. Disco from 12:30am. ◖ 10:30pm–5am.		●			■		■
La Jarra: Map 5 A3 — Carrer de la Mercè 9. ☎ 93 315 17 59. Frequented for its *jamón canario* (ham cooked on the bone served with steamed potatoes) rather than its decor, this is an essential stop on a street full of tapas bars. ◖ 11am–1:30am. ◗ Wed & mid-Aug–mid-Sep.		●	■				

TAPAS
Tapas are small snacks that may be either hot or cold and are charged for individually, allowing customers to choose as many or few as they like. A *ració* is a larger portion.
REGIONAL OR THEMED
Barcelona has many bars themed either on different regions of Spain or on other countries.
NIGHTCLUB
Most nightclubs and discos are open until 5 or 6am and charge entry fees.
OUTDOOR TABLES
In Barcelona, outdoor tables are usually on the pavement in a street or square, but cafés and bars at the Port Olímpic, Maremàgnum and Port Vell often have terraces with sea views.
LIVE MUSIC
This is played regularly, each venue indicated having its own schedule.

	CAFÉ	BAR	TAPAS SERVED	REGIONAL OR THEMED	NIGHTCLUB	OUTDOOR TABLES	LIVE MUSIC
KASPARO: Map 5 A1 Plaça de Vicenç Martorell 4. 93 302 20 72. Interesting sandwiches and snacks are served all day long at this popular bar. Sit in the sun or enjoy the shade under the arches of this quiet square just behind Plaça Catalunya. 9am–midnight (10pm in winter). Jan.		●	■			●	
LAIE: Map 3 B5 Carrer de Pau Claris, 85. 93 302 73 10. A café/restaurant with an adjacent bookshop, Laie has live jazz every Tuesday night from February to May. 9am–1am. Sun.	■						■
PASTIS: Map 2 F4 Carrer de Santa Mónica 4. 93 318 79 80. An atmospheric French bar that forms part of the history of this once seedy end of La Rambla. *Pastis* and French music on Mondays and tango music on Tuesdays. 7:30pm–2:30am Sun–Thu (3:30am Fri & Sat).		●		●			■
EL VASO DE ORO: Map 5 C4 Carrer de Balboa 6. 93 319 30 98. More a Madrileño concept than Catalan, this classic *cerveseria* (beer-cellar) hidden behind the waterfront in Barceloneta serves draught beer in three sizes and delicious seafood tapas. The crush at the bar contributes to the atmosphere. 9am–midnight. 6 Sep–6 Oct.		●	■				
EL XAMPANYET: Map 5 B3 Carrer de Montcada 22. 93 319 70 03. Famous for its *xampanyet* (sparkling wine) and anchovies, this is the perfect spot in which to relax after visiting the Picasso Museum a few doors away. One of the prettiest bars around, it is decorated with original ceramic tiles. noon–4pm & 6:30–11:30pm. Sun eve, Mon & Aug.		●	■				

EIXAMPLE

	CAFÉ	BAR	TAPAS SERVED	REGIONAL OR THEMED	NIGHTCLUB	OUTDOOR TABLES	LIVE MUSIC
LA BODEGUETA: Map 3 A3 Rambla de Catalunya 100. 93 215 48 94. A smoky wine bar full of character and atmosphere – something of an oasis in the middle of the elegant Eixample district. 7am–1:30am.		■	●	■		■	
BRACAFÉ: Map 3 B5 Carrer de Casp 2. 93 302 30 82 Seriously good coffee in a classic, bustling café. Opened in 1932, its stylish interior has remained intact. Enjoy people-watching from the attractive covered terrace. 7am–11pm Mon–Sat, 9am–11pm Sun.	■					●	

FURTHER AFIELD

	CAFÉ	BAR	TAPAS SERVED	REGIONAL OR THEMED	NIGHTCLUB	OUTDOOR TABLES	LIVE MUSIC
ANTILLA BARCELONA Carrer de Arago 141-143. 93 451 21 51. This club specializes in the sensual beat of the salsa and offers dance classes. Live music Monday to Thursday. 10:30pm–5am (6am Fri & Sat).					■		■
KITTY O'SHEA'S Carrer de la Nau Santa Maria 5-7. 93 280 36 75. The first of Barcelona's various Irish pubs. The unpromising surroundings belie the authentic decor and atmosphere within. Delicious Irish beef and Sunday brunch. Charming staff. noon–2am.		●		●			
SOL SOLER: Map 3 B1 Calle Planeta 13. 93 217 44 40. On Gràcia's most popular square, this is a tapas bar with a difference: the tapas are tasty and unusual and the decor attractive, with marble tables and mirrors. 7pm–2:30am Mon–Tue, noon–2:30am Wed–Sun.		●	■			●	

SHOPPING IN BARCELONA

A CITY WITH impeccable style, Barcelona is where you'll find the best in Catalan, Spanish and international design. For those in search of fashion, a good place to begin a tour of Barcelona is on the streets around the Passeig de Gràcia, which make up the most important shopping area, and where crowds browse among the well-known fashion and design stores. In this area there are also many

A Modernista shop window

interesting old stores such as bakeries, herbalists and pharmacies – some displaying beautiful Modernista frontages. For those who enjoy the hustle and bustle of small crowded streets, the Barri Gòtic, in the heart of the city, has something for everyone. Particularly interesting are the antiques dealers and the stores specializing in traditional crafts such as carnival masks, ceramics and handmade espadrilles.

Some of the beautifully displayed confectionery at Escribà

FOOD AND DRINK

B ARCELONA'S pastry shops are sights in themselves and, with its displays of chocolate sculptures, no *pastisseria* is more enticing or spectacular than **Escribà**. Other food stores also have a great deal of character, none more so than **Colmado Quílez** in the Eixample. This wonderful old place stocks a huge range of hams, cheeses and preserves, in addition to a comprehensive selection of Spanish and foreign wines and spirits.

DEPARTMENT STORES AND 'GALERIES'

T HE BRANCH of **El Corte Inglés**, Spain's largest department store chain, on Plaça Catalunya is a Barcelona landmark and a handy place to find everything under one roof, including plug adaptors and services like key-cutting. Other branches are located around the city. Barcelona's hypermarkets also sell a wide

range of goods. As they are on the outskirts of the city – south along the Gran Via towards the airport, and on the Avinguda Meridiana to the north – a car is the best way to reach them.

The *galeries* (fashion malls), built mostly during the affluent 1980s, are hugely popular. **Bulevard Rosa** on the Passeig de Gràcia has hundreds of stores selling clothes and accessories. On the Avinguda Diagonal is **L'Illa**, a large, lively shopping mall containing chain stores as well as specialist retailers.

FASHION

I NTERNATIONAL fashion labels are found alongside clothes by young designers on and around the Passeig de Gràcia. **Adolfo Domínguez** stocks classically styled clothes for men and women; **Armand Basi** sells quality leisure and sportswear; and discount designer fashion is available at

Contribuciones. Many stores offer traditional, fine-quality tailoring skills and **Calzados E Solé**, which is situated in the Old Town, specializes in classic handmade shoes and boots.

SPECIALITY STORES

A WALK AROUND Barcelona can reveal a wonderful choice of stores selling traditional craft items and handmade goods that in most places have now been largely replaced by the production line. **La Caixa de Fang** has a good variety of Catalan and Spanish ceramics, among them traditional Catalan cooking pots and colourful tiles. **L'Estanc** has everything for the smoker, including the best Havana cigars. **La Manual Alpargatera** is an old shoe store that specializes in Catalan-style espadrilles. These are handmade on the premises and come in all colours. The city's oldest store, **Cereria Subirà** *(see pp52–3)*, sells candles in every imaginable form.

Menswear department in Adolfo Domínguez

DESIGN, ART AND ANTIQUES

IF YOU ARE interested in modern design, or just looking for gifts, you should pay a visit to **Vinçon**, the city's famous design emporium. Situated on the Passeig de Gràcia, it has everything for the home, including beautiful fabrics and furniture. A must is **BD-Ediciones de Diseño**, which has the feel of an art gallery. Housed in a building designed by Domènech i Montaner, the store has furniture based on designs by Gaudí and Charles Rennie Mackintosh, and sells wonderful contemporary furniture and accessories.

Most of the commercial art and print galleries are found on Carrer Consell de Cent, in

Mouthwatering fruit stalls in La Boqueria market

The stylishly sparse display of furniture at Vinçon

the Eixample, while the Barri Gòtic – especially the Carrer de la Palla and Carrer del Pi – is the best place to browse around small but fascinating antiques shops. As well as fine furniture and old dolls, **L'Arca de l'Avia** sells antique silks and lace, all of which are set out in pretty displays.

BOOKS AND NEWSPAPERS

MOST CITY-CENTRE newsstands sell English-language newspapers, but the best stocks of foreign papers and magazines are at FNAC at **L'Illa** and at **Crisol**, which also sells books, videos, CDs and photographic equipment.

MARKETS

NO-ONE SHOULD miss the chance to look around **La Boqueria** on La Rambla, one of the most spectacular food markets in Europe. Antiques are sold in the Plaça Nova on Thursdays, and cheese, honey and sweets in the Plaça del Pi on the first and third Friday and Saturday of each month. On Sunday mornings coin and stamp stalls are set up in the Plaça Reial, and a craft market is held near the Sagrada Família. The city's traditional flea market, **Encants Vells** *(see p89),* takes place on Mondays, Wednesdays, Fridays and Saturdays.

DIRECTORY

FOOD AND DRINK

Colmado Quílez
Rambla de Catalunya 63.
Map 3 A4.
(93 215 23 56.

Escribà Pastisseries
La Rambla 83. **Map** 2 F4.
(93 301 60 27.

Gran Via de les Corts
Catalanes 546. **Map** 2 E1.
(93 454 75 35.

DEPARTMENT STORES AND 'GALERIES'

Bulevard Rosa
Passeig de Gràcia 55.
Map 3 A4.
(93 378 91 91.

El Corte Inglés
Avinguda Diagonal 617–19.
(93 366 71 00.
(one of several branches.)

L'Illa
Avinguda Diagonal 545 57.
(93 444 00 00.

FASHION

Adolfo Domínguez
P de Gràcia 89. **Map** 3 A3.
(93 215 13 39.

Armand Basi
Passeig de Gràcia 49.
Map 3 A3.
(93 215 14 21.

Calzados E Solé
Carrer Ample 7. **Map** 5 A3.
(93 301 69 84

Contribuciones
Riera de Sant Miquel 30.
Map 3 A2.
(93 218 71 40.

SPECIALITY STORES

La Caixa de Fang
C/ Freneria 1. **Map** 5 B2.
(93 315 17 04.

Cereria Subirà
Bajada Llibreteria 7.
Map 5 B2. (93 315 26 06.

L'Estanc
Via Laietana 4. **Map** 5 B3.
(93 310 10 34.

La Manual Alpargatera
C/ d'Avinyó 7. **Map** 5 A3.
(93 301 01 72.

DESIGN, ART AND ANTIQUES

L'Arca de l'Avia
Carrer dels Banys Nous 20.
Map 5 A2.
(93 302 15 98.

BD-Ediciones de Diseño
Carrer de Mallorca 291.
Map 3 B4.
(93 458 69 09.

Vinçon
P de Gràcia 96. **Map** 3 B3.
(93 215 60 50.

BOOKS AND NEWSPAPERS

Crisol
Rambla de Catalunya 81.
Map 3 A4.
(93 215 27 20.

MARKETS

La Boqueria
La Rambla 101. **Map** 5 A2.

Encants Vells
Calle 2 Mayo,
Catalanes. **Map** 4 F5.

ENTERTAINMENT IN BARCELONA

F EW CITIES CAN MATCH the vitality of Barcelona, and nowhere is this more evident than in its live arts scene. The stunning Palau de la Música Catalana and the new Auditori de Barcelona have keen and critical audiences. They host some of the world's greatest classical musicians, including Montserrat Caballé and Josep (José) Carreras, both of whom are *barcelonins*.

Busker in the Barri Gòtic

Equally dynamic are the many exciting contemporary theatre and dance companies performing year round at indoor and outdoor venues. Modern music fans are well provided for at numerous rock, live jazz and salsa clubs, not to mention the buskers on La Rambla or in the squares of the Barri Gòtic. A tradition of old Barcelona that continues to thrive is its brash, glittering dance halls.

The magnificent interior of the Palau de la Música Catalana

ENTERTAINMENT GUIDES

T HE MOST COMPLETE guide to what's going on each week in Barcelona is the *Guía del Ocio*, out every Thursday. It includes a cinema listings section. The Friday *El País* and *La Vanguardia* also have entertainments supplements.

SEASONS AND TICKETS

T HEATRE AND concert seasons for the main venues run from September to June, with limited programmes at other times. In general, the city's varied menu of entertainments reflects its rich multi-cultural artistic heritage. In summer the city hosts the Festival del Grec *(see p31)*, a showcase of international music, theatre and dance, held at open-air venues. There is also a wide variety of concerts to choose from during the Festa de la Mercè *(see p32)* in September. The simplest way to get theatre and concert tickets is to buy

them at the box office of the relevant venue, although tickets for many theatres can also be bought from branches of the Caixa de Catalunya or La Caixa savings banks. Tickets for the Grec *(see p31)* festival are sold at tourist offices.

CLASSICAL MUSIC

B ARCELONA'S Modernista **Palau de la Música Catalana** *(see p61)* is one of the world's most beautiful concert halls, with its stunning interior decor and world-renowned acoustic. Also inspiring is the **Auditori de Barcelona**, opened in 1999 to give the city two modern halls for large-scale and chamber concerts. Its reputation was considerably bolstered when it became the home of the Orquestra Simfònica de Barcelona.

Musical life suffered a setback when the Liceu opera house burned down in 1994. Fortunately, the city had enough credit in the bank of operatic excellence to ensure that its reputation remained

undiminished. Restoration was completed in 1999, and the Liceu is now back in operation at full-octave level.

THEATRE AND DANCE

W ORTH SEEING are Catalan contemporary theatre groups such as Els Comediants or La Cubana whose original style combines a thrilling mélange of theatre, music, mime and elements from traditional Mediterranean fiestas.

The **Mercat de les Flors** *(see p79)*, a converted former flower market in Montjuïc, is an exciting theatre presenting high-quality productions of classic and modern plays in Catalan. The new **Teatre Nacional de Catalunya** *(see p89)*, next to the Auditori de Barcelona, is another fine showcase for Catalan drama.

The main venue for classical ballet is the **Liceu** opera house. There are also many contemporary dance companies and regular performances are staged at the Mercat de les Flors in Montjuïc.

Outrageous stage show at one of Barcelona's many clubs

Auditorium of the Teatre Nacional de Catalunya

CAFÉS, BARS AND CLUBS

AMONG BARCELONA'S most famous modern sights are the hi-tech designer bars built in the prosperous 1980s, for example the **Mirablau**, which looks over the city. The **Torres de Ávila**, in the Poble Espanyol *(see p81)*, is the height of post-Modernism. **Otto Zutz** has regular DJs and the less chic but still fun **Apolo** has live music. **La Paloma** is a fine dance hall complete with a 1904 interior and its own orchestra.

Two of the best-known bars are in the old city: **Boadas** for cocktails and **El Xampanyet** *(see p132–3)* for sparkling wine and tapas. **El Bosc de la Fades** is the café of the wax museum and is imaginatively decorated like a fairy's woodland grotto.

ROCK, JAZZ AND WORLD MUSIC

BIG NAMES like David Byrne and Paul McCartney have performed at **Zeleste**. In summer, festivals and open-air concerts are held around the city. Jazz venues include the **Harlem Jazz Club** and **Jamboree**, and salsa fans will enjoy a quick slink down to **Antilla Barcelona**.

AMUSEMENT PARK

IN SUMMER, Barcelona's giant amusement park on the summit of **Tibidabo** *(see p88)* is usually open till the early hours at weekends, but also busy on other days. It is even more fun if you travel there by tram, funicular or cable car.

SPORTS

THE UNDOUBTED kings of sport in Catalonia are **FC Barcelona**, known as Barça. They have the largest football stadium in Europe, Camp Nou, and a fanatical following *(see p87)*. Barcelona also has a high-ranking basketball team.

Packed house at the gigantic Camp Nou stadium

DIRECTORY

CLASSICAL MUSIC

Auditori de Barcelona
Carrer de Lepant 150.
Map 6 E1.
📞 93 247 93 00.

Palau de la Música Catalana
Carrer de Sant Francesc de Paula 2. **Map** 5 B1.
📞 93 295 72 00.

THEATRE AND DANCE

Liceu
La Rambla 51–59.
Map 2 F3.
📞 93 485 99 13.

Mercat de les Flors
Carrer de Lleida 59.
Map 1 B3.
📞 93 426 18 75.

Teatre Nacional de Catalunya
Plaça de les Arts 1.
Map 4 F5.
📞 93 306 57 00.

CAFÉS, BARS AND CLUBS

Apolo
Carrer Nou de la Rambla 113 **Map** 2 E3.
📞 93 441 40 01.

Boadas
Carrer dels Tallers 1.
Map 5 A1.
📞 93 318 88 26.

El Bosc de les Fades
Pasaje de Banca 7.
📞 93 317 26 49.

Mirablau
Plaça Doctor Andreu.
📞 93 418 58 79.

Otto Zutz
Carrer de Lincoln 15.
Map 3 A1.
📞 93 238 07 22.

La Paloma
Carrer del Tigre 27.
Map 2 F1.
📞 93 301 68 97.

Torres de Ávila
Poble Espanyol, Avinguda del Marquès de Comillas.
Map 1 A1.
📞 93 424 93 09.

El Xampanyet
Carrer Montcada 22.
Map 5 B2.
📞 93 319 70 03.

ROCK, JAZZ AND WORLD MUSIC

Antilla Barcelona
Carrer de Aragó 141–143.
📞 93 451 21 51.

Jamboree
Plaça Reial 17.
Map 5 A3.
📞 93 319 17 89.

Harlem Jazz Club
Carrer de la Comtessa de Sobradiel 8.
📞 93 310 07 55.

Zeleste
Carrer dels Almogàvers 122. **Map** 6 F2.
📞 93 309 12 04.

AMUSEMENT PARK

Tibidabo
📞 93 211 79 42.

SPORTS

FC Barcelona
Camp Nou, Avinguda Aristides Maillol.
📞 93 496 36 00.

Sports and Outdoor Activities

FROM THE MOUNTAINS to the sea, Catalonia provides all manner of terrain for enjoying the outdoor life. The hot summer months can be filled with water activities, from fishing to white-water rafting, while skiers head for the hills with the first snowfalls of winter. Nature lovers will find spectacular wildlife habitats, while Barcelona city offers beaches and numerous sports facilities.

CITY FACILITIES

BARCELONA HAS AROUND 30 municipal pools (*piscines municipales*), including the **Piscines Bernat Picornell** next to the **Estadi Olímpic** and **Palau Sant Jordi** sports stadia on Montjuïc. The pools were the venue for the 1992 Olympic swimming events. The Estadi Olímpic is an athletics stadium and is often used for concerts. The Palau Sant Jordi is used for indoor sports, as well as musical and recreational activities. Tennis fans are well provided for and the **Centre Municipal de Tennis Vall d'Hebron** caters for younger players too. Ice-skating can be fun and the **Pista de Gel del FC Barcelona** offers skate rental and runs an ice hockey school. Golf courses within easy reach of Barcelona are **Golf Sant Cugat** and **Golf El Prat**. There are several riding stables, and the **Escola Hípica** at Sant Cugat allows day outings over the Collserola hills. Cycle shops hire by the hour, half day and full day. **Un Cotxe Menys** organizes cycle tours around Barcelona.

AIRBORNE ACTIVITIES

CATALONIA HAS several small airports where planes can be hired and parachute jumps made. One of the best known flying clubs is **Aeroclub** in Sabadell. Paragliding is popular from any high spot and **Free Evolució** offers all kinds of adventure sports for groups of 10–12 people, including bungee jumping and ballooning, as an exciting alternative way to see the sights.

BIRD-WATCHING

BIRD LIFE in Catalonia is a huge attraction for dedicated bird-watchers. Northern European visitors in particular will be thrilled by the sight of hoopoes, bee-eaters, golden orioles and pratincoles. Two major wetland areas, where migratory birds include flamingoes, are **Delta de l'Ebre** (*see p111*), south of Tarragona, with a visitor centre in Deltebre, and **Aiguamolls de l'Empordà** around Sant Pere Pescador in the Bay of Roses. Both are easy to get to, and their visitor centres supply binoculars and guide services.

Griffon vulture

The best times to visit are early morning and evening. The Pyrenees are home to many raptors, including short-toed, golden and Bonelli eagles, and Egyptian, griffon and bearded vultures. The **Parc Natural del Cadí-Moixeró** (*see p96*), in the foothills of the Pyrenees, has a visitor centre in Bagà. Look out for alpine choughs, wallcreepers and peregrine falcons, as well as black woodpeckers in the wooded areas.

An angler's paradise – fishing for trout amid spectacular scenery

FIELD SPORTS

SEA FISHING is free, but a permit (*un permís*) is required for river fishing. Permits can usually be obtained through local tourist offices.

The Noguera Pallaresa and Segre are fine trout fishing rivers and the season runs from mid-March to the end of August. The game-hunting season is generally from October to March. Short leases and permits can be obtained from the **Patrimonio Natural** in Barcelona or from a local hunting association (*associació de caça*). Travel agents specializing in hunting and fishing breaks will also readily organize licences.

HIKING

ALL THE NATIONAL PARKS and reserves publish maps and walking suggestions. Good areas close to Barcelona are the Collserola hills and the chestnut woods of Montseny. Long-distance GR (*Gran Recorrido*) footpaths criss-cross Catalonia and the walking

Paragliding above the Vall d'Aran in the eastern Pyrenees

Shooting the rapids on the white waters of the Noguera Pallaresa

possibilities in the **Parc Nacional d'Aigüestortes** *(see p95)* and the Pyrenees are particularly good, with mountain refuges *(see p115)* for serious hikers. Walkers can obtain information from the **Centre Excursionista de Catalunya** *(see p53)*. The **Llibreria Quera**, in Carrer de Petritxol (No. 2) in Barcelona's Barri Gòtic, is the best bookshop for maps and guidebooks.

All the usual rules apply to those setting off to explore the wilderness – check weather forecasts, wear appropriate clothing, take adequate provisions and let someone know where you are going.

WATER SPORTS

THERE ARE AROUND 40 marinas along Catalonia's 580 km (360 miles) of coast, and a very wide range of watersports and activities is available. In Barcelona itself, the **Centre Municipal de Vela Port Olímpic** gives sailing lessons and has a variety of craft. The Costa Brava has long been a good spot for scuba diving. The best place is around the protected Illes Medes *(see p103)*, from the resort of L'Estartit. There are also diving schools around Cadaqués and Cap Begur, notably at Calella de Palafrugell, launching point for the Illes Ullastres.

The town of Sort on the Riu Noguera Pallaresa is a centre for exciting water sports such as white-water rafting, canoeing, kayaking and cave diving. Bookings for these and other adventure activities can be made through **Yetiemotions** or **Espot Esquí Parc**.

WINTER SPORTS

THE PYRENEES offer great winter skiing just two or three hours' drive from Barcelona and at weekends the resorts fill up with city crowds. There are some 20 ski areas. La Molina is good for beginners and Baqueira-Beret *(see p95)* is where Spain's royal family skis. Puigcerdà *(see p96)* in the Cerdanya is a good base for downhill and nordic skiing within reach of 15 ski stations in Catalonia, Andorra and France. The **Associació Catalana d'Estacions d'Esquí i Activitats de Muntanya (ACEM)** supplies resort details, while **Teletiempo**, a weather hotline, provides information on current weather conditions. In Barcelona, a dry ski slope has been installed beside the Piscines Bernat Picornell on Montjuïc.

Skiing at one of the many ski stations in the Pyrenees within easy reach of Barcelona

DIRECTORY

Aeroclub de Sabadell
(93 710 19 52.

Aiguamolls de l'Empordà
(972 45 42 22.

ACEM (Associació Catalana d'Estacions d'Esquí i Activitats de Muntanya)
(93 416 01 94.

Centre Excursionista de Catalunya
(93 315 23 11.

Centre Municipal de Tennis Vall d'Hebron
(93 427 65 00.

Centre Municipal de Vela Port Olímpic
(93 225 79 40.

Un Cotxe Menys
(93 268 21 05.

Delta de l'Ebre
(977 48 96 79.

Escola Hípica
(93 589 89 89.

Espot Esquí Parc
(97 362 4058.

Estadi Olímpic/ Palau Sant Jordi
(93 426 20 89.

Free Evolució
(93 363 23 50.

Golf El Prat
(93 379 02 78.

Golf Sant Cugat
(93 674 39 08.

Llibreria Quera
(93 318 07 43.

Parc Nacional d'Aigüestortes
(973 62 40 36.

Parc Natural del Cadí-Moixeró
(93 824 41 51

Patrimonio Natural
(93 567 42 00.

Piscines Bernat Picornell
(93 423 40 41.

Pista de Gel del FC Barcelona
(93 496 36 30.

Teletiempo
(906 36 53 08 (Barcelona);
906 36 53 65 (Spain).

Yetiemotions
(97 362 22 01 (office); or
63 082 75 36.

SURVIVAL
GUIDE

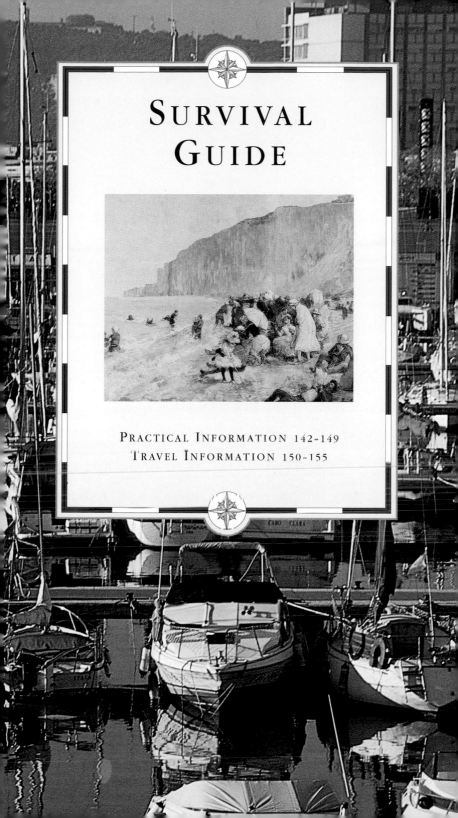

PRACTICAL INFORMATION 142–149
TRAVEL INFORMATION 150–155

PRACTICAL INFORMATION

CATALONIA has an excellent tourist infrastructure and Barcelona is particularly well organized for visitors. There are tourist offices in every town and all offer help in finding accommodation, restaurants and activities in their area. Larger offices usually have a wealth of leaflets in several languages. August is Spain's main vacation month.

Sign for a tourist office

Many businesses close for the whole month and roads are very busy at the beginning and end of this period. At any time of year, try to find out in advance if your visit will coincide with local *festes* (fiestas). Although these are attractions, they often entail widespread closures. It is a good idea to plan leisurely lunches, as most of Catalonia stops from 2pm to 4pm.

Sign to a town hall

A "closed" sign

LANGUAGE

THOUGH CATALAN is the language spoken by native Catalans, Catalonia is a bilingual country where people also speak *castellano* (Spanish). If you respond in Spanish to a question or greeting made in Catalan, the speaker will automatically switch to Spanish. All official signs and documents are in both languages. However, as Barcelona in particular regards itself as truly cosmopolitan, most tourist literature is also in English and French.

MANNERS

CATALANS GREET and say goodbye to strangers at bus stops, in lifts, in shops and in other public places. They shake hands when introduced and whenever they meet. Women usually kiss on both cheeks when they meet, and friends and family members of both sexes may kiss or embrace briefly.

VISAS AND PASSPORTS

VISAS ARE NOT required for tourists who are citizens of specified countries including the EU, Austria, Finland, Iceland, Liechtenstein, Norway, Sweden, the USA, Canada,

Australia and New Zealand. However it is always best to check visa requirements before travelling.

Spanish embassies supply a list of the other countries in the non-visa category. Tourists from these countries may stay 90 days within a continuous 180-day period. The *Oficina d'estrangers de Barcelona* (a local government office) deals with visa extensions. Proof of employment, study schedules, or sufficient funds for living are needed for a long stay.

No parking sign

TAX-FREE GOODS AND CUSTOMS INFORMATION

NON-EU RESIDENTS can reclaim *IVA* (VAT) on single items worth over 90 euros bought in shops displaying a "Tax-free for Tourists" sign. (Food, drink, cars, motorbikes, tobacco and medicines are exempt.) You pay the full price and ask the sales assistant for a *formulari* (tax exemption form), which you ask customs to stamp as you leave Spain (this must be within six months of the purchase). You receive the refund by mail or on your credit card account. Banco Exterior branches at Barcelona airport will give refunds on completed *formularis*.

TOURIST INFORMATION

BARCELONA HAS three main *oficines de turisme* providing information on the city, its attractions, transport and

places to stay and eat, all run by **Turisme de Barcelona**.

A fourth office, in the Passeig de Gràcia, run by **Turisme de Catalunya**, a department of the Generalitat (Catalonia's government), provides information on the rest of the region. Other major towns have tourist offices providing information published by the Generalitat and the province's local administration *(patronat)*.

There is a Spanish National Tourist Office in the following English-speaking cities: New York, Chicago, Miami, Los Angeles, London and Toronto.

In Barcelona during the summer, pairs of young information officers, known as Red Jackets and generally English-speaking, provide tourist information in the streets of the Barri Gòtic, La Rambla and the Passeig de Gràcia.

Turisme de Catalunya's Barcelona office

OPENING HOURS

MOST MUSEUMS and monuments close on Mondays. On other days they generally open from 10am to 2pm and, in some cases, reopen from 4 or 5pm to 8pm. Churches may only be opened for services. In smaller towns it is common for churches, castles and other sights to be kept locked. The

◁ **Boats in Barcelona's Port Olímpic with the hill of Montjuïc in the background**

Students enjoy reduced admission fees to many museums and galleries

key *(la clau)*, available to visitors on request, will be with a caretaker, kept at the town hall *(ajuntament)*, or perhaps with the owners of the local bar. Admission is charged for most museums and monuments. On Sundays, museum admission is often free.

FACILITIES FOR THE DISABLED

CATALONIA'S association for the disabled, the Federació ECOM *(see p115)*, has hotel lists and travel advice for the whole region. Spain's national association, COCEMFE, has a tour company, **Servi-COCEMFE**, that publishes guide books to facilities in Spain and will help plan vacations.

COCEMFE sign for disabled access

Tourist offices and the social services departments of town halls supply information on local facilities. A travel agency, **Viajes 2000**, specializes in vacations for disabled people.

SPANISH TIME

SPAIN IS ONE HOUR ahead of Greenwich Mean Time (GMT) in winter *(l'hivern)* and two hours in summer *(l'estiu)*, and uses the 24-hour clock. *La matinada* is the small hours, *el matí* (morning) lasts until about 1pm, while *migdia* (midday) is from 1 to 4pm. *La tarda* is the afternoon, *el vespre* the evening and *la nit* the night.

STUDENT INFORMATION

HOLDERS OF THE International Student Identity Card (ISIC) are entitled to benefits, such as discounts on travel and reduced entrance charges to museums and galleries. Information is available from all national student organizations and, in Barcelona, from **Viatgeteca**, which sells the international student card and youth hostel cards. **Unlimited Youth Student Travel** specializes in student travel.

ELECTRICAL ADAPTORS

SPAIN'S ELECTRICITY supply is 220 volts, but the 125-volt system still operates in some old buildings. Plugs for both have two round pins. A three-tier standard travel converter enables you to use appliances from abroad on both supplies. Heating appliances should be used only on 220 volts.

CONVERSION CHART

Imperial to metric
1 inch = 2.54 centimetres
1 foot = 30 centimetres
1 mile = 1.6 kilometres
1 ounce = 28 grams
1 pound = 454 grams
1 pint = 0.6 litre
1 gallon = 4.6 litres

Metric to imperial
1 millimetre = 0.04 inch
1 centimetre = 0.4 inch
1 metre = 3 feet 3 inches
1 kilometre = 0.6 mile
1 gram = 0.04 ounce
1 kilogram = 2.2 pounds
1 litre = 1.8 pints

DIRECTORY

CONSULATES

Australia
Gran Via de Carles III 98, 9°,
08028 Barcelona.
(93 330 94 96.

Canada
Calle Elisenda de Pinós 10,
08034 Barcelona.
(93 204 27 00.

Ireland
Gran Via de Carles III 94, 10°-2ª,
08028 Barcelona.
(93 491 50 21.

United Kingdom
Avinguda Diagonal 477, 13°
08036 Barcelona.
(93 366 62 00.

United States
Passeig de la Reina Elisenda 23,
08034 Barcelona.
(93 280 22 27.

TOURIST OFFICES

Turisme de Barcelona
Plaça de Catalunya 17, subterrani,
08002 Barcelona.
(906 30 12 82.

C/Ciutat 2 (Ajuntament),
08002 Barcelona.
(906 30 12 82.

Estació Sants, Pl Països Catalans,
08014 Barcelona.
(906 30 12 82.

Turisme de Catalunya
Palau Robert, Pg de Gràcia 107,
08008 Barcelona.
(93 238 40 00

DISABLED

Servi-COCEMFE
Calle Eugenio Salazar 2,
28002 Madrid.
(91 413 80 01.

Viajes 2000
Paseo de la Castellana 228-230,
28046 Madrid.
(91 323 10 29.

YOUTH/STUDENT

Unlimited Youth Student Travel & Viatgeteca
Carrer Rocafort 116–122,
08015 Barcelona.
(93 483 83 78.

Personal Security and Health

I N CATALONIA, as in most parts of western Europe, rural areas are quite safe, while towns and cities warrant more care. Keep cards and money in a belt, don't leave valuables in your car and avoid poorly lit areas at night. If you feel ill, there will always be a local *farmàcia* (pharmacy) open. In Spain, pharmacists prescribe as well as advise. Report lost documents to your consulate *(see p143)* and to the *Policia Nacional* at the local *comissaria* (police station). Emergency numbers are listed opposite.

IN AN EMERGENCY

T HE NEW NATIONAL telephone number throughout Spain for all emergency services is 112. After dialling, ask for *policia* (police), *bombers* (fire brigade) or *ambulància* (ambulance). Local numbers for the individual emergency services (opposite) still also apply. Outside Barcelona, the largely voluntary *Creu Roja* (Red Cross) often responds to 112 (or other) emergency calls for ambulances.

Ambulances take admissions to hospital *urgències* (accident and emergency) departments.

Creu Roja

Red Cross ambulance sign

URGÈNCIES

Accident and Emergency sign

MEDICAL TREATMENT

A NY EU NATIONAL who falls ill in Spain is entitled to social security cover. To claim medical treatment, UK citizens must obtain Form E111 from the Department of Health, a post office or GP surgery prior to travelling. This form must be given to anyone who treats you, so take several copies. It is normally contained within the booklet *Health Advice for Travellers*, which explains the health care you are entitled to, and where and how to claim. Not all treatments are covered by Form E111, so it is a good idea to arrange private medical insurance as well.

For private medical care in Spain ask at a tourist office, or at your consulate or hotel for the name and number of a doctor – if necessary, one who

speaks English. Visitors from the US should make sure their insurance covers medical care abroad. If payment is needed at the time of treatment, ask for an itemized bill. Some insurance companies will ask for an official translation. Extra private cover may be needed for emergency hospital care.

PHARMACIES

F OR NON-EMERGENCIES, a *farmacèutic* (pharmacist) can advise and, at times, prescribe without a doctor's consultation. The *farmàcia* sign is an illuminated green or red cross. The addresses of those open at night or at weekends are listed in all pharmacy windows or may be found in local newspapers.

PERSONAL SECURITY

V IOLENT CRIME is rare but it is wise to take sensible precautions when out and about. Always be vigilant with

Front of a high-street *farmàcia* (pharmacy) in Catalonia

handbags, wallets and cameras, especially in crowds, and take a taxi to your lodgings at night.

In Barcelona, pickpockets are more active at Plaça de Catalunya, Carrer Ferran, the cathedral, Sagrada Família and Sants station. Take extra care on La Rambla where muggings have been on the increase.

POLICE IN CATALONIA

U NTIL RECENTLY police services in Catalonia were organized into three forces as in the rest of Spain. This system still operates in some parts of Catalonia: the *Guàrdia Civil* (paramilitary Civil Guard), in olive-green, polices mainly borders, airports and rural areas; the *Policia Nacional*, in blue, deals with major crime in

Policia Nacional   Mosso d'Esquadra   Guàrdia Urbana

larger towns and national security, as well as immigration, work permits and residence documents; and the *Guàrdia Urbana,* also in blue, deals with traffic regulation and the policing of local communities.

The *Guàrdia Civil* and the *Policia Nacional* are gradually being replaced by an autonomous Catalan police force, the *Mossos d'Esquadra.* It is hoped that by 2004 the *Mossos* will have assumed all their predecessors' duties throughout the region. Girona and Llieda provinces have already achieved this, but in the city of Barcelona the *Mossos* still play a largely ceremonial role.

The current model of police car for the *Guàrdia Urbana*

A patrol car of the *Policia Nacional*

Fire engine showing the Barcelona fire service emergency number

LEGAL ASSISTANCE

SOME HOLIDAY (vacation) insurance policies cover legal costs and provide a helpline you can call.

If you are arrested, you have the right to telephone your consulate *(see p143),* which should have a list of bilingual lawyers. The *Col·legi d'Advocats* (Lawyers' Association) can guide you on getting legal advice or representation.

If you need an interpreter, ask your consulate or look in the *Pàgines Grogues* (Yellow Pages) telephone directory under *Traductors* (Translators) or *Intèrprets* (Interpreters) *Traductors oficials* or *jurats* are qualified to translate legal or official documents.

PERSONAL PROPERTY

HOLIDAY insurance is there to protect you financially in the event of the loss or theft of your property, but it is best to take preventative

An ambulance displaying the Barcelona 061 emergency number

measures – making use of hotel safes and avoiding carrying large sums of money.

Report a loss or theft straight away to the *Policia Nacional* at the local *comissaria,* as many insurance companies give you only 24 hours. You must make a *denúncia* (written statement) to the police and get a copy for your insurers.

Your consulate can replace a missing passport, but cannot provide financial assistance.

PUBLIC CONVENIENCES

PUBLIC CONVENIENCES are rare in Catalonia. Most people simply walk into a bar, café, department store or hotel and ask for *els serveis* or *el wàter* (in Catalan), or *los servicios* or *los aseos* (in Spanish). On motorways (highways), there are toilets at service stations. Women may have to ask for *la clau* (the key). Always carry toilet tissue with you, as it is often not provided.

OUTDOOR HAZARDS

CATALONIA'S HOT summers, combined with wind and bone-dry vegetation, are ideal for forest fires. To avoid the risk, extinguish cigarettes in car ashtrays and take empty bottles away with you.

If climbing or hill-walking go properly equipped and let someone know your route. Do not enter a *vedat de caça* (hunting reserve) or *camí particular* (private driveway).

DIRECTORY

EMERGENCY SERVICES

Police *(Policia)*
Fire Brigade *(Bombers)*
Ambulance *(Ambulància)*
 112 *(national number).*

Police *(local numbers)*
 091 – *Policia Nacional*
092 – *Guàrdia Urbana (Barcelona, Lleida, Girona, Tarragona).*

Fire Brigade *(local numbers)*
 080 *(Barcelona),* 085 *(Lleida, Girona, Tarragona).*

Ambulance *(local numbers)*
 061 *(Barcelona),* use 112, *(national number)* elsewhere.

Banking and Local Currency

Y OU MAY ENTER SPAIN with an unlimited amount of money, but if you intend to export more than 6,000 euros, you should declare it. Traveller's cheques may be exchanged at banks, bureaux de change (*canvi* in Catalan, *cambio* in Spanish), some hotels and some shops. Banks generally offer the best exchange rates. The cheapest exchange rate may be offered on your credit or direct debit card, which may be used in cash dispensers displaying the appropriate sign.

BANKING HOURS

A S A RULE of thumb, banks throughout Catalonia are open from 8am to 2pm on weekdays. Some open until 1pm on Saturdays, but most remain closed on Saturdays in August. Branches of some of the larger banks in the centre of Barcelona are beginning to extend their weekday opening hours, but this is not yet a widespread practice.

Bureau de change

CHANGING MONEY

M OST BANKS have a foreign exchange desk signed *Canvi/Cambio* or *Moneda estrangera/extranjera*. Always take your passport as ID to effect any transaction.

You can draw up to 300 euros on major credit cards at a bank. Several US and UK banks have branches in Barcelona, including **Citibank** and **Barclays**. If you bank with them, you can cash a cheque there.

A bureau de change, indicated by the sign *Canvi/Cambio*, or the sign "Change", will invariably charge higher rates of commission than a bank, but will often remain open after hours.

Caixes d'estalvi/Cajas de ahorro (savings banks) also exchange money. They open from 8:30am to 2pm on weekdays, and on Thursdays also from 4:30pm to 7:45pm. They have a highly visible profile, actively supporting the arts and good public works.

CHEQUES AND CARDS

T RAVELLER'S CHEQUES can be purchased at American Express (AmEx), Thomas Cook or your bank. All are accepted in Spain. If you exchange Am-Ex cheques at an AmEx office, commission is not charged. Banks require 24 hours' notice to cash cheques larger than 3,000 euros. If you draw more than 600 euros on traveller's cheques, you may be asked to show the purchase certificate.

The most widely accepted card in Spain is the **VISA** card. **MasterCard** (Access)/Eurocard and **American Express** are also useful currency. The major banks will allow cash withdrawals on credit cards.

When you pay with a card, cashiers will usually pass it through a reading machine. Sometimes, however, you will be asked to punch your PIN into a small keypad attached to the machine.

Credit card reader with PIN keypad

24-hour cash dispenser

CASH DISPENSERS

I F YOUR CARD is linked to your home bank account, you can use it with your PIN to withdraw money from cash dispensers, which are widespread. Nearly all take VISA or MasterCard (Access) cards.

When you enter your PIN, instructions are displayed in Catalan, Spanish, English, French and German. Many dispensers are inside buildings these days, and to gain access customers must run their cards through a door-entry system.

Cards with Cirrus and Maestro logos can also be widely used to withdraw money from cash machines.

DIRECTORY

FOREIGN BANKS

Barclays Bank
Ronda de la Universitat 27,
08007 Barcelona.
[93 301 52 08.

Citibank
Plaça Catalunya 1,
08007 Barcelona.
[91 657 66 13.

LOST CARDS AND TRAVELLER'S CHEQUES

American Express
[91 572 03 03.

Diners Club
[901 10 10 11.

MasterCard (Access)
[900 97 12 31 (toll free).

VISA
[900 99 12 16 (toll free).

The Euro

Introduction of the single European currency, the euro, has taken place in 12 of the 15 member states of the EU. Austria, Belgium, Finland, France, Germany, Greece, Ireland, Italy, Luxembourg, The Netherlands, Portugal and Spain chose to join the new currency; the UK, Denmark and Sweden stayed out, with an option to review the decision. The euro was introduced on 1 January 1999, but only for banking purposes. Notes and coins came into circulation on 1 January 2002. After a transition period allowing the use of both national currencies and the euro, Spain's own currency, the peseta, was completely phased out by March 2002. All euro notes and coins can be used anywhere within the participating member states.

Bank Notes

Euro bank notes have seven denominations. The 5-euro note (grey in colour) is the smallest, followed by the 10-euro note (pink), 20-euro note (blue), 50-euro note (orange), 100-euro note (green), 200-euro note (yellow) and 500-euro note (purple). All notes show the 12 stars of the European Union.

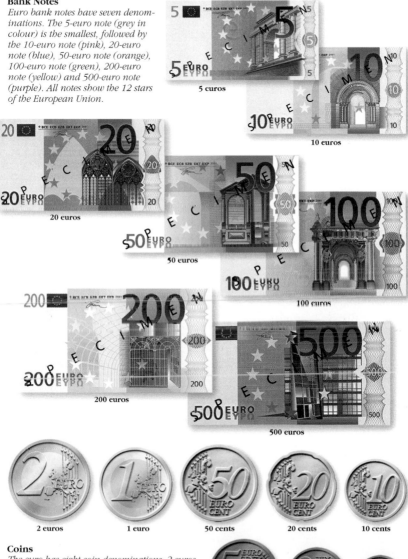

5 euros

10 euros

20 euros

50 euros

100 euros

200 euros

500 euros

2 euros

1 euro

50 cents

20 cents

10 cents

Coins

The euro has eight coin denominations: 2 euros and 1 euro (silver and gold); 50 cents, 20 cents and 10 cents (gold); and 5 cents, 2 cents and 1 cent (bronze). The reverse (number) side of euros are the same in all Euro-zone countries, but the front is different in each state.

5 cents

2 cents

1 cent

Communications

Standard issue postage stamp

Public telephones, run by the Spanish telecommunications company Telefónica, are easy to find and operate with a card or coins, but international calls have a high charge. The postal service, Correos, is identified by a crown insignia in red or white on a yellow background. Registered mail and telegrams can be sent from all Correos offices. These also sell stamps, but it is more usual, and quicker, to buy them from *estancs* (tobacconists). There are no public phones in Correos offices.

Logo of the Spanish telecom system

TELEPHONING

As well as public telephone boxes (*cabines*), bars often have payphones. Both types take coins. There is a high minimum connection charge, especially for international calls, so it is best to ensure that you have plenty of change ready. Phonecards are a more convenient option and can be bought at *estancs* and newsstands. In addition, some phones are equipped with electronic multilingual instruction displays.

Calls can also be made from *locutoris* (public telephone offices) and paid for afterwards. The cheapest offices are those run by Telefónica. Private ones, which are often located in shops, are usually much pricier.

The charges for international calls are divided into four bands: EU countries; non-EU European countries and Northwest Africa; North and South America; and the rest of the world. With the exception of local calls, using the telephone system can be expensive, especially if calling from a hotel, which may add a high surcharge. A call from a *cabina* or a *locutori* costs as much as 35 per cent more

USING A COIN AND CARD TELEPHONE

1 Lift the receiver, and wait for the dialling tone and for the display to show *Inserte monedas o tarjeta*.

2 Insert either coins *(monedas)* or a card *(tarjeta)*.

3 Key in the number firmly, but not too fast – Spanish phones prefer you to pause between digits.

4 As you press the digits, the number you are dialling will appear on the display. You will also be able to see how much money or how many units are left and when to insert more coins.

5 When your call is finished, replace the receiver. The phonecard will then re-emerge automatically or any excess coins will be returned.

Spanish phonecard

USEFUL SPANISH DIALLING CODES

- When calling within a city, within a province, or to call another province, dial the entire number. The province is indicated by the initial digits: Barcelona numbers start with 93, Lleida 973, Girona 972 and Tarragona 977.
- To make an international call, dial 00, followed by the country code, the area code and the number.
- Country codes are: UK 44; Eire 353; France 33; US and Canada 1; Australia 61; New Zealand 64. It may be necessary to omit the initial digit of the destination's area code.
- For operator/directory service, dial 1003.

- For international directory enquiries, dial 1008 for EU countries and 1005 for the rest of the world.
- To make a reversed-charge (collect) call within the EU, dial 900 99 00 followed by the country code; to the US or Canada, dial 900 99 00 followed by 11 or 15 respectively. Numbers for other countries are in the A–K telephone directory under *Comunicaciones Internacionales*.
- To report technical faults, dial 1002.
- The speaking clock is on 093, the weather on 906 36 53 08, wake-up calls on 096.

than a call made from a private telephone.

Reversed-charge (collect) calls made to EU countries may be dialled directly, but most others must be made through the operator.

Spain abolished provincial area codes in 1998, so the full number, including the initial 9, must always be dialled, even from within the area.

POSTAL SERVICE

CORREOS, Spain's postal service, is rather slow. It is better to send any urgent or important post by *urgente* (express) or *certificado* (registered) mail, or to use a private courier service.

Post can be registered and telegrams sent from all Correos offices. However, it is more convenient to buy stamps for postcards and letters from an *estanc* (tobacconist's).

Postal rates fall into four price bands: the EU, the rest of Europe, the US, and the rest of the world. Parcels must be weighed and stamped by Correos and must be securely tied with string, or a charge may be made at the counter to have them sealed by a clerk.

Main Correos offices open from 8am to 9pm from Monday to Friday and from 9am to 7pm on Saturday. Branches in the suburbs and in villages open from 9am to 2pm from Monday to Friday and from 9am to 1pm on Saturday.

ADDRESSES

IN CATALAN ADDRESSES the street name is written first, followed by the building number, the floor number, and the number or letter of the apartment. For example, C/ Mir 7, 5^e-A means apartment A on floor 5 of building number 7 in Carrer Mir. Carrer is often shortened to C/. Floor designations are: *Baixos* (ground floor), *Entresol*, *Principal*, 1^r, 2^n and so on, meaning that 2^n is in fact the 4th level above the ground.

Some of Catalonia's daily papers

Some newer buildings use the less complicated designation of *Baixos* followed by 1^r, 2^n and so on upwards. Postcodes (zip codes) have five digits; the first two are the province number.

TELEVISION AND RADIO

CATALANS HAVE a choice of watching TV3 in Catalan run by the regional government, or TVE1 and TVE2, Spain's two state television channels. There is a Catalan channel, Canal 33, which has a high cultural content and three Spanish independents: Antena 3, Tele 5 and Canal+ (Canal Plus). A regular foreign language news service is provided by Barcelona Tele-visio (BTV). Most foreign films on television (and in cinemas) are dubbed. Subtitled films are listed as *VO* (*versión original*).

Satellite channels such as CNN, Cinemanía and Eurosport and many other European channels can be received in Catalonia.

The main radio stations are Catalunya Ràdio, and COM Ràdio, the Spanish state Radio Nacional de España, and the independent stations Radio 2, broadcasting classical music, and Ser, a Spanish general-interest station.

Catalan mailbox

Catalan magazines

NEWSPAPERS AND MAGAZINES

SOME NEWSAGENTS and kiosks in Barcelona city centre stock periodicals in English. Newspapers in English available on the day of publication are the *International Herald Tribune*, the *Financial Times* and the *Guardian International*. Others can be found a day after publication. *The European* newspaper and popular weekly news magazines such as *Time*, *Newsweek* and *The Economist* are readily available.

The main Catalan-language newspapers are *Avui* and *El Periódico* (the latter also having a Spanish edition). *La Vanguardia*, in Spanish, is published in Barcelona and is widely respected. The other Spanish newspapers with large circulations are *El País*, *El Mundo* and *ABC*. *El Mundo*, aimed at young people, tends to have a lot of news features; *El País* and *ABC* are very strong on international news.

Barcelona's best weekly listings magazine for arts, leisure events and eating out is *Guía del Ocio*, published in Spanish. Lifestyle and sports magazines are also popular.

A newsstand on La Rambla in Barcelona

TRAVEL INFORMATION

CATALONIA'S three main airports – El Prat, Girona and Reus – receive international flights from all over the globe. While Barcelona's El Prat handles mainly scheduled services, Girona and Reus deal with package holiday flights. Rail networks and toll highways radiate from Barcelona to serve the

Spain's national airline

region's major towns. Barcelona has a well-developed ringroad *(ronda)* system, and a tunnel through the Collserola Hills brings the inland highways right into the city. Both its Metro and suburban train links are excellent but, as much of Catalonia is mountainous, buses or a car are the only way to see many rural sights.

Duty-free shopping at Barcelona's El Prat airport

ARRIVING BY AIR

BARCELONA IS SERVED by many international airlines. The Spanish national carrier, **Iberia**, offers daily scheduled flights to Barcelona from all west European capitals. It also offers connections with, but no direct flights from, eastern Europe. Direct flights from several other east European capitals are, however, offered by other airlines.

British Airways offers scheduled flights to Barcelona, with daily flights from London Heathrow and London Gatwick and four flights a week from Birmingham. **EasyJet** flies from Liverpool and London Luton, while Iberia offers a direct service from Manchester.

Delta Air Lines and **TWA** each offer direct flights to Barcelona from the US. Iberia operates a comprehensive service from both the US and Canada, offering regular flights from Montreal via Madrid. No airlines operate direct flights between Spain and Australasia.

Catalonia's other two international airports handle charter flights: Girona serves the Costa Brava, and Reus, near Tarragona, the Costa Daurada.

For passengers arriving from Madrid or other Spanish cities, most of Spain's domestic flights are operated by Iberia, its associated airlines **Aviaco** and **Air Nostrum**, and **Air Europa**, **Pan-Air** and **Spanair**.

The most frequent shuttle service between Madrid and Barcelona is Iberia's Pont Aeri (Puente Aéreo). It flies every quarter of an hour at peak times and passengers can buy tickets just 15 minutes in advance using a self-ticketing machine. If a flight is full, those passengers still waiting are offered a seat on the next one. The flight takes 50 minutes.

Other services between Madrid and Barcelona are less frequent but, on the whole, their prices tend to be lower.

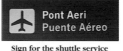

Sign for the shuttle service linking Barcelona and Madrid

The major international car rental companies *(see p155)* have desks at all three terminals of El Prat airport. Girona airport also has some of the main rental companies on site

---

DIRECTORY

AIRPORT INFORMATION

Barcelona El Prat
☎ 93 298 38 38.

Girona
☎ 972 18 66 00.

Reus
☎ 977 77 98 00.

IBERIA, AVIACO, AIR NOSTRUM

International and domestic flights
☎ 902 400 500 (Spain).

Canada
☎ (800) 772 4642.

UK
☎ 0845 601 2854.

US
☎ (800) 772 4642.

OTHER AIRLINES

Air Europa
☎ 902 401 501 (Spain).

British Airways
☎ 902 11 13 33 (Spain).
☎ 0345 222111 (UK).

EasyJet
☎ 902 29 99 92 (Spain).
☎ 0870 600 00 00 (UK).
W www.easyjet.co.uk

Delta Air Lines
☎ 901 11 69 46 (Spain).
☎ (800) 241 41 41 (US).

Pan-Air
☎ 91 746 20 38 (Spain).

Spanair
☎ 902 13 14 15 (Spain).

TWA
☎ 93 215 84 86 (Spain).
☎ (800) 221 2000 (US).

SEA TRAVEL

Atlas Cruises and Tours
☎ (800) 942 3301 (US).

Costa Cruises
☎ 93 487 56 85 (Spain).
W www.costacruceros.es

Grimaldi Group
☎ 93 443 98 98 (Spain).

Thomson Cruises
☎ 0870 550 2562 (UK).

TRAVEL TO THE BALEARIC ISLANDS

Buquebus
☎ 902 414 242 (Spain).

Trasmediterránea
☎ 902 45 46 45 (Spain).
☎ 020 7491 4968 (UK).

EL PRAT AIRPORT, BARCELONA

Barcelona's airport is currently being modified and is 12 km (7 miles) from the city centre. Terminal A handles international arrivals and foreign airlines' departures. Terminals B and C are for departures on Spanish airlines and arrivals from European Union countries. Trains to the Plaça de Catalunya in the city centre leave every 30 minutes. For inter-city rail services get off at Sants mainline station. A shuttle bus, the Aerobus, running every 15 minutes, will take you to Plaça de Catalunya.

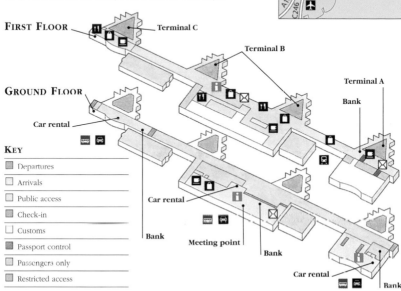

FIRST FLOOR　　Terminal C

Terminal B

Terminal A

Bank

GROUND FLOOR

Car rental

KEY

- ▣ Departures
- ▢ Arrivals
- ▢ Public access
- ▣ Check-in
- ▢ Customs
- ▣ Passport control
- ▢ Passengers only
- ▣ Restricted access

Car rental

Bank

Meeting point

Bank

Car rental

Bank

---

and cars can be delivered to Reus from nearby Tarragona. There will also be local firms offering tempting deals, but read the small print carefully.

AIR FARES

AIR FARES to Barcelona and the coastal resorts vary through the year, depending on demand. They are generally highest during the summer months. Special deals, particularly for weekend city breaks in Barcelona, are often available in the winter and may include a number of nights at a hotel. Christmas and Easter flights are almost always booked up well in advance.

Charter flights from the UK to Girona and Reus can be very cheap, but tend to be less reliable, and often fly at unsociable hours.

Flying between Barcelona and other cities in Spain is an expensive way to travel compared with other options.

SEA TRAVEL

IN 1998 THE **Grimaldi Group** established a new scheduled ferry service between Genoa and Barcelona. US travel company **Atlas Cruises and Tours** offers transatlantic cruises between the US and Barcelona, as well as cruises around the Mediterranean. **Costa Cruises** offers Mediterranean cruises starting in Barcelona, while **Thomson Cruises**, in the UK, has cruises calling at Barcelona, but starting out from Mallorca.

TRAVEL TO THE BALEARIC ISLANDS

BARCELONA IS THE main city on the Spanish mainland from which to reach the Balearic Islands. Flights are run by Iberia, Air Europa and Spanair; a passenger hydrofoil (a kind of catamaran) service, which takes three hours, by **Buquebus**; and car ferry crossings, which take about eight hours, by **Trasmediterránea**. It is wise to book in advance, especially in summer.

Trasmediterránea car ferry to the Balearic Islands in Barcelona harbour

Travelling by Train and Metro

Metro and FGC rail services sign

THERE ARE TWO PROVIDERS of rail services in Catalonia. The Spanish national **RENFE** *(Red Nacional de Ferrocarriles Españoles)* operates Spain's inter-city services including first-class Talgo trains and some of Barcelona's commuter services *(rodalies)*. The Catalan government's **FGC** *(Ferrocarrils de la Generalitat de Catalunya)* runs some suburban trains in Barcelona and a number of special-interest services in Catalonia's provinces. Barcelona also has the Metro, an efficient city-wide network of underground (subway) trains.

Escalator down to a platform (andana) at Sants mainline station in Barcelona

ARRIVING BY TRAIN

THERE ARE DIRECT international train services to Barcelona from several European cities including Paris, Montpellier, Geneva, Zurich and Milan. Long train journeys can be made more bearable by booking a sleeping compartment on an overnight train. This option is only available on direct services. All trains entering the eastern side of Spain from France go through Port Bou/Cerbère or La Tour de Carol on the Franco-Spanish border. Travelling to Barcelona from departure points not offering a direct service may mean picking up a connection here. Most international trains arrive at Sants, Estació de França or Passeig de Gràcia mainline stations, all located in the centre of Barcelona.

Services to Barcelona from other cities in Spain are fast and frequent. From Madrid, Seville, Málaga, A Coruña or Vigo there is a service called **Auto-Express** which allows you to take your car with you.

EXPLORING CATALONIA BY TRAIN

CATALONIA HAS a network of regional trains *(regionals)* covering the whole of Catalunya and run by RENFE. There are three types – the *Catalunya Exprés* linking the main towns with few stops in between, and the *Regional* and *Delta* trains which take longer and stop frequently. A high-speed Euromed service from Barcelona to Tarragona (continuing south to Castelló, València and Alacant/ Alicante) leaves from Sants station.

FGC *(Ferrocarrils de la Generalitat de Catalunya)* is a network of suburban trains run by the Catalan government in and around Barcelona. FGC also runs some other special services, such as Spain's only rack railway (cog railroad) from Ribes de Freser *(see inside back cover)* to Núria in the Pyrenees. It also runs the cable cars and funiculars at the Monastery of Montserrat *(see pp104–5)* and at Vallvidrera, as well as several historic steam trains and an electric train for tourists and enthusiasts. Details are available at the FGC station at Plaça de Catalunya or by calling the FGC number listed above.

Logo of the Spanish national rail service

BUYING TRAIN TICKETS

TICKETS FOR TALGO, inter-city and international trains and for other *llarg recorregut* (long-distance) travel by train may be bought at any of the major RENFE railway stations from the *taquilla* (ticket office). They are also sold by travel agents, plus a booking fee. Reservations for national and international journeys can be made by phone using a credit card number, not less than 24 hours in advance.

Tickets for local and regional services are purchased from station booking offices. In larger stations they can be bought from machines. Tickets for *rodalies* (local services) cannot be reserved. A one-way journey is *anada* and a round trip is *anada i tornada*.

Ticket machine for regionals trains

Ticket machine for rodalies trains

Automatic ticket barriers at one of Barcelona's Metro stations

TRAIN FARES

RENFE OFFERS a ten per cent discount on specified days to encourage people to travel. They are called *dies blaus* (blue days) and are shown in blue on timetables. Fares for rail travel depend on the speed and quality of the service. Tickets for Talgo trains are more expensive than local and regional trains. RENFE offers discounts to children and people over 60, groups of ten and through travel cards on local, regional and long-distance trains. Tourists of any nationality, normally resident outside Spain, are eligible for a tourist railcard, available at RENFE stations, which allows unlimited travel on the RENFE network.

Interrail tickets for those under 26 and Eurodomino tickets for those over 26 are available to people from EU member states and ten other European countries. The Eurail pass, Euro pass and Eurail youth pass are for people from outside Europe. All of these tickets, which offer substantial discounts on rail travel, can be purchased at Barcelona's Sants and Estació de França stations. Travel cards, available through the **Secretaria General de Juventud**, are for people under 26, of any nationality, and carry a discount of up to 40 per cent on journeys from any point in Spain to Europe. To purchase one of these cards, you will need proof of your age and identity.

THE BARCELONA METRO

THERE ARE FIVE underground Metro lines in Barcelona, identified by number and colour. Platform signs distinguish between trains and their direction by displaying the last station on

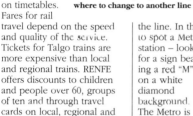

Metro interchange sign showing where to change to another line

the line. In the street it is easy to spot a Metro station – look for a sign bearing a red "M" on a white diamond background. The Metro is usually the quickest way to get around the city, especially as some tickets are now valid for the Metro and some FGC lines. A RENFE or FGC sign at a Metro station

A one-way (single) Metro ticket for Barcelona's subway

indicates a RENFE or FGC connection. Metro trains run from 5am to 11pm from Monday to Thursday, from 6am to midnight on Sunday and a weekday public holiday and from 5am to 2am on Friday, Saturday and the day before a public holiday.

BARCELONA TICKETS AND TRAVELCARDS

VISITORS TO BARCELONA will find a comprehensive range of tickets and money-saving travelcards available to suit their itineraries and length of stay. Some cover train, bus and Metro. Combined tickets now allow travellers to hop from Metro to FGC train lines without leaving the station to pay again. Tickets are as follows: *T-dia* and *T-mes* tickets are for unlimited daily and monthly travel respectively; the *T-1* ticket, for ten single journeys, can be used on Metro, bus and FGC; the *T-2*, also for ten trips, is for combining journeys on Metro, bus and FGC in one trip; the *T-50/30* is for 50 journeys within 30 days on Metro and FGC. Details of special tourist travel cards available are described on the inside back cover of this guide.

USING A METRO TICKET MACHINE

Credit cards accepted by the machine are listed here.

3 b. Insert credit card.

3 c. Insert banknote(s).

4 Collect your ticket and any change due.

Logo of **Transports Metropolitans Urbans (TMB)**, which integrates all services.

Venda de Bitllets

⊖ TMB

1 Select language: Catalan/Spanish, English, French.

2 Select ticket: *senzill* (single trip), *T-2* (10 trips), *T-50/30* (50 trips in 30 days), then quantity required.

3 a. Insert coins: the coins accepted are listed alongside.

Easy-reach language and ticket-type buttons for wheelchair users.

Travelling by Car and Bus

Barcelona road signs

DRIVING CONDITIONS in Catalonia vary enormously, from the dense road network and heavy traffic in and around Barcelona to almost empty country roads in the provinces, where villages, and in particular petrol (gas) stations, can be far apart. Toll highways *(autopistes)* are fast and free-flowing, but the ordinary main roads along the coast are usually very busy at all times of day. For tourists without private cars, joining an organized bus tour is a good way to visit well-known, but rather more remote, places of interest.

Canvi de sentit (slip or access road) 300 m (330 yd) ahead

ARRIVING BY CAR

MANY PEOPLE drive to Spain via the French motorways (highways). The most direct routes across the Pyrenees are the motorways through Hendaye in the west and La Jonquera in the east. Port Bou is on a scenic coastal route, while other routes snake over the top, entering Catalonia via the Vall d'Aran, Andorra, and Puigcerdà in the Cerdanya. From the UK, car ferries run from Plymouth to Santander and from Portsmouth to Bilbao in northern Spain.

Logo of the leading Spanish car-rental company

CAR RENTAL

INTERNATIONAL car rental companies, such as **Hertz**, **Avis** and **Europcar**, as well as some Spanish ones, such as **National ATESA**, operate all over Catalonia. You are likely to get better deals with international companies if you arrange a car from home. A hire car is *un cotxe de lloguer*. Catalonia's three main airports *(see p150)* have car rental desks. However, those at Girona and Reus have irregular opening hours, so if you need a car there, it is best to book in advance and they will meet your requirements. Avis offers deals in chauffeur-driven cars from major cities.

TAKING YOUR OWN CAR

A GREEN CARD and a bail bond from a motor insurance company are needed to extend your comprehensive cover to Spain. In the UK, the RAC, AA and Europ Assistance have sound rescue and recovery policies with European cover.

Vehicle registration, insurance documents and your driver's licence must be carried at all times. Non-EU citizens should obtain an international driver's licence; in the US, these are available through the AAA. You may also be asked for a passport or national identity card as extra identification.

A country of origin sticker must be displayed on the rear of foreign vehicles. All drivers must carry a red warning triangle, spare light bulbs and a first-aid kit. Failure to do so will incur on-the-spot fines.

DRIVING IN CATALONIA

AT JUNCTIONS give way to the right unless directed otherwise. Left turns across the flow of traffic are indicated by a *canvi de sentit* sign. Speed limits for cars without trailers

60

Speed limit 60 km/h (37 mph)

are now: 120 km/h (75 mph) on *autopistes* and *autovies* (toll and non-toll motorways/highways); 90 km/h (56 mph) on *carreteres nacionals* (main roads) and *carreteres comarcals* (secondary roads); 50 or 60 km/h (30 or 37 mph) in urban areas – look for signs. There are on-the-spot speeding fines of up to 450 euros. The blood alcohol legal limit is 0.5g per litre (0.25 mg per litre in a breath test) – tests are frequently given and drivers over the limit are fined.

Front and rear seat belts must be worn. Ordinary leaded fuel *(benzina)*, unleaded fuel *(benzina sense plom)* and diesel *(gas oil)* are all available everywhere and sold by the litre.

AUTOPISTES

ON TOLL MOTORWAYS *(autopistes)* long-distance tolls are calculated per kilometre. Over some stretches near cities a fixed toll is charged. There are three channels at the *peatge* (toll booths/plaza): *Automàtic* has machines for credit cards or the right coins; in *Manual*

A filling station run by a leading chain with branches throughout Spain

an attendant takes your ticket and money; for *Teletac* you need an electronic chip on your windscreen (windshield). *Autopistes* have emergency telephones every 2 km (1.25 miles) and service stations every 40 km (25 miles).

TAXIS

BARCELONA'S TAXIS are yellow and black, and display a green light when they are free. Most taxis are metered and show a minimum fee at the start of a journey. Rates increase after 10pm and at weekends, although the minimum fee stays the same. In unmetered taxis, such as those in villages, it is best to negotiate a price for the trip before setting off. Supplements are charged for going to and from the airport and for suitcases. **Radio Taxis** have cars adapted for disabled people, but they need to be booked a day ahead. They also have some cars that will take up to seven people.

One of Barcelona's taxis

PARKING

CENTRAL Barcelona has a pay-and-display system, with charges in force from 9am to 2pm and 4pm to 8pm Monday to Friday and all day Saturday. You can park in blue spaces for about 1–2 euros per hour. Tickets are valid for two hours but can be renewed. At underground car parks (parking lots), *lliure* means there is space, *complet* means full. Most are attended, but in automatic ones, you pay before returning to your car. Do not park where the pavement edge is yellow or where there is a private exit (*gual*). Blue and red signs saying "1–15" or "16–30" mean you cannot park on those dates in the month on the side of the street where the sign is placed.

Granollers bus station in Barcelona province

LONG-DISTANCE BUSES

SPAIN'S LARGEST inter-city bus company, **Autocares Julià**, is an agent for **Eurolines**. This runs regular services from all over Europe to Sants bus station in Barcelona. Buses from towns and cities in Spain arrive at Estació del Nord.

Julià Tours and **Pullmantur** offer tours of Barcelona. A number of companies run day trips or longer tours to places of interest in Catalonia. **Turisme de Catalunya** *(see p143)* in Barcelona has details of trips to all parts of Catalonia; in other towns, local tourist offices will know about tours in their provinces.

BUSES IN BARCELONA

AN EXCELLENT way to sightsee is by *Bus Turístic*. It runs from April through to February on two routes from Plaça de Catalunya. A ticket, bought on board, is valid for both routes and lets you get on and off or change routes as you please.

Barcelona bus stop

The main city buses are white and red. You can buy a single ticket on the bus, or a *T-1* or *T-2* ten-trip ticket at Metro stations, valid for bus, Metro and FGC *(see p153)*. Other combined tickets are described inside the back cover. The *Nitbus* runs nightly from around 10pm to 5am; the *TombBus* covers the big shopping streets from Plaça de Catalunya to Plaça Pius XII; and the *Aerobus* is an excellent service between Plaça de Catalunya and El Prat airport.

BARCELONA STREET FINDER

THE MAP REFERENCES given with the sights, shops and entertainment venues described in the Barcelona section of the guide refer to the street maps on the following pages. Map references are also given for Barcelona's hotels *(see pp116–21)*, restaurants *(see pp126–31)* and cafés and bars *(see pp132–3)*. The schematic map below shows the areas of the city covered by the *Street Finder*. The symbols for sights, features and services are listed in the key at the foot of the page.

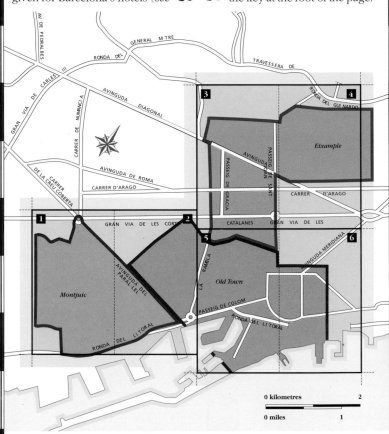

0 kilometres 2

0 miles 1

KEY TO STREET FINDER

- Major sight
- Place of interest
- Other building
- ⮑ Main train station
- Ⓢ Local (FGC) train station
- Ⓜ Metro station
- Main bus stop
- Bus station
- Golondrina boarding point
- Cable car
- Funicular station
- Taxi rank
- P Parking
- Tourist information
- Hospital with A&E unit
- Police station
- Church
- ⊠ Post office
- Railway line (railroad)
- One-way street
- Pedestrianized street

SCALE OF MAP PAGES

0 metres 250

0 yards 250

Street Finder Index

A

Abaixadors, Carrer dels 5B3
Abdó Terradas, Carrer d' 3B2
Agullers, Carrer dels 5B3
Agustí Duran i Sanpere,
  Carrer d' 2F2
Alaba, Carrer d' 6F1
Alba, Carrer de l' 3C2
Albareda, Carrer d' 2E4
Alcalde de Móstoles,
  Carrer de l' 4E1
Alcanar, Carrer d' 5C5
Aldana, Carrer d' 2E3
Alí Bei, Passatge d' 6F1
Alí Bei, Carrer d' 5C1
  & 6D1–6E1
Alió, Passatge d' 4D3
Allada, Carrer de l' 5C2
Almirall Aixada,
  Carrer de l' 5B5
Almirall Cervera,
  Carrer de l' 5B5
Almogàvers, Carrer dels 6D2
Alzina, Carrer d' 3C1
Amadeu Vives, Carrer d' 5B1
Amargòs, Carrer de N' 5B1
Ample, Carrer 5A3
Amposta, Carrer d' 1A1
Andrea Dòria, Carrer d' 5C4
Àngel, Plaça de l' 5B2
Àngels, Carrer dels 2F2
Àngel Baixeras, Carrer d' 5A3
Anníbal, Carrer d' 1C3
Antic de Sant Joan,
  Carrer 5C3
Antiga de Mataró,
  Carretera 6E2
Antóni López, Plaça d' 5B3
Antóni Maura, Plaça d' 5B2
Aragó, Carrer d' 3A4
Arai, Carrer de N' 5A3
Arc de Sant Agustí,
  Carrer de l' 2F3
Arc del Teatre,
  Carrer de l' 2F4
Arcs, Carrer dels 5A2
Argenter, Carrer de l' 5B1
Argenteria, Carrer de l' 5B2
Argentona, Carrer d' 4D1
Aribau, Carrer d' 2F1
Armada, Plaça de l' 2D5
Arolas, Carrer d'en 5A2
Arq.Sert, Carrer de l' 6F2
Assaonadors, Carrer dels 5B2
Astúries, Carrer d' 3B1
Ataúlf, Carrer d' 5A3
Atlantida, Carrer de l' 5B5
Aulèstia i Pijoan,
  Carrer d' 3A1
Aurora, Carrer de l' 2E2
Ausiàs Marc, Carrer d' 5B1
Avinyó, Carrer d' 5A3

B

Badia, Carrer de 3B1
Bailèn, Carrer de 3C2
Baix, Carrer de 1C2
Balboa, Carrer de 5C4
Balears, Moll de les 5A5
Balmes, Carrer de 3A1–3A5
Baluard, Carrer del 5C4
Banyoles, Carrer de 3C2
Banys Nous , Carrer de 5A2

Banys Vells, Carrer de 5B2
Barceloneta, Moll de la 5B4
Barceloneta, Plaça de la 5B4
Barceloneta, Platja de la 6D5
Basea, Carrer de 5B3
Beates, Carrer de les 5B2
Benet Mercadé, Carrer de 3A1
Berenguer, Passatge de 4D3
Berga, Carrer de 3A1
Bergara, Carrer de 5A1
Bergnes de las Casas,
  Carrer 4E2
Bertrellans, Carrer de 5A1
Bisbe, Carrer del 5B2
Bisbe Laguarda,
  Carrer del 2E2
Blai, Carrer de 2D3
Blanqueria, Carrer de la 5C2
Blasco de Garay,
  Carrer de 2D3
Blesa, Carrer de 2D4
Bòbila, Carrer de 1C2
Bocabella, Passatge de 4D5
Bofill, Passatge de 4E4
Bogatell, Avinguda del 6E2
Bolívia, Carrer de 6F1
Boltres, Carrer d'En 5A3
Bonavista, Carrer de 3B2
Boné, Passatge de 4E1
Bonsuccés, Carrer del 5A1
Boquer, Carrer d'En 5B2
Boqueria, Carrer de la 5A2
Boqueria, Plaça de la 5A2
Bordeta, Carretera de la 1A1
Boria, Carrer de la 5B2
Bosch, Carrer de 3A2
Bot, Carrer d'En 5A2
Botella, Carrer d'En 2E2
Boters, Carrer dels 5A2
Bou de Sant Pere,
  Carrer del 5B1
Bous les Arenes, Plaça 1B1
Bretón de los Herros,
  Carrer de 3A1
Bruc, Carrer del 3B3
Brugada, Plaça de 5C5
Bruniquer, Carrer de 3C1
Buenaventura Muñoz,
  Carrer de 6D2

C

Ca l'Alegre de Dalt,
  Carrer de 4D1
Cabanes, Carrer de 2E4
Cadena, Carrer de la 2F3
Cadena, Passatge de la 5C4
Calàbria, Carrer de 2D1
Call, Carrer del 5A2
Camprodon, Carrer de 3C3
Camps Elisis,
  Passatge dels 3B4
Canadell, Passatge de 4F3
Canó, Carrer del 3B2
Canuda, Carrer de la 5A1
Canvis Nous, Carrer dels 5B3
Capellans, Carrer dels 5A2
Carabassa, Carrer d'En 5A3
Cardenal Casañas,
  Carrer del 5A2
Carders, Carrer dels 5C2
Carles Buïgas, Plaça de 1B2
Carlos Ibáñez, Plaça de 2D4
Carme, Carrer del 2E2
Carrera, Carrer de 2E4

Carretes, Carrer de les 2E2
Carsi, Passatge de 4F3
Cartagena, Carrer de 4F1
Casanova, Carrer de 2E1
Cascades, Passeig de les 1A2
Cascades, Plaça de les 1B2
Casp, Carrer de 3B5
Castell, Avinguda del 1B4
Castella, Plaça de 2F1
Castillejos, Carrer de los 4F1
Catalunya, Plaça de 5A1
Catalunya, Rambla de 3A3
Catedral, Avinguda de la 5A2
Cendra, Carrer de la 2E2
Centelles, Passatge de 4F3
Cera, Carrer de la 2E2.
Chopin, Carrer de 1A1
Cid, Carrer del 2F4
Cigne, Carrer de 3A1
Circunval lació,
  Passeig de 5C3–6D4
Cirera, Carrer de la 5B2
Ciudad Real, Carrer de 3C2
Ciutat, Carrer de la 5A2
Clip, Passatge de 4E2
Còdols, Carrer dels 5A3
Colom, Passeig de 5A4
Colomines, Carrer de 5B2
Comerç, Carrer del 5C3
Comercial, Carrer de 5C2
Comercial, Plaça de 5C3
Comtal, Carrer de 5A1
Comte d'Urgell,
  Carrer de 2E1
Comte Borrell,
  Carrer del 2D1
Comte de Salvatierra,
  Carrer del 3A2
Comtes, Carrer dels 5B2
Concepció,
  Passatge de la 3A3
Concòrdia, Carrer de la 1C2
Congost, Carrer del 3C1
Conradí, Passatge 4D3
Consell de Cent,
  Carrer del 3A4
Consolat de Mar,
  Carrer del 5B2
Copons, Carrer d'En 5B2
Corders, Carrer dels 5B2
Còrsega, Carrer de 3A3
Cortines, Carrer d'En 5C2
Corts Catalanes,
  Gran Via de les 1A1
Cremat, Gran Carrer de 5B2
Creu dels Molers,
  Carrer de la 1C3–2D3
Cucurulla, Carrer de 5A2

D

Dàlia, Carrer de la 1A1
Dante, Plaça de 1C4
Diagonal, Avinguda de 3A2–
  3C4 & 4D4–4F5
Diluvi, Carrer del 3B2
Diputació, Carrer de la 3A5
Doctor Aiguader,
  Carrer del 5B4
Doctor Joaquim Pou,
  Carrer del 2F2
Doctor Pons i Freixas,
  Plaça del 6D4
Doctor Rizal, Carrer del 3A2
Doctor Trueta, Carrer del 6E3

Domènech, Carrer de 3B2
Domingo, Passatge de 3A4
Don Carles, Carrer de 6D4
Drassana, Carrer de la 5B5
Drassanes,
  Avinguda de les 2F3
Duc de la Victòria,
  Carrer del 5A1
Duc de Medinaceli,
  Plaça del 5A3
Duran i Bas, Carrer de 5A1

E

Egipcíaques,
  Carrer de les 2F2
Elisabets, Carrer d' 2F2
Elkano, Carrer d' 2D3
Enamorats, Carrer dels 4E4
Encarnació, Carrer de l' 4D1
Entença, Carrer d' 1C1
Erasme de Janer,
  Carrer d' 2E2
Escorial, Carrer de l' 4D2
Escudellers, Carrer dels 5A3
Escudellers,
  Passatge dels 5A3
Escudellers Blancs,
  Carrer dels 5A2
Escuder, Carrer d' 5B4
Espalter, Carrer d' 2F3
Espanya, Moll d' 5A4
Espanya, Plaça d' 1B1
Esparteria, Carrer de l' 5B3
Espaseria, Carrer de l' 5B3
Est, Carrer de l' 2F3
Estadi, Avinguda de l' 1A2
Estruc, Carrer d' 5B1
Exposició, Passeig de l' 1C3

F

Far, Camí del 1B5
Farell, Carrer del 1A1
Ferlandina, Carrer de 2E1
Ferran, Carrer de 5A2
Ferrer de Blanes,
  Carrer de 3B2
Flassaders, Carrer dels 5C2
Floridablanca, Carrer de 1C1
Flors, Carrer de les 2E3
Fonollar, Carrer del 5B2
Font, Carrer de la 2D4
Font, Passatge de 4E4
Font, Plaça de la 5C4
Font Florida, Carrer de la 1A1
Font Honrada,
  Carrer de la 1C2
Font-Trobada,
  Camí de la 2D4
Fontanella, Carrer de 5A1
Fontrodona, Carrer d'En 2D3
Franca Xica, Carrer de la 1C2
Francesc Cambó,
  Avinguda de 5B2
Francesc d'Aranda,
  Carrer de 6E2
Francisco Giner,
  Carrer de 3B2
Fraternitat, Carrer de la 3B2
Frederic Mompou,
  Carrer de 6F3
Freixures, Carrer de les 5B2
Fusina, Carrer de la 5C2
Fusta, Moll de la 5A4
Fusteria, Carrer de la 5B3

G

Gaiolà, Passatge de	4D4
Gal·la Placídia, Plaça de	3A1
Gaudí, Avinguda de	4E3
Gaudí, Plaça de	4E3
Gegants, Carrer dels	5A2
Gelí, Carrer de	5C5
General Álvarez de Castro, Carrer del	5B2
General Bassos, Passatge de	6F3
General Castaños, Carrer de	5B3
Gessamí, Carrer del	1A1
Gignàs, Carrer d'En	5A3
Gimbernat, Carrer dels	1B1
Ginebra, Carrer de	5B4
Giralt el Pellisser, Carrer d'En	5B2
Girona, Carrer de	3C3
Glòries Catalanes, Plaça de les	4F5
Gombau, Carrer de	5B2
Goya, Carrer de	3A2
Goya, Plaça de	2F1
Gràcia, Carrer de	3B2
Gràcia, Passeig de	3A2–3A5
Gràcia, Travessera de	3A2
Gran de Gràcia, Carrer	3A2
Granada del Penedès, Carrer de la	3A2
Grases, Carrer de	1C2
Grassot, Carrer d'En	4D2
Gravina, Carrer de	2F1
Gregal, Moll de	6F5
Guàrdia, Carrer de	2F3
Guàrdia Urbana, C de la	1B2
Guatla, Carrer de la	1A1
Guifré, Carrer de	2F2
Guilleries, Carrer de les	3B1
Guinardó, Ronda del	4E1
Guitert, Carrer de	5C5

H

Havana, Carrer de l'	5C5
Hipòlit Lázaro, Carrer d'	4D2
Hispanitat, Plaça de la	4E4
Hort de Sant Pau, Carrer de l'	2E3
Hortes, Carrer de les	2D3
Hospital, Carrer de l'	2E2

I

Icària, Avinguda d'	6E3
Igualada, Carrer d'	3C2
Indústria, Carrer de	3C2
Isabel II, Passatge d'	5B3
Iscle Soler, Carrer d'	4D3

J

Jaén, Carrer de	3B1
Jaume Giralt, Carrer de	5C2
Jaume Fabra, Carrer de	1C2
Jaume I, Carrer de	5A2
Jesús, Carrer de	3B2
Joan Blanques, Carrer de	3C2
Joan Casas, Passatge de	4F5
Joan d'Austria, Carrer de	6E1
Joan de Borbó, P de	5B4
Joanic, Plaça d'En	3C1
Joaquim Blume, Carrer de	1B2
Joaquim Pou, Carrer de	5B2
Joaquim Renart, Passeig de	6D2
Joaquim Ruyra, Carrer de	4D2

Joaquín Costa, Carrer de	2F2
Jonqueres, Carrer de les	5B1
Josep Anselm Clavé, Carrer de	5A3
Josep Carner, Passeig de	2E5
Josep Ciurana, Carrer de	4F1
Jovellanos, Carrer de	5A1
Judici, Carrer del	5B5
Julià, Carrer de	1C3
Julià, Passatge de	1C3
Julià Portet, Carrer de	5B1
Julian Romea, Carrer	3A2
Junta del Comerç, Carrer de	2F3

L

Laforja, Carrer de	3A1
Laietana, Via	5B1
Lancaster, Carrer de	2F3
Legalitat, Carrer de la	4D1
Leiva, Carrer de	1B1
Lepant, Carrer de	4E1
Lincoln, Carrer de	3A1
Llançà, Carrer de	1B1
Llàstics, Carrer d'En	5C2
Llavalloll, Passatge de	4D2
Lleialtat, Carrer de la	2E3
Lleida, Carrer de	1B2
Lleó, Carrer del	2F2
Lleona, Carrer de la	5A2
Llibertat, Carrer de la	3B2
Llibertat, Plaça de la	3A1
Llibreteria, Carrer de la	5A2
Llorens i Barba, Carrer de	4F1
Lluís Companys, Passeig de	5C2
Lluís Millet, Plaça de	5B1
Llull, Carrer de	6D2
Lluna, Carrer de la	2F2
Louis Braille, Carrer de	5A3
Luis Antúnez, Carrer de	3A2

M

Madrozo, Carrer dels	3A1
Magalhàes, Carrer de	1C3
Magdalenes, Carrer de les	5B1
Maiol, Passatge de	4E4
Malcuinat, Carrer del	5B3
Mallorca, Carrer de	3A4
Manresa, Carrer de	5B3
Manso, Carrer de	2D2
Manuel Ribé, Platja de	5A2
Manufactures, Passatge de les	5B1
Maquinista, Carrer de la	5B4
Mar, Carrer del	5B5
Mar, Rambla de	5A4
Mare de Déu del Remei, Carrer de la	1C2
Mare de Déu dels Desemparats, Carrer de la	3B2
Margarit, Carrer de	1C3
Maria, Carrer de	3B2
Marià Cubí, Carrer de	3A1
Marina, Carrer de la	4E2–4E5 & 6E1–6E4
Marina, Moll de	6E5
Marina, Passatge de la	4E1
Mariner, Passatge de	4D3
Mar i Terra, Passatge	2E4
Marítim de Nova Icària, Passeig	6E4
Marítim del Port Olímpic, Passeig	6E4

Marquès de Barberà, Carrer del	2F3
Marquès de Campo Sagrado, Carrer del	2D2
Marquès de Comillas, Avinguda del	1A1
Marquès de l'Argentera, Avinguda del	5B3
Marquès de la Foronda, Plaça del	1B2
Marquesa, Carrer de la	5C3
Martí, Carrer de	4D1
Martínez de la Rosa, Carrer de	3B2
Martras, Passatge de	1C3
Mas Casanovas, Carrer del	4F1
Massanet, Carrer de	5B2
Massens, Carrer de	3C1
Mata, Carrer de	2E4
Mateu, Carrer de	3B1
Meer, Carrer de	5B5
Méndez Núñez, Carrer de	5C1
Méndez Vigo, Passatge de	3B4
Mercader, Passatge de	3A3
Mercaders, Carrer dels	5B2
Mercè, Carrer de la	5A3
Meridiana, Avinguda	6D2
Mestrança, Carrer de la	5B5
Metges, Carrer dels	5C2
Mèxic, Carrer de	1B1
Migdia, Passeig del	1A4
Milà i Fontanals, Carrer de	3C3
Milans, Carrer de	5A3
Milton, Carrer de	3A1
Minerva, Carrer de	3A2
Minici Natal, Passeig de	1A3
Mirador, Plaça del	1C5
Miralles, Carrer dels	5B2
Miramar, Avinguda de	1B3
Miramar, Carretera de	2D5
Miramar, Passeig de	2D4
Mistral, Avinguda de	1C1
Moianès, Carrer del	1A1
Moles, Carrer de les	5B1
Molí, Camí del	1A5
Molí Antic, Camí del	1A5
Mònec, Carrer d'En	5C1
Monistrol, Carrer de	3C2
Montalegre, Carrer de	2F2
Montanyans, Avinguda dels	1A2
Montcada, Carrer de	5B3
Montjuïc, Camí de	1C5
Montjuïc, Parc de	1C3
Montjuïc, Passeig de	2D4
Montmany, Carrer de	3C1
Montseny, Carrer del	3B1
Montserrat, Passatge de	2F4
Montsió, Carrer de	5A1
Morabos, Carrer dels	1A1
Moscou, Carrer de	6D4
Mosques, Carrer de les	5B3
Mossèn Jacint Verdaguer, Plaça de	3C3
Mozart, Carrer de	3B2
Muntaner, Carrer de	2F1
Murillo, Carrer de	2D3

N

Nacional, Passeig	5B5
Nàpols, Carrer de	4D2–4D5 & 6D1–6D2
Narcis Oller, Plaça de	3A2

Navas, Plaça de las	1C2
Neptú, Carrer de	3A2
Niça, Carrer de	4F1
Nogués, Passatge de	4E2
Nord, Carrer del	1A1
Notariat, Carrer del	2F2
Nou de la Rambla, Carrer	2D4
Nou Sant Francesc, Carrer	5A3
Nova, Plaça	5A2

O

Obradors, Carrer dels	5A3
Ocata, Carrer d'	5C3
Olímpic, Passeig	1A4
Olivera, Carrer de l'	1C2
Olles, Plaça de les	5B3
Om, Carrer de l'	2E3
Or, Carrer de l'	3B1
Oreneta, Carrer d'	3A1
Ortigosa, Carrer de	5B1

P

Pablo Neruda, Plaça de	4E4
Padilla, Carrer de	4F1
Pagès, Passatge de	4D5
Palau, Carrer del	5A3
Palaudàries, Carrer de	2E4
Palla, Carrer de la	5A2
Pallars, Carrer de	6E2
Palma, Carrer de la	1C3
Palma de Sant Just, Carrer de la	5B3
Paloma, Carrer de la	2E1
Pamplona, Carrer de	4F5 & 6F1–6F3
Paral·lel, Avinguda del	1B1–1C2 & 2D2–2F5
Parc, Carrer del	5A3
Pare Eusebi Millan, Plaça del	1A2
Pare Laínez, Carrer del	4D2
Parlament, Carrer del	2D2
Parlament, Passatge del	2D2
Patriarca, Passatge del	5A1
Pau, Passatge de la	5A3
Pau Claris, Carrer de	3B3
Pedreres, Carrer de les	1C2
Pedró, Plaça del	2E2
Pelai, Carrer de	2F1
Penedès, Carrer del	3B2
Pere Costa, Carrer de	4F1
Pere IV, Carrer de	6E2
Pere Serafí, Carrer del	3B1
Perill, Carrer del	3B2
Perla, Carrer de la	3B1
Permanyer, Passatge de	3B5
Pescadors, Carrer dels	5B5
Pescadors, Moll dels	5A5
Petons, Carrer dels	5C2
Petritxol, Carrer de	5A2
Peu de la Creu, Carrer del	2F2
Pi i Margall, Carrer de	4D1
Pi, Carrer del	5A2
Pi, Plaça del	5A2
Picasso, Passeig de	5C3
Pintor Fortuny, Carrer del	2F2
Piquer, Carrer de	2D3
Pizarro, Carrer de	5C4
Plata, Carrer de la	5A3
Poeta Boscà, Plaça del	5B4
Poeta Cabanyes, Carrer del	2D3
Polvorí, Camí del	1A1
Pompeu Gener, Plaça de	5C4

Portaferrissa,
  Carrer de la   5A2
Portal de l'Angel,
  Avinguda del   5A1
Portal de la Pau,
  Plaça del   2F4
Portal de Santa Madrona,
  Carrer del   2F4
Portal Nou, Carrer del   5C2
Prat, Rambla del   3A1
Princep d'Astúries,
  Avinguda del   3A1
Princep de Viana,
  Carrer del   2E2
Princesa, Carrer de la   5B2
Progrés, Carrer del   3B2
Provença, Carrer de   3A3
Providència,
  Carrer de la   4D1
Prunera, Passatge de   1C2
Puig i Xoriguer,
  Carrer de   2E4
Puigmartí, Carrer de   3B2
Pujades, Carrer de   6F2
Pujades, Passeig de   6D2
Puríssima Concepció,
  Carrer de la   1C3

Q

Quevedo, Carrer de   3C2

R

Rabí Rubén, Carrer del   1A1
Radas, Carrer de   1C3
Rambla, La   5A1
Ramis, Carrer de   3C2
Ramon Turró, Carrer de   6E3
Ramon y Cajal,
  Carrer de   3B2
Raspall, Plaça del   3B2
Ratés, Passatge de   6F1
Rauric, Carrer d'En   5A2
Rec, Carrer del   5C3
Rec Comtal, Carrer del   5C2
Rector Oliveras,
  Passatge del   3D4
Regàs, Carrer de   4A1
Regomir, Carrer del   5A3
Reial, Plaça   5A3
Reig i Bonet, Carrer de   4D1
Reina Amàlia,
  Carrer de la   2F3
Reina Cristina,
  Carrer de la   5B3
Reina Maria Cristina,
  Avinguda de la   1B2
Rellotge, Moll del   5B5
Revolució de Setembre
  de 1868, Plaça de la   3B1
Ribera, Carrer de la   5C3
Ribes, Carrer de   4E5 & 6D1
Ricart, Carrer de   1C2
Riera Alta, Carrer de la   2E2
Riera Baixa, Carrer de la   2F2
Riera de Sant Miquel,
  Carrer de la   3A2
Riereta, Carrer de la   2E2
Ripoll, Carrer de   5B2
Rius i Taulet,
  Avinguda de   1B2
Rius i Taulet, Plaça de   3B2
Robador, Carrer d'En   2F3
Robí, Carrer del   3B1
Roca, Carrer d'En   5A2
Rocafort, Carrer de   2D1
Roger de Flor, Carrer de 4D2–
                  4D5 & 6D1–6D2

Roger de Flor,
  Passatge de   4D3
Roger de Llúria,
  Carrer de   3B3
Roig, Carrer d'En   2F2
Romans, Carrer de   4D1
Ros de Olano, Carrer de   3B1
Rosa, Carrer de la   5A3
Rosa Sensat, Carrer de   6F3
Rosalía de Castro,
  Carrer de   4F2
Roser, Carrer del   2D3
Rosselló, Carrer del   3A3
Rull, Carrer d'En   5A3

S

Sadurní, Carrer de   2F3
Sagrada Família,
  Plaça de la   4D3
Sagristans, Carrer dels   5B2
Salamanca, Carrer de   5C5
Salvà, Carrer de   2D3
Salvador, Carrer del   2E2
Salvador Espriu,
  Carrer de   6E4
Sancho de Ávila,
  Carrer de   6E1
Sant Agustí, Carrer de   3B3
Sant Agustí, Plaça de   2F3
Sant Agustí Vell,
  Plaça de   5C2
Sant Antoni, Ronda del   2E2
Sant Antoni Abat,
  Carrer de   2E2
Sant Antoni Maria Claret,
  Carrer de   4D2
Sant Benet, Passatge de   5C1
Sant Bertran, Carrer de   2E4
Sant Carles, Carrer de   5B4
Sant Climent, Carrer de   2E2
Sant Cristòfol, Carrer de   3A1
Sant Domènec,
  Carrer de   3B2
Sant Domènec del Call,
  Carrer de   5A2
Sant Elm, Carrer de   5B5
Sant Ferriol, Carrer de   1A1
Sant Francesc de Paula,
  Carrer de   5B1
Sant Fructuós, Carrer de   1A1
Sant Gabriel, Carrer de   3A1
Sant Germà, Carrer de   1A1
Sant Gil, Carrer de   2E2
Sant Honorat, Carrer de   5B2
Sant Isidre, Carrer de   1C3
Sant Jaume, Plaça de   5A2
Sant Jeroni, Carrer de   2F3
Sant Joan, Passeig de 3C2–3C5
                      & 5C1
Sant Joaquim, Carrer de   3B2
Sant Josep Oriol,
  Carrer de   2F3
Sant Lluís, Carrer de   3C1
Sant Marc, Carrer de   3A1
Sant Martí, Carrer de   2E3
Sant Miquel, Baixada de   5A2
Sant Miquel, Carrer de   5B5
Sant Oleguer, Carrer de   2F3
Sant Pacià, Carrer de   2E3
Sant Pau, Carrer de   2E3
Sant Pau, Ronda de   2E2
Sant Paulí de Nola,
  Carrer de   1A1
Sant Pere, Passatge de   4E1
Sant Pere, Plaça de   5C1
Sant Pere, Ronda de   5A1

Sant Pere d'Abanto,
  Carrer de   1A1
Sant Pere Martir,
  Carrer de   3B2
Sant Pere Mes Alt,
  Carrer de   5B1
Sant Pere Mes Baix,
  Carrer de   5B2
Sant Pere Mitja,
  Carrer de   5B1
Sant Rafael, Carrer de   2F3
Sant Ramon, Carrer de   2F3
Sant Roc, Carrer de   1A1
Sant Sebastià, Platja de   5B5
Sant Sever, Carrer de   5A2
Sant Vicenç, Carrer de   2E2
Santa Anna, Carrer de   5A1
Santa Carolina, Carrer de   4F2
Santa Dorotea, Carrer de   1A1
Santa Elena, Carrer de   2E3
Santa Eugènia, Carrer de   3A1
Santa Eulàlia, Carrer de   3C2
Santa Madrona,
  Carrer de   2E3
Santa Madrona,
  Passeig de   1B3
Santa Magdalena,
  Carrer de   3B1
Santa Mònica, Carrer de   2F4
Santa Rosa, Carrer de   3B1
Santa Tecla, Carrer de   3B3
Santa Teresa, Carrer de   3B3
Saragossa, Carrer de   3A1
Sardana, Plaça de la   2D4
Sardenya, Carrer de 4E2–4E5
                 & 6E1–6E2
Seca, Carrer de la   5B3
Secretari Coloma,
  Carrer del   4D1
Sedata, Jardí de la   4D2
Segons Jocs Mediterranis,
  Carrer dels   1B2
Seneca, Carrer de   3A2
Sepúlveda, Carrer de   1C1
Serra, Carrer d'En   5A3
Sert, Passatge de   5C1
Sevilla, Carrer de   5B8
Sicília, Carrer de   4D2–4D5
                     & 6D1
Sidé, Carrer de   5B2
Sils, Carrer de   5A3
Simó, Passatge de   4E3
Simó Oller, Carrer de   5A3
Siracusa, Carrer de   3B2
Sitges, Carrer de les   5A1
Sol, Carrer del   3B1
Sol, Plaça del (Gràcia)   3B1
Sol, Plaça del (Montjuïc)   1B3
Sombrerers, Carrer dels   5B3
Sòria, Carrer de   5C5
Sortidor, Plaça del   2D3
Sota Muralla, Pas de   5B3
Sots-tinent Navarro,
  Carrer del   5B2

T

Tallers, Carrer dels   2F1
Tamarit, Carrer de   1C2
Tànger, Carrer de   4D5
Tantarantana, Carrer d'En   5C2
Tàpies, Carrer de les   2E3
Tapineria, Carrer de la   5B2
Tapioles, Carrer de   2D3
Tarròs, Carrer d'En   5B2
Tasso, Passatge de   4D5
Taxdirt, Carrer de   4E1
Templaris, Carrer dels   5A3

Terol, Carrer de   3B1
Tigre, Carrer del   2E1
Til·lers, Passeig dels   5C2
Topazi, Carrer del   3B1
Tordera, Carrer de   3B2
Torrent de les Flors,
  Carrer del   3C1
Torrent de l'Olla,
  Carrer del   3B3
Torrent d'en Vidalet,
  Carrer del   3C2
Torres, Carrer de   3B2
Torres, Passatge de les   4E3
Torres i Amat, Carrer de   2F1
Torrevella, Carrer de   6D4
Torrijos, Carrer de   3C2
Trafalgar, Carrer de   5C1
Tragí, Carrer de   5B2
Traginers, Plaça dels   5B3
Trelawny, Carrer de   6D4
Tres Pins, Carrer dels   1B4
Tres Senyores,
  Carrer de les   3C1
Unió, Carrer de la   2F3
Univers, Plaça de l'   1B1
Universitat, Plaça de la   2F1
Universitat, Ronda de la   2F1
Utset, Passatge d'   4E4

V

València, Carrer de   3A4
Valldonzella, Carrer de   2F1
Vallfogona, Carrer de   3B1
Vallhonrat, Carrer de   1C2
Ventalló, Carrer de   4D2
Venus, Carrer de   3B2
Verdaguer i Callís,
  Carrer de   5B1
Verdi, Carrer de   3B1
Vermell, Carrer   5C2
Verntallat, Carrer de   3C1
Viada, Carrer de   3C1
Vicenç Martorell,
  Plaça de   5A1
Victòria, Carrer de la   5C1
Vigatans, Carrer del   5B2
Vila de Madrid,
  Plaça de la   5A1
Vila i Vilà, Carrer de   2E3
Viladecols, Baixada de   5B2
Viladomat, Carrer de   2D1
Vilafranca, Carrer de   3C1
Vilamarí, Carrer de   1C1
Vilanova, Avinguda de   6D1
Vilaret, Passatge de   4F3
Villarroel, Carrer de   2E1
Villena, Carrer de   6D3
Vinaròs, Carrer de   5C5
Vinyassa,
  Passatge de la   6F2
Vinyeta, Passatge de la   2D4
Virtut, Carrer de la   3B1
Vistalegre, Carrer de   2E2
Voluntaris Olímpics,
  Plaça dels   6E4

W

Wellington, Carrer de   6D3

X

Xaloc, Moll de   6F5
Xiquets de Valls,
  Carrer dels   3B2
Xuclà, Carrer d'En   5A1

Z

Zamora, Carrer de   6F1

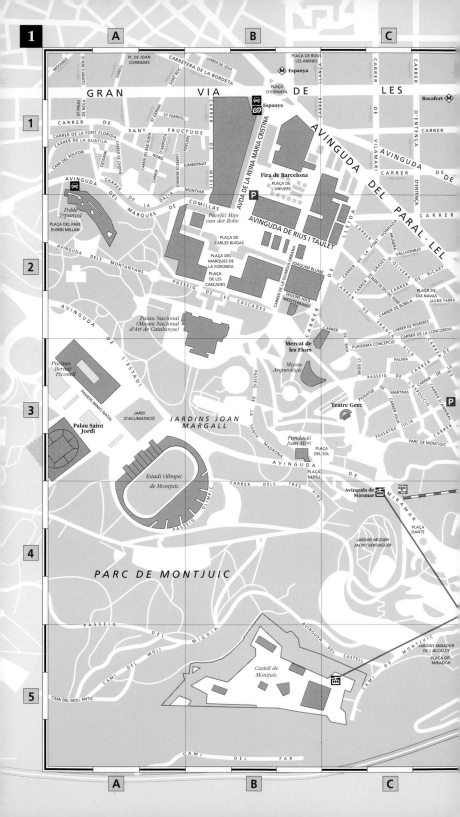

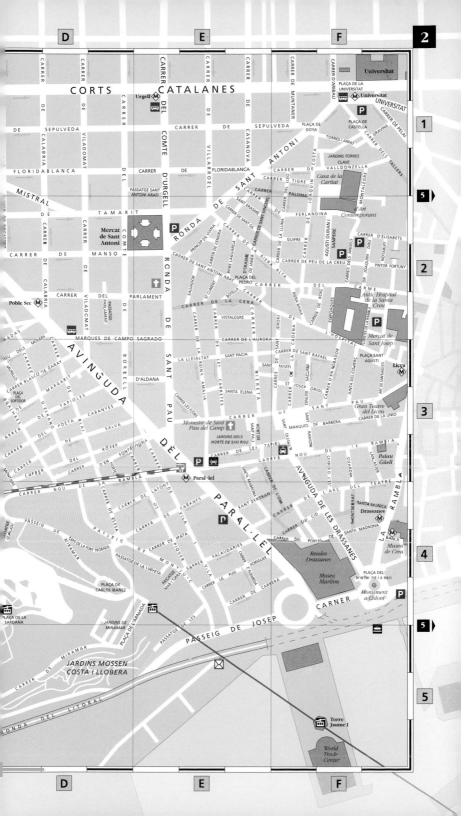

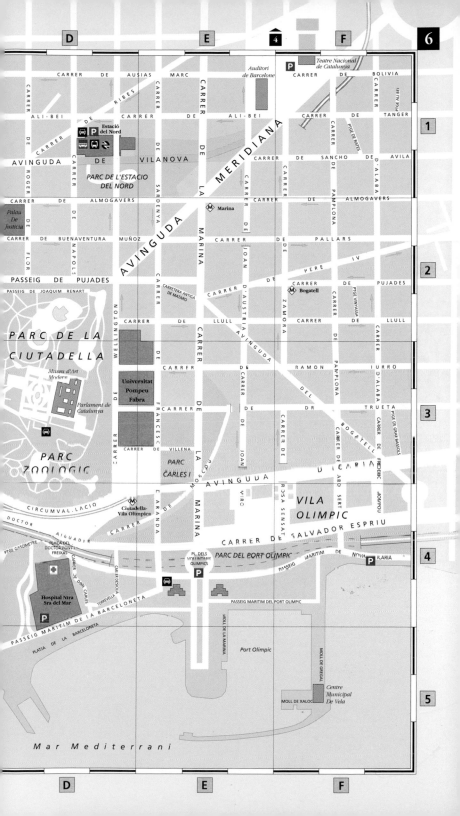

General Index

Page numbers in **bold** refer to
main entries

A

Addresses **149**
Adolfo Domínguez (Barcelona) 135
Adventure sports 138
Aeroclub de Sabadell 139
Agua (Barcelona) 126
Agut (Barcelona) 126
Aïguamolls de l'Empordà 139
Air Europa 150
Air Nostrum 150
Air travel **150–51**
Airborne activities **138**
Akhila, King of the Visigoths 38
Al Limón Negro (Barcelona) 132
Albéniz, Isaac 17
Alexandra Hotel (Barcelona) 118
Alfonso II, King of Aragón
  Monestir de Poblet 108
  Puigcerdà 96
Alfonso III, King of Aragón
  conquest of Mallorca 39
Alfonso XIII, King of Spain 87
Almodóvar, Pedro 16, 17
Almogàvers 39
Altafulla
  restaurants 129
Amargós, Josep 63
Amaya (Barcelona) 126
Ambulances 144, 145
American Express 146
Amposta 111
Amusement Park 137
Andorra **96**
Andorra la Vella 96
  hotels 119
  restaurants 129
Angelico, Fra 87
Antiga Casa Figueres
  (Barcelona) 48
Antilla Barcelona (Barcelona) 137
Antiques shops 135
Any Nou (New Year) 32
Apolo (Barcelona) 137
Aqüeducte de les Ferreres
  (Tarragona) 111
Arc de Berà (Tarragona) 111
Arc del Triomf (Barcelona) **62**
L'Arca de l'Àvia (Barcelona) 135
Archaeological Museum (Barcelona)
  see Museu Arqueològic
Arché, Rafael 65
Architecture
  Gaudí and Modernisme **22–3**
  Romanesque Art and
    Architecture **20–21**
  La Ruta del Modernisme **48–9**
Arenys de Mar
  restaurants 129
Aribau, Bonaventura 41
Armand Basi (Barcelona) 135
Arribas, Alfredo 81
Art
  Catalan Painting **24–5**
  Romanesque Art and
    Architecture **20–21**
  stores 135
  see also Museums and galleries
Art Cristià workshops 24
Arties 94
  hotels 119
  restaurants 129
Arts Hotel (Barcelona) 117

Associació de Campings de
  Barcelona 115
Associació Catalana d'Estacions
  d'Esquí i Activitats de Muntanya
  (ACEM) 139
Associació Fondes de Catalunya 115
Assumpció (Assumption Day) 32
Atlantis Hotel (Barcelona) 116
Atlas Cruises and Tours 150
Auditori de Barcelona
  (Barcelona) 137
Augustus, Emperor 37
Australian Consulate 143
Auto-Express 152
Autocares Julià 155
Autopistes (motorways/highways)
  154–5
Autumn in Catalonia **32**
Aviaco 150
Avinyonet de Puigventós
  hotels 119
Avis 155

B

Balaguer 91
Balearic Islands
  sea travel 150, **151**
Bank notes 147
Banking **146**
Banyoles 97
Baqueira-Beret 95
  hotels 119
Bar Ra (Barcelona) 132
Barcelona
  airport **150–51**
  cafés and bars **132–3**
  Eixample **67–75**
  entertainment **136–7**
  festes 30–33
  Further Afield **85–9**
  hotels **116–18**
  maps 12–13, 46–7, **159–65**
  Metro **153**
  Montjuïc **77–83**
  Old Town **51–65**
  Quadrat d'Or **68–9**
  restaurants **126–8**
  shopping **134–5**
  trains **152**
Barcelona, Counts of 38
Barcelona Football Club **87**, 137
  Museu del Futbol Club
    Barcelona 86
Barceloneta **64**
Barclays Bank 146
Barri Gòtic (Barcelona) 51
  Street-by-Street map 52–3
Barruera 95
Bars **122**, **132–3**
  designer bars **137**
Bartomeu, Mestre 24
Basílica de Santa Maria del Mar
  (Barcelona) **60**
Bassa, Ferrer 24, 87
BD-Ediciones de Diseño
  (Barcelona) 135
Beaches
  Costa Brava 103
  Costa Daurada 110
Beatus of Liébana, St 96
Bed and breakfast 115
Beget 97
Begur 103
  hotels 119
  restaurants 129

Berenguer, Francesc 89
Berga
  festes 30
  restaurants 129
Berga i Boix, Josep 24
Besalú 97
Beuda
  hotels 119
Bicycling 138
Bilbao Restaurant (Barcelona) 127
Bird-watching **138**
Black Virgin **105**
Blai, Pere 55
Blanes **102**
  restaurants 129
Blay, Miquel
  Museu d'Art Modern
    (Barcelona) 63
  Museu Comarcal de la Garrotxa
    (Olot) 97
  Palau de la Música Catalana
    (Barcelona) 61
  Plaça d'Espanya (Barcelona) 81
Boadas (Barcelona) 132, 137
Boats
  golondrinas (Barcelona) **65**
  Museu Marítim (Barcelona) **65**
  sailing 139
  sea travel 150, **151**
Bodega La Palma (Barcelona) 132
La Bodegueta (Barcelona) 133
Bofill, Guillem 98
Bofill, Ricard 81, 89
Bolvir de Cerdanya
  hotels 119
  restaurants 129
Bonaparte, Joseph 41
Bookshops 135
La Boqueria (Barcelona) 135
Borrassà, Lluís 24
Bossòst 94
Bourbon dynasty
  Carlist Wars 42
  Castell de Montjuïc (Barcelona) 81
  War of the Spanish Succession
    40–41
Bracafé (Barcelona) 133
British Airways 150
Buigas, Carles 79, 81
Buigas, Gaietà 65
Bulevard Rosa (Barcelona) 135
Buquebus 150
Buses **155**
Butterflies of the Vall d'Aran **94**

C

Caballé, Montserrat 17
Cadaqués 91, **102**
  Costa Brava 103
  hotels 119
Cadí-Moixeró 96
Caesar, Julius 102
Cafè de l'Acadèmia
  (Barcelona) 126
Café Marès (Barcelona) 132
Café Zurich (Barcelona) 132
Cafés **132–3**, **137**
La Caixa de Fang
  (Barcelona) 135
Cal Pep (Barcelona) 126
Cal Ros 130
Calafell Platja
  restaurants 129
Caldes de Boí 95
Calzados E Solé (Barcelona) 135

Cambrils 110
    restaurants 129
Camp Nou stadium 86
Camp sites **115**
Camprodon 97
Can Culleretes (Barcelona) 126
Can Majó (Barcelona) 127
Canadian Consulate 143
Canaletto 87
Canary Islands
    map 11
Cantada d'havaneres 31
Los Caracoles (Barcelona) 127
Carballeira (Barcelona) 127
Cardona **106**
Cardona, Dukes of 106, 108
Carlist Wars (1833–9) 37, 41, 42
Carlos IV, King of Spain 108
Carnestoltes 33
Carnival 33
Carrer Montcada
    (Barcelona) **60–61**
Carreras, Josep (José) 17, 136
Cars **154–5**
Carthage 37
Casa de l'Ardiaca (Barcelona) **54**
    Street-by-Street map 52
Casa Batlló (Barcelona) 22, 23, 72
Casa de la Ciutat (Barcelona) **55**
    Street-by-Street map 52
Casa Leopoldo (Barcelona) 127
Casa Lléo Morera (Barcelona) 48
    Street-by-Street map 68
Casa Milà (Barcelona) 46, 72, **73**
    Street-by-Street map 69
Casa-Museu Castell Gala Dalí
    (Figueres) 99
Casa-Museu Salvador Dalí
    (Cadaqués) 102
Casa Terrades (Barcelona) 73
    Street-by-Street map 69
Casa Vicens (Barcelona) 48
Casals, Pau 17
    Museu Pau Casals (Sant
    Salvador) 110
Casas, Ramon 25, 63
    *Procession outside Santa Maria
    del Mar* 24
Cases de Pagès 115
Cash dispensers 146
Castell de Montjuïc (Barcelona) 46, **81**
Castell-Platja d'Aro
    restaurants 130
Castelldefels
    hotels 119
Casteller festivals 31, 107
Castelló d'Empúries
    hotels 119
Castells (Barcelona) 132
Castles
    Cardona 106
    Castell de Montjuïc (Barcelona)
    46, **81**
    Torre Bellesguard (Barcelona) **88**
Catalan language 16–17, **142**
Catalonia **91–111**
    Catalan painting **24–5**
    history **37–43**
    hotels **119–21**
    maps 10–11, 13, 92–3
    Portrait of Catalonia **15–17**
    restaurants **129–31**
Catalunya Plaza Hotel
    (Barcelona) 117
The Cathedral of the Poor (Mir) 25

Cathedrals
    Barcelona 47, 52, **56–7**
    Girona 98–9
    La Seu d'Urgell 96
    Lleida 106
    Tarragona 111
    Vic 106
Cava Country **28–9**
Central de Reservas 115
Centre d'Art Perrot-Moore
    (Cadaqués) 102
Centre Bonastruc Ça Porta (Girona) 98
Centre Excursionista de Catalunya
    (Barcelona) 139
    Street-by-Street map 53
Centre Municipal de Tennis Vall
    d'Hebron 139
Centre Municipal de Vela Port
    Olímpic 139
Cercle de Pessons 96
Cerdà i Sunyer, Ildefons 22, 42
    Eixample (Barcelona) 67
    Plaça de les Glòries Catalanes
    (Barcelona) 89
Cerdanya 96
Cereria Subirà (Barcelona) 135
Cervantes, Miguel de 39
Chagall, Marc 102
Charlemagne, Emperor 38, 98–9
Charles the Bald, King of the
    Franks 96
Charles Martel, King of the Franks 38
Cheques 123, 146
Christmas 32, 33
Churches in Barcelona
    opening hours 142–3
    Basílica de Santa Maria del Mar **60**
    Sagrada Família 22, 47, 67, 72, **74–5**
    Temple Expiatori del Sagrat Cor
    85, 88
    "Gistercian triangle" 107, 108
Citibank 146
City Museum (Barcelona) *see* Museu
    d'Història de la Ciutat
Claris Hotel (Barcelona) 118
Clavé, Josep Anselm 61
Climate 19, **30–33**
Climbing, safety 145
Clothes
    in restaurants 122
    stores **134**, 135
Cloud and Chair (Tàpies) 68
Clubs **137**
Coins 147
Coll 95
Col·legi de les Teresianes 23
Collet, Charles 105
Colmado Quílez (Barcelona) 135
Colón Hotel (Barcelona) 117
Columbus, Christopher 40
    Barcelona Cathedral 56
    Dia de la Hispanitat 32
    Monument a Colom (Barcelona)
    46, 58, **65**
    Palau Reial Major (Barcelona) 54
Communications **148–9**
Companys, Lluís
    arrest and imprisonment 42
    Castell de Montjuïc (Barcelona) 81
    execution 43, 81
Concert season (Barcelona) 31
Condes de Barcelona Hotel
    (Barcelona) 118
Consulates 143
Contribuciones (Barcelona) 135

Convergència i Unió 16, 43
Conversion chart 143
Corpus Christi 30
El Corte Inglés (Barcelona) 135
Les Corts
    hotels 118
Costa Brava 91, **103**
Costa Cruises 150
Costa Daurada **110**
Un Cotxe Menys 139
Credit cards 123, 146
Crime **144–5**
Crisol (Barcelona) 135
Cubelles
    hotels 119
Currency **146–7**
Currency exchange 146
Cycling 138

D
Dalí, Gala 99
Dalí, Salvador 17, 25, **99**
    Cadaqués 102
    Casa-Museu Castell Gala Dalí
    (Figueres) 99
    Casa-Museu Salvador Dalí
    (Cadaqués) 102
    Centre d'Art Perrot-Moore
    (Cadaqués) 102
    Rainy Taxi (Dalí) 99
    Museu d'Art Moderne (Barcelona) 63
    Teatre-Museu Dalí (Figueres) 99
Dalmau, Lluís 24, 80
Dance **136**, 137
    sardana **111**, 117
Delta Air Lines 150
Delta de l'Ebre **111**, 139
Department stores **134**, 135
Desclot, Bernard 39
Design shops 135
Dia de la Constitució 32
Dia de la Hispanitat 32
Diada de Catalunya 32
Dialling codes **148**
Dijous Sant (Maundy Thursday) 30
Dilluns de Pasqua
    (Easter Monday) 32
Diners Club 146
Disabled travellers **143**
    in hotels 115
    in restaurants 123
Diumenge de Rams (Palm Sunday) 30
Divendres Sant (Good Friday) 32
Diving 139
Doctors 144
Dolça of Provence 38
Domènech i Montaner, Lluís
    Casa de l'Ardiaca (Barcelona) 54
    Casa Lléo Morera (Barcelona) 68, 72
    Fundació Antoni Tàpies
    (Barcelona) 68, 72
    Hospital de la Santa Creu i de Sant
    Pau (Barcelona) 67, **73**
    Modernisme 22
    Museu de Zoologia (Barcelona) 62
    Palau de la Música Catalana
    (Barcelona) 61
Domènech i Montaner, Pere 73
Domènech i Roura, Pere 81
Dona i Ocell (Miró) 86
Drassanes (Barcelona) **65**
Ducs de Bergara Hotel
    (Barcelona) 118
Durro 95
Dusk on the River Loing (Sisley) 63

E

Easter 30, 32
EasyJet 150
Ebre, Riu 111
Eco-Museu (Delta de L'Ebre) 111
Efficiencies *see* Self-catering
Egipte (Barcelona) 126
Eixample (Barcelona) 13, **67–75**
    area map 67
    cafés and bars 133
    hotels 117–18
    Quadrat d'Or: Street-by-Street
    map 68–9
    restaurants 127–8
    Sagrada Família **74–5**
Eixample Esquerra
    restaurants 128
El Bosc de les Fades (Barcelona) 137
El Prat airport (Barcelona) **150–51**
El Vendrell 110
Electrical adaptors 143
Elisenda de Montcada de Piños 87
Emergencies **144**
Empúries 37, **102**
Encants Vells (Barcelona) 135
Entertainment **136–7**
Erill-la-Vall 95
L'Escala 103
Escola Hípica 139
Escribà Pastisseries (Barcelona) 135
Escunhau 94
España Hotel (Barcelona) 116
L'Espluga de Francolí
    hotels 119
Estació del Nord (Barcelona) **89**, 155
Estació de Sants 155
Estadi Olímpic de Montjuïc
    (Barcelona) **81**, 139
L'Estanc (Barcelona) 135
L'Estartit 103
Estevet (Barcelona) 127
Etiquette 142
Eulàlia, St 56, 57
Eurocheques 146
Eurolines 155
Europcar 155
European Union 43

F

Falqués, Pere 68, 89
Falset
    restaurants 130
Fashion stores **134**, 135
Faust, Karl 102
Federació ECOM 115
Federació d'Entitats Excursionistes
    de Catalunya 115
Felipe II Hotel (Barcelona) 117
Felipe IV, King of Spain 40
Felipe V, King of Spain
    Castell de Montjuïc (Barcelona) 81
    Diada de Catalunya 32
    Parc de la Ciutadella (Barcelona) 62
    La Seu Vella (Lleida) 106
    War of the Spanish Succession 41
Felix, St 98
Fernando II, King of Catalonia-
    Aragon 40, 54
Ferrer, Pere 55
Festa del Treball 32
Festa major de Gràcia (Barcelona) 31
Festa major de Sants (Barcelona) 31
Festa major de Vilafranca del
    Penedès 31

Festes 30–33
Festes de Sarrià i de Les Corts
    (Barcelona) 32
Festival del Grec 31
Festivals **30–33**
    casteller 107
FGC Information 152
Field sports **138**
Fiestas *see Festes*
Figueres **99**
    restaurants 130
Fira de Sant Ponç (Barcelona) 30
Fire Brigade 145
Fires, forest 145
Fishing 138
Fiveller, Joan 55
Flags
    Les Quatre Barres **96**
Flame in Space and Naked Woman
    (Miró) 80
Flor, Roger de 39
La Floresta
    restaurants 130
Flowers of the Matollar **18–19**
Flying clubs 138
Foix, Counts of 96
Folguera, Francesc 104
Fonda Senyor Parellada
    (Barcelona) 127
Font de Canaletes (Barcelona) 59
Font Màgica (Barcelona) 77
    Street-by-Street map 79
Fontseré, Josep
    Museu de Geologia (Barcelona) 63
    Parc de la Ciutadella
    (Barcelona) 62
Food and drink
    Cava Country **28–9**
    The Food of Catalonia **26–7**
    A Glossary of Typical Dishes
    124–5
    The Other Wines of Catalonia 28
    stores **134**, 135
    see also Restaurants
Football
    Barcelona Football Club **87**, 137
    Barcelona *v* Real Madrid **87**
    Museu del Futbol Club Barcelona
    (Barcelona) **86**
Forest fires 145
Forestier, Jean 62
Forment, Damià 109
Fortuny i Marsal, Marià 25, 63
Foster, Norman 87
Franco, General Francisco 43
Franks 38
Free Evolució 139
Fundació Antoni Tàpies
    (Barcelona) **72**
    Street-by-Street map 68
Fundació Joan Miró (Barcelona) **80**
    Street-by-Street map 79

G

'Galeries' **134**, 135
Galleries *see* Museums and galleries
Gallery Hotel (Barcelona) 118
Galters, Charles 56, 57
Game hunting 138
Gandesa 93
Gardens *see* Parks and gardens
The Gardens at Aranjuez
    (Rusiñol) 24
Gargallo, Pau 61, 73
Garona, Riu 94

Garraf, coast 91
La Garriga
    hotels 119–20
Gas *see* Petrol
Gaudí, Antoni 17, 42, **72**
    Casa Battló (Barcelona) 22, 23, 72
    Casa Milà (Barcelona) 46, 69,
    72, **73**
    Casa Vicens (Barcelona) 48
    death 58
    Gaudí and Modernisme **22–3**
    Palau Güell (Barcelona) 22–3
    Palau Reial de Pedralbes
    (Barcelona) 87
    Parc de la Ciutadella
    (Barcelona) 62
    Parc Güell (Barcelona) **88–9**
    Plaça Reial (Barcelona) 59
    Sagrada Família (Barcelona) 22, 47,
    67, 72, **74–5**
    Torre Bellesguard (Barcelona) 88
Gaudí Hotel (Barcelona) 116
Generalitat 15, 16, 43
    Palau de la Generalitat
    (Barcelona) 55
Geology Museum (Barcelona) *see*
    Museu de Geologia
George, St 30
Girona 91, **98–9**
    airport 150
    map 98
    restaurants 130
Golf 138
Golf El Prat 139
Golf Sant Cugat 139
Golondrinas (Barcelona) **65**
Gothic art **24**
Goya, Francisco de 24
Gràcia
    restaurants 128
Gran Hotel Calderón (Barcelona) 118
Gran Hotel Havana (Barcelona) 118
Gran Teatre del Liceu (Barcelona) 59
Gran Via Hotel (Barcelona) 117
Granados, Enric 17
Granja M Viader (Barcelona) 132
Granollers
    hotels 120
El Greco 24, 80, 110
Grimaldi Group 150
Grup Aeri 139
Güell, Count Eusebi 42
    Palau Reial de Pedralbes
    (Barcelona) 87
    Parc Güell (Barcelona) 23, 88
Guies del Pirineu 139
Guifré el Pelós (Wilfred the Hairy),
    Count of Barcelona 38
    Les Quatre Barres 96
    Ripoll 96
    Sant Joan de les Abadesses 97

H

Habsburg dynasty 40
Hamil Barca 37
Hannibal 37
Harlem Jazz Club (Barcelona) 137
Health **144**
Hertz 155
Highways *see* Motorways
Hiking **138–9**
Hiring cars **154**, 155
History **37–43**
Holidays, public 32
Holy Week 30

Homar, Gaspar 48
Homenatge a Picasso
(Barcelona) **63**
Horse riding 138
Hospital de la Santa Creu i de Sant
Pau (Barcelona) **73**
Hospitals 144
Hostal Ciudad Condal (Barcelona) 117
Hotels **114–21**
Barcelona 116–18
booking and check-in 114
Catalonia 119–21
disabled travellers 115
grading and facilities 114
Paradors 114
prices and paying 114
rural accommodation 115
Huguet, Jaume
Museu Nacional d'Art de Catalunya
(Barcelona) 80
Palau Reial Major (Barcelona) 55
St George and the Princess 24
Human towers **107**
Hunting 138

I
Iberia 150
Iberians 37
Ice-skating 138
L'Illa (Barcelona) 135
Illa de la Discòrdia (Barcelona) **72**
Street-by-Street map 68
Immaculada Concepció 32
Individual Travellers' Spain 115
Inquisition 54
Insurance
holiday (vacation) 145
motor 154
Internacional de Cotxes d'Època 33
International Exhibition (1929) 42
Montjuïc 77
Museu Nacional d'Art de Catalunya
(Barcelona) 80
Pavelló Mies van der Rohe
(Barcelona) 81
Poble Espanyol (Barcelona) 81
Irati (Barcelona) 132
Irish Consulate 143
Isabel of Castile 40, 54
Isozaki, Arata 81
IVA *see* VAT

J
Jamboree (Barcelona) 132, 137
Jardí Botànic Mar i Murtra
(Blanes) 102
Jardí Hotel (Barcelona) 116
La Jarra (Barcelona) 133
Jaume I the Conqueror, King of
Aragón 39, 55
Jaume II, King of Aragón 87
Barcelona Cathedral 56, 57
court painter 24
Monestir de Santes Creus 107
Jazz **137**
Terrassa Jazz Festival 30
Jews **54**
Besalú 97
Centre Bonastruc Ça Porta
(Girona) 98
expulsion of 40
Joan, Pere 111
Juan, Don of Austria 65
Juan II, King of Aragón 108
Juan Carlos, King of Spain 43

Jujol, Josep Maria 73
Parc Güell (Barcelona) 89
Plaça d'Espanya (Barcelona) 81
Julià Tours 155

K
Kasparo (Barcelona) 133
Keytel International 115
Kitty O'Shea's (Barcelona) 133
Kolbe, Georg 78
Morning 81

L
Language 16–17, **142**
Lavatories, public **145**
Legal assistance 145
Lichtenstein, Roy 64
Lithograph (Tàpies) 25
Llafranc 103
Lleida 91, **106–7**
restaurants 130
Llibreria Quera 139
Lliga de Catalunya 42
Llimona, Josep 62, 63
Llívia 96
Lloret de Mar 103
festes 31
hotels 120
restaurants 130
Lloret Hotel (Barcelona) 116
La Llotja (Barcelona) **60**
Llúria, Roger de 39
Lotto, Lorenzo 87
Luke, St 105
Lull, Ramon 39
Luminists 25
Luna, Bigas 17

M
Macià, Francesc 42
Magazines **149**
Magic Fountain (Barcelona) *see* Font
Màgica
Majestic Hotel (Barcelona) 118
Mancomunitat 42
Manners 142
La Manuel Alpargatera
(Barcelona) 135
Maps
Barcelona 46–7, **159–65**
Barcelona: City Centre 12–13
Barcelona: Further Afield 85
Barcelona: Quadrat d'Or 68–9
Barri Gòtic (Barcelona) 52–3
Canary Islands 11
Catalonia 13, 92–3
Cava Country 28–9
Eixample (Barcelona) 67
Europe and North Africa 11
Girona 98
Montjuïc (Barcelona) 77, 78–9
Old Town (Barcelona) 51
La Rambla (Barcelona) 59
La Ruta del Modernisme 48–9
Spain 10–11
Maragall, Pasqual 43
Marès i Deulovol, Frederic **54**, 109
Maresme, coast 91
Mariscal, Javier 17, 81
Maritime Museum (Barcelona) *see*
Museu Marítim
Marketing Ahead 115
Markets 135
Mercat de San Josep (Barcelona) 59
Martí the Humanist 55, 88

Martín de Cermeño, Juan 64
Martinet
restaurants 130
Martorell, Bernat
The Transfiguration 57
Martorell, Joanot 39, 40
Mas i Fontdevila, Arcadi 25
MasterCard 146
Mateu, Pau 55
Matollar
Flowers of the Matollar **18–19**
Wildlife of the Matollar 19
Medi Natural 139
Medical treatment **144**
Meier, Richard 58
Las Meninas (Picasso) 61
Menus 123, **124–5**
Mercat de les Flors (Barcelona) 137
Mercat de Sant Josep (Barcelona) 59
La Mercè (Barcelona) 32
Le Meridien Hotel (Barcelona) 117
Mesón Castilla (Barcelona) 116
Metro **153**
Mies van der Rohe, Ludwig
Pavelló Mies van der Rohe
(Barcelona) 81
Milà family 73
Mir, Joaquim 63
The Cathedral of the Poor 25
Mirablau (Barcelona) 137
Miró, Joan 25, 17, 78
Barcelona School of Fine Arts 60
Dona i Ocell 86
*Flame in Space and Naked
Woman* 80
Fundació Joan Miró (Barcelona)
79, **80**
Museu d'Art Moderne
(Barcelona) 63
Museu de Ceràmica (Barcelona) 87
Parc de Joan Miró (Barcelona) 86
Plaça de la Boqueria (Barcelona) 59
Miró, Toni 17
Mitjans, Francesc 86
Modernisme 17
Eixample (Barcelona) 67
Gaudí and Modernisme **22–3**
Illa de la Discòrdia (Barcelona) **72**
La Ruta del Modernisme **48–9**
Mompou, Frederic 17
Monasteries
"Cistercian triangle" 107, 108
Monestir de Montserrat **104–5**
Monestir de Poblet **108–9**
Monestir de Santa Maria (Ripoll)
20, 96
Monestir de Santa Maria de
Pedralbes (Barcelona) **87**
Monestir de Santes Creus 107
Sant Joan de les Abadesses 97
Moneo, Rafael 89
Money **146–7**
Mont-Ras
restaurants 130
Montblanc **107**
Montjuïc (Barcelona) **12, 77–83**
area map 77
Street-by-Street map 78–9
Castell de Montjuïc 46, **81**
Montseny
hotels 120
Montserrat **104–5**
Monturiol i Estarriol, Narcís 99
Monument a Colom (Barcelona) 46,
58, **65**

Moors 38, 40
  Tortosa 111
La Moreneta **105**
Morning (Kolbe) 81
Motor insurance 154
Motorways (highways) **154–5**
Murals, Gothic art 24
Murillo, Bartolomé Esteban 24
Museums and galleries (general)
  admission charges 143
  opening hours 142
Museums and galleries (individual)
  Barcelona Cathedral 57
  Casa-Museu Castell Gala Dalí
    (Figueres) 99
  Casa-Museu Salvador Dalí
    (Cadaqués) 102
  Castell de Montjuïc (Barcelona) 81
  Centre d'Art Perrot-Moore
    (Cadaqués) 102
  Centre Bonastruc Ça Porta
    (Girona) 98
  Eco-Museu (Delta de L'Ebre) 111
  Fundació Antoni Tàpies
    (Barcelona) **72**
  Fundació Joan Miró (Barcelona)
    79, **80**
  Girona Cathedral 99
  Monestir de Montserrat 104
  Museu Arqueològic (Barcelona)
    79, **80**
  Museu d'Art (Girona) 99
  Museu d'Art Contemporani
    (Barcelona) **58**
  Museu d'Art Modern (Barcelona) **63**
  Museu de Arts Decoratives
    (Barcelona) **87**
  Museu d'Autòmats (Barcelona) 88
  Museu Cau Ferrat (Sitges) 110
  Museu Comarcal de la Conca de
    Barberà (Montblanc) 107
  Museu Comarcal de la Garrotxa
    (Olot) 97
  Museu de Cera (Barcelona) 59
  Museu de Ceràmica (Barcelona) 87
  Museu de la Ciència (Barcelona) **88**
  Museu del Cinema (Girona) 99
  Museu Diocesà (La Seu d'Urgell) 96
  Museu Diocesà i Comarcal
    (Solsona) 106
  Museu Episcopal de Vic (Vic)
    20, 106
  Museu Etnològic (Barcelona) 79
  Museu Frederic Marès (Barcelona)
    53, **54**
  Museu del Futbol Club Barcelona
    (Barcelona) **86**
  Museu Ganivets (Solsona) 106
  Museu de Geologia (Barcelona) **63**
  Museu d'Història de la Ciutat
    (Barcelona) 53, **55**
  Museu d'Història de la Ciutat
    (Girona) 99
  Museu de Joguets (Figueres) 99
  Museu de la Romanitat (Tarragona)
    110–111
  Museu Marítim (Barcelona) **65**
  Museu Municipal (Tossa de Mar) 102
  Museu de la Música (Barcelona) 69
  Museu Nacional Arqueològic
    (Tarragona) 111
  Museu Nacional d'Art de Catalunya
    (Barcelona) 78, **80**
  Museu Pau Casals (Sant
    Salvador) 110

Museums and galleries (cont.)
  Museu Picasso (Barcelona) **61**
  Museu Têxtil i d'Indumentária
    (Barcelona) 61
  Museu de la Vall d'Aran (Vielha) 94
  Museu del Vi (Vilafranca del
    Penedès) 107
  Museu de Zoologia (Barcelona) **62**
  Sagrada Família (Barcelona) 74
  Teatre-Museu Dalí (Figueres) 99
Music
  classical music 31, **136**, 137
  Museu de la Música (Barcelona) 69
  Palau de la Música Catalana
    (Barcelona) **61**
  rock, jazz and world music **137**
  Terrassa Jazz Festival 30

N
Nadal (Christmas) 32, 33
Nagel, Andrés 86
Napoleon I, Emperor 32, 41
Narcissus, St 98
National ATESA 155
National parks
  hiking **138–9**
  Parc Nacional d'Aigüestortes **95**
Newspapers **149**
  stores 135
Noche negra 43
Nonell, Isidre 63
  Waiting for Soup 25
Nouvel Hotel (Barcelona) 117

O
Old Town (Barcelona) 13, **51–65**
  area map 51
  Barcelona Cathedral 56–7
  cafés and bars 132–3
  hotels 116–17
  La Rambla **58–9**
  restaurants 126–7
  Street-by-Street: Barri Gòtic 52–3
Oliva, Abbot 38, 106
Olot **97**
Olot School 24, 97
Olympic Games (1992) 43
  Estadi Olímpic de Montjuïc
    (Barcelona) 81
  Montjuïc (Barcelona) 77
  Port Olímpic (Barcelona) **64**
  Torre de Collserola
    (Barcelona) 87
Opening hours
  banks 146
  churches 142
  museums 142
  restaurants 122
Oriente Hotel (Barcelona) 116
Otto Zutz (Barcelona) 137
Outdoor hazards **145**

P
Painting, Catalan **24–5**
Palamós 103
Palau Baró de Quadras
  (Barcelona) 48
Palau de la Generalitat (Barcelona) **55**
  Street-by-Street map 52
Palau Güell (Barcelona) 22–3, 59
Palau Macaya (Barcelona) 59
Palau Moja (Barcelona) 59
Palau de la Música Catalana
  (Barcelona) **61**, 137
Palau Nacional (Barcelona) 46, 78, 80

Palau Reial Major (Barcelona) **54–5**
  Street-by-Street map 53
Palau Reial de Pedralbes
  (Barcelona) **87**
Palau Sant Jordi (Barcelona) 81
Palau de la Virreina (Barcelona) 59
Pallarès Grau, Manuel 60
Palm Sunday 30
La Paloma (Barcelona) 137
Pan-Air 150
Parachute jumps 138
Paradors **114**, 115
Paragliding 138
Paral·lel any 1930 (Roger) 10
Parc d'Atraccions (Barcelona) 88
Parc de la Ciutadella (Barcelona)
  47, **62**
Parc de l'Espanya Industrial
  (Barcelona) **86**
Parc Güell (Barcelona) **88–9**
Parc de Joan Miró (Barcelona) **86**
Parc Nacional d'Aigüestortes **95**, 139
Parc Natural del Cadí-Moixeró 96, 139
Parc Natural del Delta de L'Ebre 111
Parc Zoòlogic (Barcelona) **63**
Park Hotel (Barcelona) 116
Parking **155**
Parks and gardens
  Jardí Botànic Mar i Murtra
    (Blanes) 102
  Palau Reial de Pedralbes
    (Barcelona) 87
  Parc de la Ciutadella (Barcelona)
    47, **62**
  Parc de l'Espanya Industrial
    (Barcelona) **86**
  Parc Güell (Barcelona) **88–9**
  Parc de Joan Miró (Barcelona) **86**
Pasqua (Easter) 30
Passeig de Gràcia (Barcelona)
  Street-by-Street map 68
Passports 142
Pastis (Barcelona) 133
Pavelló Mies van der Rohe
  (Barcelona) **81**
  Street-by-Street map 78
Pedralbes
  hotels 118
  restaurants 128
Pelegrí de Tossa (Tossa de Mar) 33
Peña Ganchegui, Luis 86
Peninsular Hotel (Barcelona) 116
Peninsular War (War of
  Independence, 1808–14) 41
Pepper, Beverley 89
Peralada
  restaurants 130
Peramola
  hotels 120
Peratallada
  restaurants 130
Pere IV the Ceremonious, King of
  Aragon 39, 108
Personal security **144–5**
Peter, St 105
Petrol (gas) 154
Petronila of Aragon 38
Pharmacies **144**
Picasso, Jacqueline 61
Picasso, Pablo 17, 25
  Barcelona School of Fine Arts 60
  Centre d'Art Perrot-Moore
    (Cadaqués) 102
  Homenatge a Picasso (Barcelona) **63**
  Las Meninas 61

Picasso, Pablo (cont.)
  Museu d'Art Moderne (Barcelona) 63
  Museu de Ceràmica (Barcelona) 87
  Museu Picasso (Barcelona) **61**
  Pablo Picasso in Barcelona **60**
Piscines Bernat Picornell 139
Pista de Gel del FC Barcelona 139
Pla, Francesc 24
Pla de la Garsa (Barcelona) 126
Plaça de la Boqueria (Barcelona) 59
Plaça d'Espanya (Barcelona) 81
Plaça de les Glòries Catalanes
  (Barcelona) **89**
Plaça Reial (Barcelona) 59
Platja d'Aro 31, 103
  festes 33
Poble Espanyol (Barcelona) **81**
  Street-by-Street map /8
Poblenou **89**
  restaurants 128
Poblet *see* Monestir de Poblet
Police **144–5**
Porrera
  restaurants 130
Port Aventura 110
Port Olímpic (Barcelona) **64**
Port Vell (Barcelona) **64–5**
Postal services **149**
Prim, General 62
Primo de Rivera, Miguel 42
*Procession outside Santa Maria del
  Mar* (Casas) 24
Public conveniences **145**
Public holidays 32
Puig i Cadafalch, Josep
  Casa Amatller (Barcelona) 72
  Casa Macaya (Barcelona) 49
  Casa Terrades (Barcelona) 69, **73**
  Modernisme 22
  Museu de la Música 69
  Palau Barò de Quadras
    (Barcelona) 48
Puigcerdà **96**
Pujol, Jordi 16, 43
Pullmantur 153
Pyrenees 96

Q

Quadrat d'Or (Barcelona)
  Street-by-Street map 68–9
Les Quatre Barres **96**
Les Quinze Nits (Barcelona) 126

R

Radio **149**
Radio Taxis 155
Rainfall 32
Rainy Taxi (Dalí) 99
La Rambla (Barcelona) 47, **58–9**
  map 59
Ramon Berenguer I, Count of
  Barcelona 38, 57
Ramon Berenguer III, Count of
  Barcelona 38
Ramon Berenguer IV, Count of
  Barcelona 38
  Monestir de Poblet 108
  Monestir de Santes Creus 107
El Raval (Barcelona) **58**
Raventós, Josep 28
Raventós, Ramon 81
Real Madrid Football Club 87
Rebull, Joan
  Three Gypsy Boys 52
Reccared, King of the Visigoths 37

Regente Hotel (Barcelona) 117
Reial Acadèmia de Ciències i Arts
  (Barcelona) 59
Reial Club Marítim de Barcelona 127
Reis Mags 32, 33
Rembrandt Hotel (Barcelona) 116
Renaixença 41–2
RENFE 152
Restaurants **122–31**
  Barcelona 126–8
  Catalonia 129–31
  eating hours 122
  A Glossary of Typical Dishes
    124–5
  how to dress 122
  prices and paying 123
  reading the menu 123
  smoking in 123
  wheelchair access 123
  wine choices 123
  see also Food and drink
Reus
  airport 150
  restaurants 131
Revellón 33
Revetlla de Sant Joan 31
Reynés, Josep 62
Ribera, José de 24
Riding 138
Rigalt, Lluís 48
Ripoll **96**
Ritz Hotel (Barcelona) 118
Rivoli Ramblas Hotel (Barcelona) 117
Road signs 154
Rock music **137**
Rogent, Elies 64–5
Roger, Emili Bosch
  Paral·lel any 1930 10
Roig i Soler, Joan 25, 63
Roig Robí (Barcelona) 128
Roman remains 37
  Barri Gòtic (Barcelona) 52
  Empúries 102
  Museu d'Història de la Ciutat 55
  Tarragona 110–111
  Vic 106
Romanesque Art and Architecture
  20–21
Romesco (Barcelona) 126
Romeu, Pere 63
Ros i Güell, Antoni 48
Roses 103
  restaurants 131
Royal Hotel (Barcelona) 117
Royal Palace *see* Palau Reial Major
Rural accommodation **115**
Rusiñol, Santiago 25
  The Gardens at Aranjuez 24
  Museu d'Art Modern
    (Barcelona) 63
  Sitges 110
La Ruta del Modernisme **48–9**

S

Sa Tuna
  hotels 120
Sabartés, Jaime 61
Safont, Marc 55
S'Agaró
  hotels 120
Sagnier, Enric 88
Sagrada Família (Barcelona) 47, 67,
  72, **74–5**
  Gaudí and Modernisme 22
Sailing 139

St George and the Princess
  (Huguet) 24
Salardú 94
El Salón (Barcelona) 127
Salou 110
San Agustín Hotel (Barcelona) 116
Sant Carles de la Ràpita 111
  restaurants 131
Sant Celoni
  restaurants 131
Sant Climent de Taüll 20, 95
Sant Cristòfol de Beget 21
Sant Feliu de Guíxols
  restaurants 131
Sant Gervasi
  restaurants 128
Sant Jaume de Frontanyà 20, 96
Sant Joan 32
Sant Joan de les Abadesses **97**
Sant Jordi 30
Sant Josep 30, 32
Sant Martí 96
Sant Medir (Barcelona) 30
Sant Miquel 32
Sant Pere de Besalú 21
Sant Pere de Camprodon 21
Sant Pere de Galligants 21
Sant Pere de Ribes
  hotels 120
Sant Pere de Rodes 21, 99
Sant Sadurní d'Anoia
  cava 28–9
  restaurants 131
Santa Cristina (Lloret de Mar) 31
Santa Cristina d'Aro
  hotels 120
Santa Eulàlia (Barcelona) 33
Santa Maria (Ripoll) **20**, 95
Santa Maria (Taüll) 95
Santa Pau
  hotels 120
Santes Creus **107**
Sants
  restaurants 129
Saportella, Francesca 87
Sardana (dance) **111**
Sarria-Sant Gervasi
  hotels 118
Science Museum (Barcelona) *see*
  Museu de la Ciència
Sea travel 150, **151**
Self-catering (efficiencies) **115**
Sert, Josep Lluís
  Fundació Joan Miró (Barcelona)
    79, 80
Sert, Josep-Maria 25, 106
  Casa de la Ciutat (Barcelona) 55
  Cathedral (Vic) 106
Servi-COCEMFE 143
Set Portes (Barcelona) 127
Setmana Santa (Easter week) 30
La setmana tràgica (1909) 42
La Seu d'Urgell 92, **96**
  hotels 120
  restaurants 131
Shopping
  Barcelona **134–5**
Sisley, Alfred
  Dusk on the River Loing 63
Sitges 93, **110**
  festes 30, 33
  hotels 121
  Luminists 25
  restaurants 131
Skating 138

Skiing 139
  Baqueira-Beret 95
Smoking
  in restaurants 123
Sol Soler (Barcelona) 133
Soler, Frederic 62
Solsona 106
Spain
  map 10–11
Spanair 150
Spanish Civil War (1936–9) 43, 111
Speciality stores **134**, 135
Speed limits 154
Sports **137**, **138–9**
Spring in Catalonia **30**
Student travellers 143
Subirachs, Josep Maria 74
Suizo Hotel (Barcelona) 117
Summer in Catalonia 31
Sunshine 31
Super Esport 139
Swimming pools 138
Synagogues 54

T

Talaia Mar (Barcelona) 127
Tapes (tapas – snacks) **124**
Tàpies, Antoni 17, 25
  Cloud and Chair 68
  Fundació Antoni Tàpies
    (Barcelona) 68, **72**
  Homenatge a Picasso
    (Barcelona) **63**
  Lithograph 25
  Museu d'Art Moderne
    (Barcelona) 63
Tarragona 91, **110–111**
  hotels 121
  restaurants 131
Tavérnoles
  hotels 121
Tavertet
  hotels 121
  restaurants 131
Taxes
  in restaurants 123
  tax-free goods 142
Taxis **155**
Teatre Grec (Barcelona)
  Street-by-Street map 79
Teatre-Museu Dalí (Figueres) 99
Teatre Nacional de Catalunya
  (Barcelona) 137
Telephones **148–9**
  emergencies **144**
Teletiempo 139
Television **149**
Temperatures 33
Temple Expiatori del Sagrat Cor
  (Barcelona) 85, 88
Tennis 138
Terrassa Jazz Festival 30
Theatre **136**, 137
Theft **145**
Theme parks
  Port Aventura 110
Thirty Years War (1618–59) 40
Thomson Cruises 150
Three Gypsy Boys (Rebull) 52
Tibidabo (Barcelona) **88**
  amusement park 137
  restaurants 131
Tiepolo, Giovanni Battista 87
Time zone 143
Tipping 123

Titian 87
TMB Information 152
Toilets, public **145**
Torre Bellesguard (Barcelona) **88**
Torre de Collserola (Barcelona) **87**
Torrent
  hotels 121
Torres de Ávila (Barcelona) 137
Tortosa **111**
  hotels 121
Tossa de Mar 17, **102**, 103
  festes 33
Tots Sants (All Saints' Day) 32
Tourist offices 115, **142**, 143
El Tragaluz (Barcelona) 128
Trains **152–3**
The Transfiguration (Bernat) 57
Trasmediterránea 150
Travel **150–55**
  air travel **150–51**
  buses **155**
  cars **154–5**
  Catalonia 92
  golondrinas (Barcelona) **65**
  Metro **153**
  sea travel 150, **151**
  taxis **155**
  trains **152–3**
Traveller's cheques 146
  in restaurants 123
Tredòs
  hotels 121
Els Tres Tombs (Barcelona) 33
Turisme de Barcelona 143
Turisme de Catalunya 143
Turisverd 115
Tusquets, Oliver 17
TWA 150

U

United Kingdom Consulate 143
United States Consulate 143
Universal Exhibition (1888) 22, 42
  Arc del Triomf (Barcelona) 62
  Monument a Colom (Barcelona) 65
  Museu de Zoologia (Barcelona) 62
    85*5
Unlimited Youth Student Travel &
    Viatgeteca 143
Usatges (Constitution) 38

V

Vall d'Aran **94**
  Butterflies of the Vall d'Aran **94**
Vall de Boí **95**
Vallmitjana, Agapit and Venanci 105
Valls
  festes 31
  restaurants 131
Van Eyck, Jan 24
Van Gogh, Vincent 64
El Vaso de Oro (Barcelona) 133
VAT
  in restaurants 123
  tax-free goods 142
Vayreda i Vila, Joaquim 24, 97
Velázquez, Diego de 24, 61
  Monestir de Santa Maria de
    Pedralbes 87
  Museu Nacional d'Art de Catalunya
    (Barcelona) 80
Verboom, Prosper 62
Verdaguer, Jacint 41
Veronese, Paolo 87
La Veronica (Barcelona) 126

Vespucci, Amerigo 65
Viajes 2000 143
Vic **106**
  hotels 121
  restaurants 131
Vielha **94**
  hotels 121
Viladomat, Antoni 24
Viladrau
  hotels 121
Vilafranca del Penedès 29, **107**
  festes 31
Vilanova
  festes 33
Vilanova i la Geltrú 110
  hotels 121
Vilaseca i Casanovas, Josep 62
Villar i Lozano, Francesc de Paula 75
Vinçon (Barcelona) 135
Virgen del Carmen (Barcelona) 31
Virgin of Montserrat **105**
VISA 146
Visas 142
Visigoths 37–8, 96

W

Waiting for Soup (Nonell) 25
Walking
  hiking **138–9**
  La Ruta del Modernisme **48–9**
  safety 145
War of the Spanish Succession 40–41
Water sports **139**
Waxwork museum (Barcelona) *see*
    Museu de Cera
Weather 19, **30–33**
Wheelchair access *see* Disabled
    travellers
Wildlife
  bird-watching **138**
  Butterflies of the Vall d'Aran **94**
  Parc Nacional d'Aigüestortes 95
  Parc Natural del Delta de L'Ebre 111
  Wildlife of the Matollar 19
Wine
  Cava Country **28–9**
  Museu del Vi (Vilafranca del
    Penedès) 107
  The Other Wines of Catalonia 28
  in restaurants 123
Winter in Catalonia **33**
Winter sports **139**
Wirtzia, King of the Visigoths 38
World music **137**

X

El Xampanyet (Barcelona) 133, 137
Xarxa d'Albergs de Catalunya 115

Y

Young People's Tourist Office 152

Z

Zelestre (Barcelona) 137
Zoological Museum (Barcelona) *see*
    Museu de Zoologia
Zoos
  Parc Zoològic (Barcelona) **63**
Zurbarán, Francisco de 24
  Monestir de Santa Maria de
    Pedralbes 87
  Museu Nacional d'Art de Catalunya
    (Barcelona) 80

Acknowledgments

DORLING KINDERSLEY would like to thank the following people whose contributions and assistance have made the preparation of this book possible.

MAIN CONTRIBUTOR

ROGER WILLIAMS contributed to the *Eyewitness Travel Guide to Spain* and has written Barcelona and Catalonia titles for Insight Guides. He was also the main contributor to the *Eyewitness Travel Guide to Provence. Lunch with Elizabeth David*, set around the Mediterranean, is his latest novel.

ADDITIONAL CONTRIBUTORS

Mary Jane Aladren, Pepita Arias, Emma Dent Coad, Rebecca Doulton, Josefina Fernández, Nick Rider, David Stone, Judy Thomson, Clara Villanueva.

DESIGN AND EDITORIAL ASSITANCE

Special thanks are due to Amaia Allende, Queralt Amella Miró (Catalan Tourist Board), Gillian Andrews, Imma Espuñes i Amorós, Alrica Green, Elly King, Kathryn Lane, Barbara Minton, Mary Scott, Alicia Ribas Sos, Lola Carbonell Zaragoza.

PROOFREADER

Stewart J Wild.

INDEXER

Hilary Bird.

SPECIAL PHOTOGRAPHY

Max Alexander, D. Murray/J. Selmes, Dave King, Clive Streeter.

PHOTOGRAPHY PERMISSIONS

© Obispado de VIC; © Cabildo de la Catedral de Girona; Teatre Nacional de Catalunya (Barcelona); Institut Mpal. del Paisatge Urba i la Qualitat de Vida, Ajuntament de Barcelona.

Dorling Kindersley would like to thank all the churches, museums, restaurants, hotels, shops, galleries and other sights too numerous to thank individually.

PICTURE CREDITS

KEY: t=top; tl=top left; tlc=top left centre; tc=top centre; trc=top right centre; tr=top right; cla=centre left above; ca=centre above; cra=centre right above; cl=centre left; c=centre; cr=centre right; clb=centre left below; cb=centre below; crb=centre right below; bl=bottom left; b=bottom; bc=bottom centre; bcl=bottom centre left; br=bottom right; bcr=bottom centre right; d=detail.

Works of art have been reproduced with the permission of the following copyright holders:

Dona i Ocell Joan Miró © ADAGP, Paris & DACS, London 1999; *Morning* George Kolbe © DACS 1999; IOC/Olympic Museum Collections; Tapestry of the Foundation Joan Miró 1975 © ADAGP, Paris & DACS, London; *Rainy Taxi* © Salvador Dalí - Foundation Gala - Salvador Dalí/DACS 1999.

The publisher would like to thank the following individuals, companies and picture libraries for their kind permission to reproduce their photographs:

ACE PHOTO LIBRARY: Mauritius 17t; AISA, Barcelona: 12b, 16b, 21bl, *San Jorge* Jaume Huguet 24c, 36, 37c, 40cb, 42c, 42bl, 144bc; AQUILA PHOTOGRAPHICS: Adrian Hoskins 94bla; 94bl; James Pearce 19b; NATIONAL ATESA: 154cr.

JAUME BALANYA: 75crb; MIKE BUSSELLE: 93b, 94t.

CODORNIU: 29t, 29c; BRUCE COLEMAN COLLECTION: Erich Crichton 18tr; José Luis González Grande 19tr; Norbert Schwirtz 19tl; Colin Varwdell 19 cra; COCEMFE: 134c; COVER, Madrid: Pepe Franco 134c; Matias Nieto 139b.

FREIXENET: 28c, 29b; FUNDACION COLLECTION THYSSEN-BORNEMISZA: *Madonna of Humility* Fra Angelico 87t;

FUNDACIO JOAN MIRO, Barcelona: *Flama en l'espai i dona nua* Joan Miró 1932 © ADAGP, Paris and DACS, London 1999 80t.

GODO PHOTO: 111t, José Luis Dorada 107t.

ROBERT HARDING PICTURE LIBRARY: 23tr, 57ca, 68ca, 80b, 81b.

THE ILLUSTRATED LONDON NEWS PICTURE LIBRARY: 43t; INDEX, Barcelona: CJJ.17b, 40t, 43c; IMAGE BANK: 22b, 69b; Andrea Pistolesi 84; IMAGES COLOUR LIBRARY: 22c, 151b; AGE Fotostock 76, 95b, 100–101, 135t, 135c, 138cr; NICK INMAN: 18b.

LIFE FILE PHOTOGRAPHIC: Xabier Catalan 23c; Emma Lee 23cra.

MAS SALVANERA: Ramón Ruscalleda 115t; MARY EVANS PICTURE LIBRARY: 45 (inset); JOHN MILLER: 90; MUSEU NACIONAL D'ART DE CATALUNYA: J. Calveras J. Sagrista 82-83; *La Compañia de Santa Barbara* 1891 Ramon Marti Alsina 41t, *El Tombant del Loing* Alfred Sisley 63t; MUSEU PICASSO: *Auto Retrato* Pablo Ruiz Picasso © DACS 1999 60bl, *Las Meninas* Pablo Ruiz Picasso 1957 © DACS 1999 61b; ABADIA DE MONTSERRAT (BARCELONA) 104br.

NATURAL SCIENCE PHOTOS: C Dani & I Jeske 138c; NATURPRESS, Madrid: 15b; Oriol Alamany 30c, 33b; Walter Kvaternik 33c, 44–45, 145b; Carlos Vegas 146t, 148tr; Jose A Martinez 91b.

ORONOZ, Madrid: 37b, 38t, 38c, 41bl, 42t.

PICTURES COLOUR LIBRARY: 70–71;

PRISMA,Barcelona: 4t, *Paralelo Año 1930* Roger Bosch 8–9, 9 (inset), 16t, *Procesión en Santa María del Mar* Carbo Cases 24t, *Jardines de Aranjuez* 1907 Rusiñol y Prats 24b, *Esperando la Sopa* 1899 Isidro Monell y Monturiol 25t, *La Catedral de los Pobres* Mir Trinxet 25c, *Litografía* Tàpiés © ADAGP, Paris & DACS, London 1999 25b, 34–35, 41cb, 42 cra, 113 (inset), 134b, 137c, 141 (inset), 150ca, 155t; Carles Aymerich 20bl, 32c; A. Bofill 17c; Barbara Call 15t; Jordi Cami 30b; Albert Heras 2–3, 32b; Kuwenal 39t, 39c; Mateu 31c.

RAIMAT: 28cb; RED-HEAD: 50; REX FEATURES: 99cb; ELLEN ROONEY:1.

M ANGELES SÁNCHEZ: 31b; SCIENCE PHOTO LIBRARY: Geospace 10; SPECTRUM COLOUR LIBRARY: 22tr; STOCKPHOTOS, Madrid: 138b; Campillo 139t.

JACKET
Front – CORBIS: David G. Houser main image; DK PICTURE LIBRARY: Max Alexander crb; Heidi Grassley bl; Clive Streeter clb.
Back - DK PICTURE LIBRARY: Heidi Grassley t; Alan Keohane b. Spine – CORBIS: David G. Houser.

FRONT END PAPER: clockwise John Miller; Image Bank Andrea Pistolesi; Red-Head; Images Colour Library/ AGE Fotostock.

All other images © DORLING KINDERSLEY. For further information see www.DKimages.com

English–Catalan Phrase Book

IN AN EMERGENCY

Help!	Auxili!	ow-**gzee**-lee
Stop!	Pareu!	pah-**reh**-oo
Call a doctor!	Telefoneu un metge!	teh-leh-fon-**eh**-oo oon **meh**-djuh
Call an ambulance!	Telefoneu una ambulància!	teh-leh-fon-**eh**-oo oo-nah ahm-boo-**lahn**-see-ah
Call the police!	Telefoneu la policia!	teh-leh-fon-**eh**-oo lah poh-lee-**see**-ah
Call the fire brigade!	Telefoneu els bombers!	teh-leh-fon-**eh**-oo uhlz boom-**behs**
Where is the nearest telephone?	On és el telèfon més proper?	on-ehs uhl tuh-leh-fon **mehs** proo-**peh**
Where is the nearest hospital?	On és l'hospital més proper?	on-ehs looss-pee-**tahl mehs** proo-**peh**

COMMUNICATION ESSENTIALS

Yes	Sí	see
No	No	noh
Please	Si us plau	sees plah-oo
Thank you	Gràcies	**grah**-see-uhs
Excuse me	Perdoni	puhr-**thoh**-nee
Hello	Hola	**oh**-lah
Goodbye	Adéu	ah-they-**oo**
Good night	Bona nit	bo-nah neet
Morning	El matí	uhl muh-**tee**
Afternoon	La tarda	lah **tahr**-thuh
Evening	El vespre	uhl **vehs**-pruh
Yesterday	Ahir	ah-**ee**
Today	Avui	uh-voo-**ee**
Tomorrow	Demà	duh-**mah**
Here	Aquí	uh **kee**
There	Allà	uh-**lyah**
What?	Què?	keh
When?	Quan?	kwahn
Why?	Per què?	puhr keh
Where?	On?	ohn

USEFUL PHRASES

How are you?	Com està?	kom uhs-**tah**
Very well, thank you.	Molt bé, gràcies.	mol **beh grah**-see-uhs
Pleased to meet you.	Molt de gust.	mol duh **goost**
See you soon.	Fins aviat.	feenz uhv-**yat**
That's fine.	Està bé.	uhs-tah beh
Where is/are …?	On és/són?	ohn ehs/**sohn**
How far is it to …?	Quants metres/ kilòmetres hi ha d'aquí a …?	kwahnz meh-truhs/kee-loh-muh-truhs yah dah-**kee** uh
Which way to …?	Per on es va a …?	puhr **on** uhs bah ah
Do you speak English?	Parla anglès?	**par** luh àn-**glehs**
I don't understand	No l'entenc.	noh luhn-**teng**
Could you speak more slowly, please?	Pot parlar més a poc a poc, si us plau?	pot par-**lah mehs** pok uh **pok** sees plah-oo
I'm sorry.	Ho sento.	oo **sehn**-too

USEFUL WORDS

big	gran	gran
small	petit	puh-**teet**
hot	calent	kah-**len**
cold	fred	fred
good	bo	boh
bad	dolent	doo-**len**
enough	bastant	bahs-**tan**
well	bé	beh
open	obert	oo-**behr**
closed	tancat	tan-**kat**
left	esquerra	uhs-**kehr**-ruh
right	dreta	**dreh**-tuh
straight on	recte	**rehk**-tuh
near	a prop	uh **prop**
far	lluny	**lyoon**yuh
up/over	a dalt	uh **dahl**
down/under	a baix	uh **bah**-eeshh
early	aviat	uhv-**yat**
late	tard	**tahrt**
entrance	entrada	uhn-**trah**-thuh
exit	sortida	**soor**-tee-thuh
toilet	lavabos/ serveis	luh-**vah**-boos sehr-**beh**-ees

SHOPPING

more	més	mess
less	menys	**men**yees
How much does this cost?	Quant costa això?	kwahn **kost** ehs-**shoh**
I would like …	M'agradaria …	muh-grad-uh-**ree**-ah
Do you have?	Tenen?	**tehn**-un
I'm just looking, thank you	Només estic mirant, gràcies.	**noo**-mess ehs-**teek** mee-**rahn grah**-see-uhs
Do you take credit cards?	Accepten targes de crèdit?	ak-**sehp**-tuhn tahr-**zhuhs** duh **kreh**-deet
What time do you open?	A quina hora obren?	ah **keen**-uh oh-ruh **oh**-bruhn
What time do you close?	A quina hora tanquen?	ah **keen**-uh oh-ruh **tan**-kuhn
This one.	Aquest	ah-**ket**
That one.	Aquell	ah-**kehl**
expensive	car	kahr
cheap	bé de preu/ barat	**beh** thuh **preh**-oo/ bah-**rat**
size (clothes)	talla/mida	**tah**-lyah/**mee**-thuh
size (shoes)	número	**noo**-mehr-oo
white	blanc	**blang**
black	negre	**neh**-gruh
red	vermell	vuhr-**mel**
yellow	groc	**grok**
green	verd	**behrt**
blue	blau	**blah**-oo
antique store	antiquari/botiga d'antiguitats	an-tee-**kwah**-ree/ boo-**tee**-gah/dan-tee-**ghee**-tats
bakery	el forn	uhl **forn**
bank	el banc	uhl **bang**
book store	la llibreria	lah lyee-bruh-**rée**-ah
butcher's	la carnisseria	lah kahr-nee-suh-**ree**-uh
pastry shop	la pastisseria	lah pahs-tee-suh-**ree**-uh
chemist's	la farmàcia	lah fuhr-**mah**-see-ah
fishmonger's	la peixateria	lah peh-shuh-tuh-**ree**-uh
greengrocer's	la fruiteria	lah froo-ee-tuh-**ree**-uh
grocer's	la botiga de queviures	lah boo-**tee**-guh duh keh-vee-**oo**-ruhs
hairdresser's	la perruqueria	lah peh-roo-**kuh**-**ree**-uh
market	el mercat	uhl muhr-**kat**
newsagent's	el quiosc de premsa	uhl kee-**ohsk** duh **prem**-suh
post office	l'oficina de correus	loo-fee-**see**-nuh duh koo-**reh**-oos
shoe store	la sabateria	lah sah-bah-tuh-**ree**-uh
supermarket	el supermercat	uhl soo-puhr-muhr-**kat**
tobacconist's	l'estanc	luhs-**tang**
travel agency	l'agència de viatges	la **jen** soo uh duh vee-**ad**-juhs

SIGHTSEEING

art gallery	la galeria d' art	lah gah-luh **ree**-yuh **dart**
cathedral	la catedral	lah kuh-tuh-**thrahl**
church	l'església	luhz-**gleh**-zee-uh
garden	la basílica	lah buh-**zee**-lee-kuh
library	el jardí	uhl zhahr-**dee**
	la biblioteca	lah bee-blee-oo-**teh**-kuh
museum	el museu	uhl moo-**seh**-oo
tourist information office	l'oficina de turisme	loo-fee-**see**-nuh thuh too-**reez**-muh
town hall	l'ajuntament	luh-djoon-tuh-**men**
closed for holiday	tancat per vacances	tan-**kat** puhr bah-**kan**-suhs
bus station	l'estació d'autobusos	luhs-tah-see-**oh** dow-toh-**boo**-zoos
railway station	l'estació de tren	luhs-tah-see-**oh** thuh **tren**

STAYING IN A HOTEL

Do you have a vacant room?	¿Tenen una habitació lliure?	teh-nuhn oo-nuh ah-bee-tuh-see-**oh lyuh**-ruh

double room with	habitació doble amb	ah-bee-tuh-see-oh doh-bluh am
double bed	llit de matrimoni	lyeet duh mah-tree-moh-nee
twin room	habitació amb dos llits/ amb llits individuals	ah-bee-tuh-see-oh am dohs lyeets/ am lyeets in-thee-vee-thoo-ahls
single room	habitació individual	ah-bee-tuh-see-oh een-dee-vee-thoo-ahl
room with a bath	habitació amb bany	ah-bee-tuh-see-oh am bahnyuh
shower	dutxa	doo-chuh
porter	el grum	uhl groom
key	la clau	lah klah-oo
I have a reservation	Tinc una habitació reservada	ting oo-nuh ah-bee-tuh-see-oh reh-sehr-vah-thah

EATING OUT

Have you got a table for...	Tenen taula per...?	teh-nuhn tow-luh puhr
I would like to reserve a table.	Voldria reservar una taula.	vool-dree-uh reh-sehr-vahr oo-nuh tow-luh
The bill please.	El compte, si us plau.	uhl kohm-tuh sees plah-oo
I am a vegetarian	Sóc vegetarià/ vegetariana	sok buh-zhuh-tuh-ree-ah buh-zhuh-tuh-ree-ah-nah
waitress	cambrera	kam-breh-ruh
waiter	cambrer	kam-breh
menu	la carta	lah kahr-tuh
fixed-price menu	menú del dia	muh-noo thuhl dee-uh
wine list	la carta de vins	lah kahr-tuh thuh veens
glass of water	un got d'aigua	oon got dah-ee-gwah
glass of wine	una copa de vi	oo-nuh ko-pah thuh vee
bottle	una ampolla	oo-nuh am-pol-yuh
knife	un ganivet	oon gun-ee-veht
fork	una forquilla	oo-nuh foor-keel-yuh
spoon	una cullera	oo-nuh kool-yeh-ruh
breakfast	l'esmorzar	les-moor-sah
lunch	el dinar	uhl dee-nah
dinner	el sopar	uhl soo-pah
main course	el primer plat	uhl pree-meh plat
starters	els entrants	uhlz ehn-tranz
dish of the day	el plat del dia	uhl plat duhl dee-uh
coffee	el cafè	uhl kah-feh
rare	poc fet	pok fet
medium	al punt	ahl poon
well done	molt fet	mol fet

MENU DECODER *(see also pp26–7 & 124–5)*

l'aigua mineral	lah-ee-gwuh mee-nuh-rahl	mineral water
sense gas/amb gas	sen-zuh gas/am gas	still/sparkling
al forn	ahl forn	baked
l'all	lahlyuh	garlic
l'arròs	lahr-roz	rice
les botifarres	lahs boo-tee-fah-rahs	sausages
la carn	lah karn	meat
la ceba	lah seh-buh	onion
la cervesa	lah-sehr-ve-sah	beer
l'embotit	lum-boo-teet	cold meat
el filet	uhl fee-let	sirloin
el formatge	uhl for-mah-djuh	cheese
fregit	freh-zheet	fried
la fruita	lah froo-ee-tah	fruit
els fruits secs	uhlz froo-eets seks	nuts
les gambes	lahs gam-bus	prawns
el gelat	uhl djuh-lat	ice cream
la llagosta	lah lyah-gos-tah	lobster
la llet	lah lyet	milk
la llimona	lah lyee-moh-nah	lemon
la llimonada	lah lyee-moh-nah-thuh	lemonade
la mantega	lah mahn-teh-gah	butter
el marisc	uhl muh-reesk	seafood
la menestra	lah muh-nehs-truh	vegetable stew
l'oli	loll-ee	oil
les olives	luhs oo-lee-vuhs	olives
l'ou	loh-oo	egg

el pa	uhl pah	
el pastís	uhl pahs-tees	
les patates	lahs pah-tah-tuhs	
el pebre	uhl peh-bruh	
el peix	uhl pehsh	
el pernil salat serrà	uhl puhr-neel suh-lat sehr-rah	
el plàtan	uhl plah-tun	
el pollastre	uhl poo-lyah-struh	
la poma	la poh-mah	
el porc	uhl pohr	
les postres	lahs pohs-truhs	
rostit	rohs-teet	
la sal	lah sahl	
la salsa	lah sahl-suh	
les salsitxes	lahs sahl-see-chuh	
sec	sehk	
la sopa	lah soh-puh	
el sucre	uhl-soo-kruh	
la taronja	lah tuh-rohn-djuh	
el te	uhl teh	
les torrades	lahs too-rah-thuhs	
la vedella	lah veh-theh-lyuh	
el vi blanc	uhl bee blang	
el vi negre	uhl bee neh-gruh	
el vi rosat	uhl bee roo-zaht	
el vinagre	uhl bee-nah-gruh	
el xai/el be	uhl shahee/uhl be	
el xerès	uhl shuh-rehs	
la xocolata	lah shoo-koo-lah-t	
el xoriç	uhl shoo-rees	

NUMBERS

0	zero
1	un (masc)
	una (fem)
2	dos (masc)
	dues (fem)
3	tres
4	quatre
5	cinc
6	sis
7	set
8	vuit
9	nou
10	deu
11	onze
12	doce
13	tretze
14	catorze
15	quinze
16	setze
17	disset
18	divuit
19	dinou
20	vint
21	vint-i-un
22	vint-i-dos
30	trenta
31	trenta-un
40	quaranta
50	cinquanta
60	seixanta
70	setanta
80	vuitanta
90	noranta
100	cent
101	cent un
102	cent dos
200	dos-cents (masc)
	dues-centes (fem)
300	tres-cents
400	quatre-cents
500	cinc-cents
600	sis-cents
700	set-cents
800	vuit-cents
900	nou-cents
1,000	mil
1,001	mil un

TIME

one minute	un minut
one hour	una hora
half an hour	mitja hora
Monday	dilluns
Tuesday	dimarts
Wednesday	dimecres
Thursday	dijous
Friday	divendres
Saturday	dissabte
Sunday	diumenge

Rail Transport Maps

The main map shows the whole of Barcelona's Metro which has 115 stations on five lines. It also shows the suburban lines, funiculars and tram *(see pp152–3)*. Pub port in Barcelona is modern and efficient, and the driv more integrated system is progressing rapidly – combine now allow interchange between different modes of tran special ticket for tourists is the *Barcelona Card*, availabl day to five-day values, which offers unlimited travel o and bus, and discounts at leading sights and museums. map shows Catalonia's mainline rail network, which is RENFE, the Spanish state system. The stations selected sion here are those closest to sights described in this g

KEY

▬ Metro Line 1	▬ RENFE airport-rail conn
▬ Metro Line 2	✚ Funicular
▬ Metro Line 3	═ Tramvia Blau (Blue Tra
▬ Metro Line 4	◯ Interchange station
▬ Metro Line 5	⮀ RENFE mainline train s
▬ FGC train service (Ferrocarrils de la Generalitat de Catalunya)	

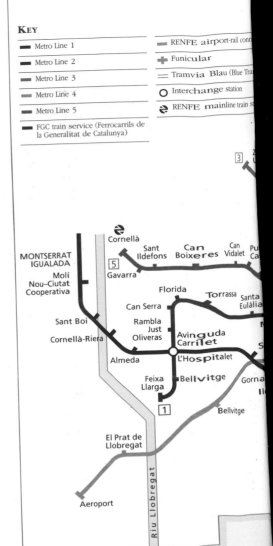